THE ART OF LEADERSHIP
Volume 2

BY OBA T'SHAKA

*AUTHOR OF THE ART OF LEADERSHIP VOLUME
I
AND
THE POLITICAL LEGACY OF MALCOLM X*

**Pan Afrikan Publicatons, Richmond, California
94804**

THE ART OF LEADERSHIP
Volume 2

First Edition 1991   First Printing 1991

ISBN Number:
1-878557-02-5

Printed in the United States of America
Pan Afrikan Publicatons, Richmond, California 94804

CONTENTS

CHAPTER ELEVEN

FREE THE MIND..**445**

CHAPTER TWELVE

ORGANIZING STRATEGIES............................499

CHAPTER 13

THE BLACK CHURCH AND BLACK THEOLOGY IT'S AFRICAN ROOTS 550

CHAPTER FOURTEEN

ALLIANCES AND COALITIONS

BROADENING YOUR BASE 624

CHAPTER FIFTEEN

PROPAGANDA, PUBLICITY AND PUBLIC THINKING CAMPAIGNS

PROPAGANDA, PUBLICITY, AND PERSUASION.........................647

CHAPTER SIXTEEN

SECURITY COUNTER INSURGENCY......... 683

CHAPTER SEVENTEEN

1. Political Education materials:

    a. Orientation Schedule

    b. Cycles of African Consciousness

    c. Introductory Reading List

    d. Basic Family Bibliography on African and African-AmericanHistory and Culture (compiled by Dr. Asa Hilliard)

    e. Sample Cadre Training Outline

2. Intelligence Section:

    President Reagan's Memorandum on Intelligence Activities

"*In every negro there is a potential BLACK MAN...*"

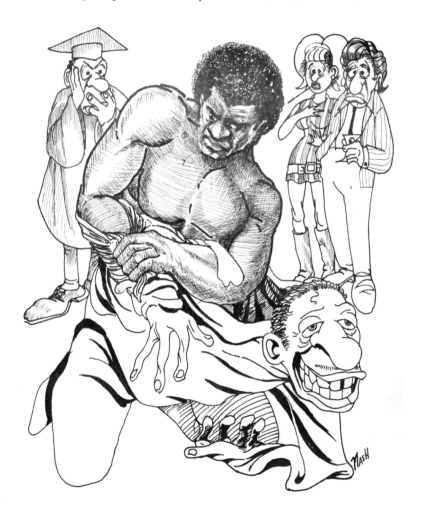

CHAPTER ELEVEN

FREE THE MIND

Organizational programs are a reflection of how the organization sees the world, itself, its people, and the future. The political outlook of an organization is the vision that gives the group a sense of purpose and direction. Without a vision of the future, our groups will grope in the alleys of confusion and despair. The political outlook of a group should be both moral and political. It should spell out standards of honesty and self-respect. It should also define the long term, political objectives of the group, and hopefully the race.

SPIRITUAL POLITICAL OUT LOOK

According to European thought, political ideas have nothing to do with considerations of honesty and morality. Only power considerations are of concern to the European political theorists. Many of us have been infected with the same disease, which treats politics as amoral. This is a bankrupt position. The outlook of a group should deal with the whole person, and the person is physical, mental, spiritual, and political. These areas are not separate, they represent a whole. The head is not separate from the body, nor is the body separate from the spirit.

Politics is not separate from economics, nor is the spirit separate from political struggle.

SUIT YOUR EDUCATION PROGRAM TO THE GROUP

A good organizer has to be both honest and clear-sighted. If the organizer is honest, the people will trust him; if the organizer has a sense of direction, he will have a good chance of achieving success.

The type of political education program you shape for your group depends upon the nature of your organization. If your organization is a cadre organization, then it is a disciplined group and should have a clear long-range objective and a clearly defined set of ideas on the nature of the new society that it wants to construct. A correct political ideology must exist before cadres can be created because this ideology determines your long-term and overall strategies for achieving the objective. Where the line is incorrect, the chances are good that the people will be channeled into suicidal or losing positions. If there is no line or it is fuzzy, the membership will be confused in its direction, and political education will only heighten that confusion.

Similarly, it is incorrect for a cadre organization to think that a statement of principles represents a political line. A statement of principles represents a minimum set of ideas. A correct political line enables the leadership to create a "like-minded collective" around itself. A body that does not share a common outlook is not a "cadre organization." A political education program that balances theory and work is the basis for creating common thought patterns, common communications, and common behavior patterns in the organization.

Where a group is an organization of organizations and individuals, a political line is not the problem. The need is for toleration of different ideologies. A Black United Front has to fight to see that no single line is imposed on the BUF. The national Black United Front is tied together by a set of principles, a basic set of values, and programs of action.

THE HISTORICAL CULTURAL EDUCATION PROGRAM

In structuring your political education program, work to strike a balance between theory and work. The practice of keeping a balance between theory and work develops organizers that are both practical and theoretical.

This type of balance is necessary for your training program, because organizers in the Black liberation movement tend to be either theory-oriented or action-oriented. Those organizations that are strong on the theory level, usually are unable to organize a popular mass base. Often the organizations that have a mass base don't have a theoretical orientation.

To develop a successful Black liberation movement you need organizers who unite theory and action. You also need cadres that carry out group decisions, and display initiative in carrying out those decisions. Organizing training must stress the importance of members of the group being fully involved in organizational decisions. The consensus method is the best decision-making approach because it enables each member to participate in shaping group decisions. However, when the group cannot reach a consensus, and decide to follow the will of the majority, members must carry out the decisions whether they agree with them or not. A good organizer carries out decisions he/she disagrees with, with the same enthusiasm that is executed with decisions he/she agrees with, and raises any objections to the decisions at organizational meetings. An organizer, who only carries out the decisions he/she agrees with, is a poor organizer, because of their inability to place group interests above individual views.

CREATING RESPONSIBLE MEMBERS

Organizing training encourages the organizer to assume responsibility. The heart of organizing, the heart of leadership, is responsibility, and a good organizer assumes unpleasant responsibilities without being told to. Within the Black liberation movement, too many of our organizers will only take responsibility to mop a floor, or try to resolve a problem when they are forced to. A good organizer sees that dirt is swept up before it piles up into a big mess, and that problems are addressed before they mushroom into big problems.

A good way to develop organizing skills is by transferring individuals from easier to more difficult jobs within the organization and promoting them to higher leadership positions when they show growth. Organizers are developed by moving them through three levels: local organizing, national organizing, and international organizing. Organizers who display ability on the local level should be gradually given national assignments. When they display national skills, they should be allowed to take on international responsibilities. This type of step-by-step approach creates seasoned organizers.

Organizers must learn that organizing is detailed work. To organize a block, school, or political support group, means paying attention to tedious, often boring, details. Only through taking care of small details will big things emerge. Often we make the mistake of wanting to build a big organization, a big rally, or a big fundraising project, without paying attention to all of the little details that go into a good organizing effort. Big things come from small things; organizing training starts with the nuts and bolts of organization building, which make up the ideas that tie the group together.

CREATING AFRO-CENTRIC ATTITUDES, THOUGHTS AND BEHAVIOR PATTERNS

Above and beyond everything else, a successful political education program depends on your commitment to build on the strengths of the culture of African people, and the lessons of the Black liberation movement, in order to create a "new African." "Negro" thought and behavior patterns have to be overturned so that we can create the "New African." A stable cadre is the seed of a new people, and a new way of life. The day-to-day struggle is the water that nourishes the seed of consciousness and commitment. The political education process is the beginning of this new transformation.

FRANTZ FANON'S CYCLES OF AWAKENING

In creating the "New African," those conducting the political education sessions should take the new members through the cycles of African consciousness. The cycles of African consciousness are an adaptation of the threefold stages of consciousness discussed by Franz Fanon in his book, *The Wretched of the Earth.* Here, Fanon analyzes the transformation of the native intellectual as he responded to the culture of the colonial power:

If we wanted to trace in the works of native writers the different phases which characterize this evolution we would find spread out before us a panorama on three levels. In the first phase, the native intellectual gives proof that he has assimilated the culture of the occupying power. His writings correspond point by point with those of his opposite numbers in the mother country. His inspiration is European and we can easily link up these works with definite trends in the literature of the mother country. This is the period of unqualified assimilation. We find in this literature coming from the colonies of the Parnasians, the Symbolists and the Surrealists.

In the second phase we find the native is disturbed; he decides to remember what he is. This period of creative work approximately corresponds to that immersion which we have just described. But since the native is not a part of his people, since he only has exterior relations with his people, he is content to recall their life only. Past happenings of the by-gone days of his childhood will be brought up out of the depths of his memory; old legends will be reinterpreted in the light of a borrowed estheticism and of a conception of the world which was discovered under other skies.

....Finally in the third phase, which is called the fighting phase, the native, after having tried to lose himself in the people and with the people, will on the contrary shake the people. Instead of according the peoples' lethargy an honored place in his esteem, he turns himself into an awakener of the people; hence comes a fighting, a revolutionary literature, and a national literature. During this phase a great many men and women who up till then would never have thought of producing a literary work, now that they find themselves in exceptional circumstances -- in prison, with the Maquis or on the eve of their execution -- feel the need to speak to their nation, to compose the sentence which expresses the heart of the people and to become the mouthpiece of a new reality in action.63

ADAPTING FANON'S THEORY TO AFRICANS IN THE DIASPORA

Experiences in the Black Liberation movement in the U.S. reveal that this framework, with some modifications, has application to our situation.   Fanon's framework described the transformation of consciousness among the colonized African intellectual. The Black liberation movement experience in America shows that this framework applies with modifications to the masses of African people in the United States.

The Black intellectual in the U.S., has undergone a process similar to the one described by Fanon. In fact, our intellectuals have produced an assimilationist literature, which parallels white themes and values in much the same way that the African intellectual has.   Similarily, some of our intellectuals have moved into the fighting phase (Garvey, Malcolm, DuBois in his *Dusk of Dawn* phase, Delaney, Turner, etc.) calling on our people to fight for their liberation.

Where the Fanonian model has to be modified is in how it applies to the situation of the masses of Africans in the U.S. Fanon did not attempt to apply his model to the masses of continental Africans. In other places in his book, he pictures the masses as being in possession of a culture of resistance, where the heroes who fought the European were presented as legendary figures. Of course, we know that African people today are undergoing a transformation, where many of the traditional values are giving way to European values. The African novelists have best described this process.

THE SYNTHESIS OF AFRICAN AND EUROPEAN CULTURE

As for Africans in the U.S., the cultural experience was different. Traditional African culture underwent a kind of attack unknown in any other part of the world. Unlike Africans in the Caribbean or on the continent, Africans in the U.S. did not retain traditional African religion generally. The Obeah man persisted on many plantations in the U.S., but the dominant religious force was Christianity, and in time, the Christian minister. The drum, which could not be stamped out in the Caribbean or Africa where Blacks were a majority, was stamped out as a medium of communication in America. This is not to say that African culture was entirely wiped out as the assimilationist historians and sociologists contend, but rather the culture underwent unique and deep transformations, with core elements of the African culture being reworked into the Euro-American setting. Black slaves and rural Blacks of the 19th and early 20th centuries developed this tradition, creating Spirituals and the Blues. As Blacks moved into urban areas, the Black classical music, or so-called jazz, was created.

Moreover, African approaches to life that could not be stamped out by slave masters were retained. These retentions included an approach to life where decisions were made on a collective basis, and leadership was charged with being responsible for voicing the decisions of the group. This collective system was highly democratic and sought to draw the best ideas from the group. Under this system the elders were highly respected; the oral tradition was maintained as the primary vehicle for passing on knowledge; Christianity was mixed with faith healing and the belief that Africa would rise again an expression of Ethiopianism.

Today the "New African" culture of the masses of our people is undergoing destruction, which is reflected in the weakening of the extended family, the undermining of the nuclear two-parent family, the rise in Black suicides, drug addiction, and a massive level of self-hatred. This crisis, which can best be described as a crisis of culture, has many complex causes. Some of the causes behind this general breakdown in Black life are integration; television, which has promoted the rise of a new mass culture; changes in the economy, which have pushed many more Blacks into the ranks of the poor; a government supported campaign to wage war on Black youth, especially Black male youth, through drugs; and the lack of a national movement among Blacks to turn all of this around. But the underlying cause of this general state of disorientation is the crisis of identity, the crisis of culture.

Fanon's threefold cycle of consciousness provides a path for overturning self-hatred and creating a sense of African identity pride and self-confidence among Black people. When the organizer creatively adapts this model to African-American realities the organizer will find that profound changes in identity can be produced.

THE CYCLES OF AFRICAN CONSCIOUSNESS

In applying Fanon's model, whether we are applying it on the mass movement level, or through a well organized political education system, it is important to understand that this system will only work when we combine our efforts to change individual thought and behavior patterns with organized campaigns to produce change on the political, educational, economical, and shelter levels.

Put another way, our consciousness as individuals is influenced by the consciousness of the larger group. Many of the negative forces just described work to produce a low level of individual consciousness among Blacks as a whole. Yet, at the very time when the Black community is facing so many serious crises', there are Blacks who have a high level of political consciousness. This demonstrates that the individual has the power to produce deep changes in the level of identity and in the larger society, in spite of the negative attitudes and behaviors produced by the larger society and by Blacks who are conditioned by the larger society.

So society has the power to influence thought and behavior, and the individual has the power to influence thought and society. Political education has to recognize this dual truth. On the group level, the political education process works to transform thoughts and behavior from white identity to African identity, so that the individual will have the strength to challenge mass "menticide," and white control of Black lives. The transformed individual uses his or her consciousness to build movements that challenge the existing white power center for Black power, the power to control our lives, communities, economies, politics, culture, religions, and way of life.

In applying the Fanonian system to Black people there are four stages: assimilation, disturbance, identity, and social transformation. For the sake of understanding, we will examine these stages separately; however, while people experience stages separately, parts of other stages will also overlap. For example, a person who is going through the stage of African identity may still have some negative attitudes about their color, the size of their lips, or the natural quality of their hair. In some cases these negative attitudes may be subconscious and may occasionally slip out with some revealing statement such as "that fair-skinned sister," or that "nappy-haired brother." These statements reveal that the person has not shed some important negative attitudes about their Blackness. Still, this person may display some very positive African values. So one stage is often mixed with another, yet the person, by his or her attitude, words, and actions will reveal his or her general level of consciousness.

THE ASSIMILATIONISTS STAGE OF CONSCIOUSNESS

Whether conducting a small political orientation session, or organizing a mass movement, we have to recognize that a society run by whites inevitably works to produce an assimilationists mentality among many Blacks. This white Euro-centric mentality is built on cultural rape carried out through slavery. Today the white Euro-centric view grows out of the mass media, the public school, the university, the church, and political and economic systems that are rooted in Greek, Roman, French, British, and German historical, philosophical, political, and religious tradition. This European centered tradition conditions Blacks to worship white and hate Black.

SEEING OURSELVES THROUGH THE EYES OF OTHERS'

The European centered view of history conditions Blacks to adopt an assimilationists outlook, through conditioning us in DuBois' words to "see ourselves through the eyes of others." Convinced that Blacks have no history, Blacks become conditioned to the idea that the only intellectual food we can digest is European intellectual food. The acceptance of the Europeans estimation of us represents cultural and historical surrender. Turning our backs on our past we take on the attitudes, thoughts and behavior patterns of whites.

It is the organizers job to expose how this conditioning system works. You have to expose this conditioning system so that Black people can see self hatred is based upon a negative image of themselves, manufactured by a negative picture of Africa, and a distorted positive view of Europe.

The foundation of the assimilationist's mentality rests on the false European historical assumption that Africans (Blacks) have never been anything and therefore will never be anything. This view will exist as long as Blacks who hold it are ignorant of their ancient and recent past. Self-knowledge is the only cure to ignorance of self. The organizers job is to expose people to the truth about their great past. What is often difficult to accept is that Blacks will not move out of this white state of consciousness until their assimilationists ideas are exposed, and their faith in white superiority questioned.

OVERTURNING NEGATIVITY

In exposing the assimilationist ideas that affect us, the organizer should be honest. You should be willing to share with your people your deepest "white hangups," and you should discuss how you are struggling to overcome them. A good organizer understands that hangups are human and that people learn from human examples. This was Malcolm's great strength, he did not attempt to appear to be a perfect person. He let people know that he had done something to change his Negro ways. Some of the things you should discuss with your people is how a negative view of their past leads them to have a negative view of themselves and our people today. A basic quality of assimilation is negativity. The assimilationist minded Black person doesn't see the positives and negatives in Black people, they see mainly the faults. Although the assimilated Black person may have been hired by Blacks, promoted by Blacks, and praised by Blacks, one negative act by another Black person can serve to erase all the good that Blacks have done. Their view of Blacks is the white persons view, that Blacks are simply messed up. Many negative minded Blacks think that their (whites) judgment of the race is fair, and further, many also confuse their occasional criticism of white racism, with being Black. If you tell the negative minded Black person that their views are anti-Black, most will protest that they are Blacker than most Blacks. Actually, the pitiful thing about the negative Blacks is that their wholesale criticism of the race is made as though they were white. Since they never can be white their negative views of the race represent a negative view of themselves. Still, many negative Blacks honestly believe that they and they alone are the only true hope for the race.

COUGHING UP EUROPEAN STANDARDS OF BEAUTY

Another phase of "seeing ourselves through the eyes of others," is the acceptance of European standards of beauty, as the sole standards of beauty. Conditioned to see beauty as blonde hair, blue eyes, and white skin, Blacks measure themselves ugly accordingly. Black is perceived as ugly also because it has been portrayed in a distorted, Aunt Jemmimah, Black Sambo, shiftless, lazy, humorous image. The negative historical image of Blacks combined with mass media that portrays whites as beautiful and Blacks as ugly conditions Blacks to imitate whites. As organizers we have to get our people to measure ourselves according to our own standards of beauty.

SEEING OUR BLACK BEAUTY

A Black skin, natural hair, and thick lips are beautiful. The melanin pigment not only gives us beautiful shades of color, but it slows down aging. As a sister once said, "if its Black it don't crack." That melanin makes for a youthful look, long after most folks with little melanin have started to show wrinkles. A natural head of hair complements our Black features and accents our natural Black beauty. Our thick lips and wide noses look good when we don't try to straighten them out and decrease their size. Blacks who get nose jobs are trying to look like Europeans, and because they go against nature they look ridiculous. Similarily, whether Blacks have naturally wide noses, or thin ones, thick lips, or thin ones, light skin or dark they are beautiful. They will see their beauty when they are able to see their own historical image. When we are able to see our history through our own eyes we will begin to gain a new measure of ourselves physically, emotionally, intellectually, and spiritually. Then we will be able to look in the mirror, see our own reflection, and appreciate what we see.

SYNTHESIZING EMOTION WITH REASON

When we take on the Euro-centric view of us, we try to act the way they do, so they will accept us. The assimilated Black, as

Malcolm said, is taught to be unemotional because whites generally don't display their emotions. Generally, the more educated Blacks become, the less emotional they become. Many lose their Black taste for emotional Blues, Spirituals, and Rhythm and Blues. Some forget how to holler, and tragically some even forget how to fight. They become cool, calm, collected "negroes" who calmly, cooly express their watered down views. Whites usually label these types of negroes as "responsible negroes" and Blacks are encouraged to imitate them. When Blacks become this cool they often lose their soul and even find it hard to shake their hips soulfully. The organizer has the responsibility to explain that Black behavior includes being emotional. Whether we are listening to emotional music, engaging in emotional talk, or listening to emotional preaching, emotional expression is a part of what moves us no matter how much we try to keep from tapping our feet when we hear moving music. In African-American and traditional African culture, emotion and reason go hand in hand. When we understand the history and culture of African people we will understand that this is an important trait of our people. Instead of trying to imitate the white unemotional trait, we will understand why we behave the way we do, and feel comfortable with it.

THE MYTH OF REVERSE SEGREGATION

Another way in which we see ourselves through the eyes of others, is in our view that all Black groups are segregation in reverse. Again the problem is that we are "seeing these groups through the eyes of others." Often we don't know anything about the groups that we label as being segregation in reverse, neither do we understand the meaning of the label "reverse segregation." The label is designed to make us think that an all-Black group is no different in its objectives than the Ku Klux Klan, which excludes Blacks because the Klan believes that Blacks are inferior. Of course this is ridiculous. The Black Panther Party was an all Black group that organized Blacks to fight Ku Klux Klan type activity. More important, when Blacks organize on a voluntary basis they aren't practicing segregation or reverse segregation. Segregation is a system that forces one race to live in certain neighborhoods, attend certain schools, eat in certain restaurants, etc. All Black organizations aren't trying to segregate other races, they are simply coming together on an all Black basis to solve Black problems, just as other ethnic groups do. But whites label all Black groups as segregationists in reverse to discourage Blacks from organizing on an all Black basis. Without organization Blacks will remain powerless and subject to the power of the real segregationists who run the country. As long as we see Black organizations through the eyes of others, we find ourselves dependent upon other races for our basis needs.

LOSS OF SELF CONFIDENCE

Through "seeing ourselves though the eyes of others," we are robbed of a sense of self-confidence. The assimilationist mentality encourages us to think the thoughts of others rather than to think our own thoughts. This kind of conditioning leads us to lose confidence in our own ability to think and evaluate the world through our own eyes. Accepting the European view of us, we are left with a lot of humiliating judgments about our race. Accepting the negative historical judgment of Blacks without question we find ourselves operating on remote control, without even knowing it.

THEORY AND PRACTICE

The organizer has the task of challenging our people to think and to believe in themselves, partially through exposing them to the truth about our ancient past, and partially through encouraging the people to take control of their own lives through organized struggle. So political education has both a theory and practice side to it. We have to be encouraged to return to the past to gain a sense of our potential in the present. We also have to change the present conditions if we are to have confidence in our ability to shape the future. As organizers, one of the best ways we can overcome negative, self-hatred, individualism, and the overall white viewpoint is to let the people see their enemies on the school board, on the job, in the redevelopment agency, in the police department, as the people organize against racist school boards and police departments. This confrontation with white racism is absolutely necessary because it teaches the people who the enemy is and it allows the people to "see the enemy through their own eyes."

THE SECOND STAGE: DISTURBANCE OR CONTACT WITH WHITE RACISM

Following the Fanonian model, contact with white racism occurs during the disturbance stage of development. The Black victim may be exposed to racism on an individual or a group level. Racist assaults may occur on the job, in school in the military, in court, or it may be experienced in some other place. On a collective level Blacks may be exposed to racist insults through political struggles for jobs, housing or education. Whether racism is experienced on the individual or collective level, it is the condition for the individual returning to his roots.

CONFRONTATION WITH WHITE RACISM

Contact with white racism, when it is extreme, can teach the Black victim that no matter how much they try to think white, feel white, and act white, to the system they are still "niggers." The exposure to white racism, can teach the Black victim that trying to be white is not only futile, but it is also degrading. A lot of supportive political education is needed to drive this point home. Through political education, and the mass struggle the organizer needs to show how racism is built into every segment of society. Individual experiences with racism are not accidental, they are not the result of the behavior of a few bad whites. American society is structured to keep Blacks on the bottom and whites on top. Assimilation into a racist society is no more possible for Blacks as a whole, than a mouse is capable of integrating with an elephant, or a dog integrating with a cat.

BLACK RAGE

The confrontation with a racist cop, teacher, or employer can trigger one of a number of reactions. The feeling of rage can lead the victim to take instant action against the racist. This crisis reaction is a perfectly natural reaction. The danger is that when the anger has subsided the victim will try to go back to business as usual without questioning the system of racism that produced the racist attack. The organizer uses individual racist attacks to exposé the racist nature of the system, and to organize specific campaigns against the racist police or racist employers.

SPONTANEOUS REACTIONS

Sometimes Black rage is expressed through spontaneous uprisings, often triggered by police violence against Blacks. The strength of spontaneous uprisings is that they express a collective attitude that an attack on one is an attack on all Black people. The weakness of the spontaneous uprising is that they lack organization and theoretical direction. Without organization sooner or later the spontaneous uprising will die out.

On other occasions, the Black victim of racism may verbally attack "whitey," the "honkey," or the "devil," with stinging indictments.

Whatever the victims response to racism, the disturbance stage is a necessary but potentially dangerous, contradictory stage. The danger of the stage arises from the victims ignorance of the enemy that he or she wants to fight. Where the victim does not understands the organized system of racism they are up against, they may strike out in individual, futile ways that either don't produce anything or endanger their lives.

The disturbance stage is also a confusing contradictory one. The head-on experience with a policeman's nightstick may lead the victim to examine many of their own beliefs about whites. When this happens Blacks find themselves torn between their old beliefs and the sense that many of these white oriented beliefs don't make sense. As Black victims begin to angrily question white authority, their anger is too often interpreted by Blacks and whites as "Black racism." Sometimes Black victims, in their confusion, even accept the label that they are Black racists. When they see themselves this way, they simply reflect the fact that their eyesight is still derived from some one else.

In truth the contact with white racism unleashes the Black victim's hatred of the enemy. Rather than this hatred being racist, it is a healthy reaction to the violence and insults that Blacks experience. This hatred of the oppressor is also part of the process of demystifying whites. The brutal white racist is hard to place on a mantle of supreme power, wisdom, and civilized authority. The hatred of racism is necessary if the Black victim of racism is going to come to a point where they love and respect themselves. Knowledge of the enemy is necessary for knowledge of self.

LOVE HATE ATTITUDES

But the disturbance stage is not clear cut. The Black victim of racism reveals during this stage a love-hate attitude toward whites. Whites are denounced, but their perceptions of Blacks are still a basic part of how disturbed Blacks see the world and most importantly themselves. Because Black victims have not yet internalized an African value system, Blacks going through this cycle may confuse anti-whiteness with pro-

Blackness.   During this stage Blacks may confuse arrogance with self confidence.

CONFORMING TO WHITE SUPREMACY

Some Blacks who experience racism may decide to put up with it for fear of losing their job or in some cases their life. In some cases the lack of an organized alternative, may force many Black victims of racism to put up with it. Where the people have a movement or the opportunity to organize against racist attacks, they may be more willing to strike out against the insults and assaults.

In some cases, Blacks are economically comfortable and simply assume that racism is part of what they have to put up with. Some Blacks who may tolerate racism on the job, may still fight racism when they return home to their communities after work.

For those Blacks who are moved to examine the enemy, themselves, and the need to do something to change a system based on racism, knowing the enemy provides the basis for seeing the oppressor and not wanting to identify with him. Demystifying the oppressor is the reverse side of the struggle for self-knowledge.

THE THIRD STAGE: AFRICAN IDENTITY

The third phase of the Fanonian cycle of consciousness is the stage of African identity. The individual's experience with racism leads to a new evaluation of the enemy. Personal or collective experiences with racism reveal to many Blacks that there is something basically wrong with how they see themselves and how they see whites. During periods of mass political struggle such as the Civil Rights and Black Power movements, the daily sight of racist police beating Blacks may be the thing that triggers this re-evaluation of the enemy and themselves. During periods when political movements are in decline more Blacks will attempt to escape from being Black. The organizer has the responsibility to expose the people to the truth about their history and culture. Information about their ancient past needs to be linked to their daily organizing campaigns in order to encourage their awakening.

DISCOVERY OF THE AFRICAN PAST

The stage of African identity is one where Black people have an intense concern about their ancient African past and their African-American past. The Black people's connection to the past gives them a sense of direction in the present and in the future. The study of ancient Kemet (Egypt) Nubia, Kush, Ghana, Mali, Songhay, Zimbabwe, the Zulus, Moors, Dravidians of India and the Olmecs of America (to name a few) is necessary to provide vision, so that we can see ourselves through our own historical eyes.

PHYSICAL OR PSYCHOLOGICAL WITHDRAWAL FROM WHITES

The period of identification involves some kind of withdrawl from whites. For some Blacks the withdrawl from whites may be psychological. These Blacks may experience the desire to withdraw from white thoughts, white approval, and white attitudes. Other Blacks may physically and psychologically withdraw from whites. Whatever form the withdrawl takes, withdrawl is necessary so Blacks can deeply examine their historical roots.

BALANCED STUDY OF THE AFRICAN AND AFRICAN-AMERICAN PAST

African identification is the product of deep study of our ancient African past. But if this examination is to be useful, it must be balanced. Study of our ancient African past is the key to everything else. This kind of study is root study. Here, by studying the history and cultures of ancient Africa we discover the true origins of African people. Our ancient history tells us of our past achievements, failures, strengths, and weaknesses. The study of our African past has to be balanced with a serious study of our African-American past, and the history of Africans throughout the world. As we begin to seriously undertake a study of our past, we must use the perspective we gain from this examination, to study the history of the world, especially the history of Europeans. This is necessary because a balanced study of history is one that examines the history of ourselves and our oppressors.

USING THE POSITIVE VALUES FROM OUR AFRICAN PAST TO TRANSFORM EUROCENTRIC VALUES TO AFRO-CENTRIC VALUES

The study of our past cannot be surface, it must be deep. This is a lifelong pursuit. Serious historical study is not simply rote study, where we remember facts. Serious study of the past is a study of the lessons and values of our past, and this study forces us to examine our innermost values. When the positive aspects of our past are internalized we begin to transform our attitude, thought, and behavior patterns, from European centered, to African-American centered attitudes, thoughts, and behaviors.

A return to our ancient past is a return to old time-tested values that seem new but are suprising because of our ignorance of our rich past. As we begin to study the achievements and values of ancient Africa we begin to gain a sense of having a foundation in life. This understanding provides the basis for creative thought and action.

Each person, when going through the identity stage, has to confront their own individual past, which is a part of the collective past of African people. Each person has to draw on the lessons and values of the past while at the same time examining their own values both positive and negative. At this stage, when African identity is applied through the political education process, the organizer needs to describe how the study of the past led him or her to examine and cough-up some of their own hangups. On the collective level of the mass movement, mass rallies, and other kinds of mass organizing, the organizer should explore African ancient history showing how it reveals important values that can help them survive today. When this is discussed on the individual, or collective level, the people have to be encouraged to deeply study their rich African African-American past.

FEELING GOOD ABOUT YOUR AFRICAN PAST

One of the first reactions of a person who, for the first time, has received a dose of historical truth, such as how human life began in Africa, or how civilization began in Africa, or how the Egyptians were Black and had the most advanced ancient civilization on earth, is a feeling of disbelief combined with a feeling like you are on cloud nine. Learning about past historical greatness makes you feel good like a Black man or Black woman should. While you feel good, you also wonder why you had to go so long before finding out the truth about your past. You have a feeling that you have been robbed of this knowledge, and if you are serious you will take up the study of the past the way a starving person consumes food.

THE SEARCH FOR SELF KNOWLEDGE

It doesn't seem possible to get enough information about your ancient past. Each thing you read raises more questions. If the Egyptians (people of Kemet) had a fully developed civilization when the first dynasty was established, where did Egypt's civilization come from? If you dig deeply you may discover that the Egyptian civilization was preceded by the Nubian civilization that established the Pharaohnic system. You may also discover that the civilization of Kush or Nubia was the mother civilization of the world. The examination of your African past takes you back to a period of time when Black people ruled themselves and a large part of the world. You see Blacks ruling nations, running educational systems, making medical and scientific discoveries. You see Blacks building great architectural monuments such as the great pyramids and you see a set of values that are opposed to the Euro-centric values that you have been taught to worship.

IDENTIFYING AND INTERNALIZING AFRO-CENTRIC VALUES

As you study your ancient past you see that these ancient societies placed a high value on morality. They didn't simply talk honesty, they practiced honesty. You read with astonishment that in ancient Ghana when a European trader died his property was preserved until someone could claim it. Or with equal amazement you discover that in ancient African civilizations people could move from one end of Egypt or Ghana to another without fear of being robbed or murdered. You will also discover that there was no conception of land or water being private property. The natural resources, the land, the water, and the mineral wealth did not belong to individuals; this wealth was used by the people under a communal system, where the user has the responsibility to preserve these resources and pass them on to future generations.

CENTRAL ROLE OF THE AFRICAN WOMAN

When you start to dig deeper, you also discover that ancient African societies were centered around the woman. These ancient societies, as Diop pointed out, were matrileneal. A child's last name and their inheritance rights came from the mothers eldest brother. Mother-right guaranteed equality between men and women. Contrary to the picture of Africa presented by the European, you discover that the African woman was highly respected, and even more important, her role in society was the basis for African social organization.

AFRICAN SPIRITUALITY

An examination of our ancient past also reveals why Blacks all over the world are religious. Ancient Africans were a spiritual people who did not separate the spiritual from the material. The creator and the spiritual forces were believed to be aids in assisting African people to achieve the good life, provided that the people lived truthful lives and respected God.

THE NEED FOR A DEEP STUDY OF OUR AFRICAN PAST

As you begin to face these and many more truths from your past, it causes you to re-evaluate your view of yourself and the world. An understanding of your past achievement creates a great sense of pride. How deep this sense of pride becomes depends upon how deeply you study and internalize the positive aspects of the past. If your study of the past is surface, then the sense of pride will be a surface temporary feeling, that will leave you as quickly as it came. If, on the other hand, your study of the achievements and values of ancient Africa is deep then you will find that you are undergoing continual transformation and growth that is both painful and rewarding.

THE ROMANTIC PHASE

Whether your study of the past is deep or surface there is a tendency in the first phase of returning to your past, to romanticize the past. Because the European has portrayed such a negative picture of our past, when we discover our own history we tend at first to only see the positive. During this phase an either/or situation develops where Africans can do no bad and the European can do no good.

DEVELOP A BALANCED APPROACH TO THE PAST

Our view of the past also influences how we approach the present. In time we have to learn to balance the positive with the negative. We discover that ancient civilizations had many strengths but they also had some key weaknesses. For example, we learn that while the communal system of sharing was a great strength, when this system was applied to strangers (Europeans) that did not share communal values, the strangers began to take control of what we only intended to share.

So the process of internalization requires that we separate the positive aspects of our past from the negative ones. We also have to be prepared to compare these positive values and achievements with our own values. For example, our examination of the great achievements of our people leads us to new attitudes of pride that begin to undermine the attitudes of self-hate. Yet it would be a mistake to think that simply knowing facts and values arising out of our past will drive out a lifetime of conditioning that subconsciously tells us that Black is ugly, evil, and nothing of value. Many Blacks who dig into their past fool themselves into thinking that they have overturned their sense of self-hatred when they have not. If we are to cough up the attitudes and thoughts as well as the behaviors of self-hatred then we have to understand how we internalized negative attitudes about our color as children. We have to examine how our attitudes about color and beauty influence our selection of mates, and how it conditions our behavior in life. If our parents instilled in us the idea that we were too dark to be beautiful, or too light to be Black, then we first have to identify these influences and begin to change our attitudes, thoughts, and behaviors on these subjects. This can be painful because it may mean that we will honestly have to face why, for example, we choose a particular mate. Did we select our mate because we truly loved them, or was it because they reflected our negative self-concept? Did we choose our current occupation because we really believed that we were suited for the work, or because it fulfilled a white fantasy implanted in our heads by our parents, teachers, or the mass media. Has our choice of an occupation revealed a sense of self-confidence or did we choose an occupation because we lacked confidence in our ability to do better?

EXAMINE OUR INNERMOST VALUES AND AMBITIONS

The cycle of African identity forces us to examine our innermost values and ambitions. Where these values and ambitions do not grow naturally from our own interests and gifts and loves, the truth tell us to go inside ourselves and find our true identity and true mission in life. If my ambitions were based on pure considerations of what would benefit me and me alone, a serious examination of our past will force me to consider how my ambitions will advance or hold back the race. Ancient African values are collective values that teach that the strength of the individual is derived from the group. A return to the past is a return to collective values, and it calls for us to take a collective approach to life. This isn't easy since we live in a society that programs us to follow the individual path and go for self.

RESTORING THE CONCEPT OF AFRICAN NATIONHOOD

A return to our past also gives us a new understanding of power. Ancient African history is a history of African nations and smaller ethnic societies ruled by African people. When we see our past through our own eyes then we see that African equality and freedom was based on Black people running their own societies in their own way. This part of the study of the past calls for some of the deepest re-examination of ourselves that we can possibly conceive. The idea of Africans running governments provides the seeds for Blacks conceiving how we can gain national power in the future.

It is here especially that the connection between our ancient African past and our African-American past becomes particularly important. For it is through the thinking of people such as Martin R. Delaney, Henry Highland Garnett, Bishop Henry McNeal Turner, Marcus Garvey and Malcolm X that we gain an appreciation of Blacks running governments and ruling nations. These men applied the past national achievements of African people to the present. They help us to understand the need for Blacks to achieve the kind of power that will take racial and economic oppression off of our backs.

AFRICAN COMMUNALISM

It is also necessary to balance a study of ancient Africa with a study of Afro-America as well as Africans throughout the world. On the level of values, as we examine the traditional values of ancient Africa, we also need to examine the positive African-American values that are carryovers and adaptations of African values. Communalism, or sharing, was not only practiced in traditional Africa, it is also a value that rural Blacks practiced during and after slavery. Our value for sharing food, labor, and material things is a major reason why poor Blacks could survive the ravages of share cropping that kept us continually in debt to the landowner. In drawing on traditional African and African-American history and culture we are able to synthesize the positive aspects of African and African-American history and culture.

SEEING BEYOND EUROPE AND EURO-AMERICA

The internalization of the positive aspects of our African and African-American past creates a new historical and cultural center that enables us to see beyond Europe and Euro-America, to an African past, which is the foundation for a great African future. The transformed African does not see Europe as the center of their world. An African, African-American historical and cultural center offers a framework for an old/new worldview and an old/new society that is based on the best of traditional African and African-American values.

COMBINE HISTORICAL STUDY WITH POLITICAL STRUGGLE

As we blend together the best from our past we have the responsibility to translate those values and lessons into programs that address the real needs of African people. Studying the past is only part of the process that we have to undergo to create the new African. We also have to combine a study of the past with a struggle to make history in the present and the future. The example of Black unity, Black organizational power, and creative Black programs will instill examples of power and pride in our people. So the organizer must inspire our people to make the past serve the present, through learning from the past and organizing for full liberation.

GIVING BIRTH TO THE NEW AFRICAN

The degree to which the individual undergoes deep transformation of values will determine the consistency and creativity of these new Africans in the organizations and movements that they build. The political education process is the key ingredient for creating new Africans who are committed to truth, are consistent, and are able to take initiative on their own because they have confidence in themselves. The cycles of African consciousness provide the path for the internal transformation of values and commitment.

ANCIENT KEMET'S (EGYPT'S) SYSTEM OF SELF-CULTIVATION

Ancient Kemet's system of self-cultivation, which was used by mystery system candidates, and initiation is a useful way to continually apply new African values.

INTERNALIZING MAAT (HARMONY, TRUTH AND JUSTICE)

The central goal of political education is to internalize Maat or harmony, truth and justice in our attitudes, thoughts, words, and actions. The system of self-mastery that we will use is derived from the great Kemetic mystery system. Our ancestors understood that we could only raise ourselves to the God level or good level by working on our characters every night. To internalize Maat, it is not enough for us to think and talk Maat day and night, it is also necessary that we live Maat. Like the good farmer, the cultivator of Maat works each day to uproot the weeds of self-hate, the weeds of inconsistency, and the weeds of dishonesty. Through daily cultivation of the character, the farmer of Maat keeps the weeds of disorder under control, and ultimately the follower of Maat uproots the weeds of injustice entirely from his or her character.

THE STEPS OF KEMETIC SELF-CULTIVATION: THE PATH TO SELF MASTERY

Just as the farmer tends to his fields regularly, we must apply Kemet's system of self-mastery every night. Before going to bed each night, we should find a quiet place so that we can commune with ourselves in a three-fold way. Every part of this system is to be said to ourselves it is not to be written down.

> First, we review all of our actions during the day, in the order in which they occurred. As we review each activity of the day, we should make a

mental note of important activities.

Next, we should note our weaknesses, or where we went wrong and what we omitted that we should have done. Then we should review the lessons learned from the day.

Finally, we should spell out our activities for the following day. Our activities should seek to weed out our weaknesses through basing our words and actions on Maat.[64]

This system of self-mastery will not work if we arbitrarily evaluate ourselves according to just any values that may cross our minds. Self-cultivation must be based on eternal divine principles that derive from supreme wisdom. When we apply divine principles to our daily actions, and our daily self-evaluation, we are able to commune with our souls and seek divine directions.

This system of daily self-cultivation is designed to perfect our memories so that they are as perfect as the scales of Maat. In the beginning, many will find it hard to remember everything that happened in the correct order during the course of the day. Through consistently using this system of self-mastery we will sharpen our memories so that it reflects like clear glass. By practicing this system every night we are able to discipline our minds to follow a consistent line of thought without wavering. As we acquire the mastery of our thoughts, we gain the key to mastering our actions. For some, it will be difficult keeping the mind focused on a single path; allowing the mind to wander into detours, away from the path of truth. Through practice we will be able to gain mastery of our minds and be able to discipline ourselves to follow a true path without deviation.

FORTY-TWO CONFESSIONS OF INNOCENCE

Self-cultivation or self-mastery is based on eternal principles. The *Confessions of Innocence* (known as the *Negative Confessions*) provide the central basis for this system of self-cultivation. In selecting central principles from the *Confessions of Innocence*, we should certainly focus on the most basic ones; and should definitely concentrate on the ones that reflect our weaknesses. In reviewing where we went wrong, or where we omitted doing what was right, we can ask ourselves....

> did I speak the truth;
> was I fair in judgments and actions;
> was I arrogant
> or did I display humility in words and actions;

was I evil minded or was my
mind
focused on good;
did I lose my temper or did I
control
my words and actions?

In addition , while we are determining whether we did good or wrong, through commission or ommission we should ask if we have extended reverence to God.

We should also ask ourselves if we have shown respect and love to or parents, our nearest relatives, and our family members.

Also, have we selected friends who are virtuous; have we shown respect for ourselves in public and private; have our actions been based on reason and truth; have we maintained virtue and justice in our words and actions; have we thought before acting?

Self-cultivation is the path to self-mastery. Self-mastery cannot be achieved in a day, a week or a year. To attain self-mastery, we must dedicate ourselves to the life long pursuit of Maat. In so doing, we seek to reflect in our thoughts, words, and actions the God that dwells within.

APPLYING THE KEMETIC SELF-CULTIVATION SYSTEM EVERY NIGHT

Having used this system, I can speak from experience when I say that this system is a powerful tool of self-purification. It is a way to gain self-mastery by being totally honest with yourself. By reviewing your actions and thoughts each night, you are able to stay on top of yourself. As you note excesses, weaknesses or missed opportunities, you condition your mind to correct those mistakes, or oversights. When reviewing your weaknesses be hard on yourself, be self-critical. On the other hand, praise yourself for your strengths. Through identifying your weaknesses and strengths, you are able to develop a constructive course of action.

By correcting your weaknesses and building on your strengths you come to know yourself, and to think the truth, speak the truth, and act the truth. By being true to your inner ideal, you come to live a true and just life. This is the path to self-knowledge, which is the key to all knowledge.

The people who conduct political education sessions should have a personal experience with the cycles of African consciousness, and the Kemetic system of self-cultivation.

GROUND RULES FOR POLITICAL EDUCATION

Care should be taken to select people who are suited for orienting new members. The people who are selected to conduct political education should be disciplined, well-read, hard working, good listeners, and able to fire people up.

ORIENTATION SHOULD ALLOW FOR TWO WAY DISCUSSIONS

Experience indicates that the best political education sessions are two-way sessions where there is a relaxed, balanced, free exchange between those being oriented, and those conducting the orientation.

The best way to open up new members is for those conducting the orientation to open themselves up by showing how the ideology and program have changed their outlook and commitment to struggle for African liberation. Those conducting the orientation should be honest, freely discussing the hang-ups they are facing or have overcome. When new members see that older members are going through the same struggles that they are facing, they will be more willing to open up.

When the cycles of African consciousness are covered, new members should learn the basic political concepts of the organization's historical analysis.

MAKING FRIENDS WITH NEW MEMBERS

Those conducting the orientation should make a special effort to form friendships with the prospective members. Friendship ties are often stronger than ideological commitment, so you have a better chance of holding onto a member if strong bonds of friendship are created. Various social events can be held so that new members can get acquainted with the older members. Every effort should be made to help new members with their personal problems.

One method used by the House of the Lord Church in Brooklyn, New York is the buddy system. New members are paired off with older members who they have something in common with. The buddy is a person with whom the new member feels comfortable, and can talk to about things that they would not discuss with just any member. As Reverend Daughtry, former chairman of the National Black United Front, says, "people don't join organizations, they join people." So one can see that the buddy system allows new members to get support from people they relate to.

The atmosphere of the orientation should also be sociable. Try to get a potluck lunch or dinner going, so you can feed the stomach while you are feeding the mind.

WORK PROJECTS

New members should be encouraged to get involved in organizational work projects before the orientation is completed. The new member's work habits tell you a lot about their seriousness. Those, who only show up occasionally for work during the orientation period can be expected to be inconsistent workers when they become members. Make consistent work, and consistent attendance at political education sessions a condition for membership, since you want consistent members. By having new members work and socialize with other members, a sense of organizational unity is created, and organizational values are reinforced through work. Work projects are the real school for molding organizers, and each new member should be encouraged to work in the area he/she is best suited for.

MEASURING THE EFFECTIVENESS OF POLITICAL EDUCATION

Throughout the political education program the prospective members should be evaluated for positive work habits, internalization of values and ideology, and their personal qualities and skills. A background check should be made of each new member in the early stages of the orientation. At the end of the political education session, the prospective members should be examined to see how well they have understood the areas covered.

POLITICAL EDUCATION FOR NEW NATIONAL BLACK UNITED FRONT MEMBERS

National Black United Front is an organization of individuals some of whom are members of other groups. NBUF is tied together by a statement of principles, a constitution, and local and national programs of action. Each local BUF has the right to shape a political education program that is suited to their needs. Since local BUF's are a part of a national organization there are key national documents that every local will include in their political education program. These include the national constitution and by-laws; the national program of NBUF developed at the national convention; the paper on BUF direction delivered by Reverend Daughtry; the article, "Strategies and Tactics for Building A Mass Based Black United Front," local chapter reports, etc.

Each BUF is empowered to shape their own political education program. However, in developing a Political Education program, local BUF's should be careful not to turn BUF political education into a forum for a particular ideology in the front.

POLITICAL EDUCATION FOR STANDING MEMBERS

Continuous political education is necessary, otherwise standing members will lose sight of organizational objectives and philosophy. The political education program for standing members should be shaped to suit the needs of the organization. One way to shape a political education program for standing members is to develop a questionnaire that asks your members and community people to assess the strengths and weaknesses of the organization. Political education should be shaped to overcome the outstanding weaknesses of the organization.

If your organizational survey shows that the bulk of your standing members are new to the movement, then you may want to bring them up-to-date on the history of the Black liberation movement, the programs and ideologies of different Black groups, and the strengths and weaknesses of movement organizations. If your survey shows that the organization is weak in fundraising and recruitment, you will probably want to shape a training program that trains members in fundraising and recruitment skills.

If a number of your members displays a lack of self-confidence in their ability to defend or push an organizational position, you can set up a training program where members defend the organization's position in debates.

In the case of a BUF that is made up of a mixture of groups and individuals, you can have forums where the different groups explain their positions, and BUF representatives explain the BUF statement of principles and the program for action.

When your members are weak on leadership skills, then you may want to allow them to chair meetings, supervise the work of individual members, and chair committees in the organization.

Political education programs for the new and old members should balance theory with practical work projects. New members should be integrated into the organizational work, and old members should develop projects during the training program that can be used in the organization. An example of this would be fundraising training, where those taking part develop a fundraising program for their local group.

National Black organizations should conduct national and regional training on a regular basis to consolidate the gains of the organization and to overcome outstanding weaknesses. The national Black United Front has developed regional organizing training to overcome major organizational weaknesses. Organizational weaknesses were identified at the third National NBUF convention by having local BUF representatives answer questions pertaining to the strengths and weaknesses of their organizations. Once these questions were answered, a list of strengths and weaknesses was drawn up. Seven areas were listed for regional training based on leading organizational weaknesses. The regional organizing training program covered the following areas:

SAMPLE TRAINING PROGRAM

I. Fundraising

    A. How to organize an effective fundraising program

II. How to recruit new members

    A. Individual
    B. Communication

III. Strategic Planning

    A. Developing program and issues
    B. Building your organization
    C. Developing community support
    D. Building coalitions
    E. Organizational structure
    F. Threats and opportunities

IV. BUF theory and practice

    A How do we define the purpose and makeup of the Black United Front?

    B. What can we learn about what the BUF is and should be from examining our work?

V. Media

A How do you layout a leaflet?
B. How do you write a press release?
C. How do you layout a poster?
D. How do you hold a press conference?
E. How do you layout a newspaper?
F. How do you develop a newsletter?

VI. Internal Security

A How do counterintelligence programs work?
B. How can BUF chapters and NBUF nationally counteract COINTELPRO actions?
C. How to set up BUF security sections locally and nationally.

VII. Organizing

A Leadership development
B. Management skills
C. Community organizing skills
D. Developing community organizing strategies
E. Training and development

The national Black United Front central committee agreed that a local BUF chapter in each region should host the regional training program. In each region, people with organizing skills were identified as regional trainers. They were given the responsibility for identifying specialists in various areas including propaganda, fundraising, security, administration, public speaking, etc.

Regional training programs should be theoretical and practical. Every training session should have a project built into the training with each local BUF representative required to take the local project back to their chapter for implementation. At the next regional training session, the projects would be evaluated.

Regional training programs should not over extend themselves by trying to accomplish more than is possible in a single session. Regional trainers should establish a training agenda and time lines for training. For the first training session three agenda items were outlined for regional training, which were fundraising, recruitment, and theory of BUF. NBUF's move to establish organizing training on the regional and national level shows a maturity for the Black liberation movement.

Regional and national training proposals provide a forum for strengthening local fronts, by spreading out skills and political consciousness to BUF members.

The political education process provides the basis for members internalizing positive African values that create inner transformations enabling members to carryout a struggle for external transformation of their families, communities and society as a whole. The inner cultural transformation of attitudes, thoughts, and behavior patterns from Euro-centric to Afro-centric is the basis for creating consistent members who will be able to organize struggles for African liberation on a long term basis. Political education, which is based on positive African values provides the spiritual and political foundation for New Africans who embody the New African in thoughts, words, and actions. Poltical education is also a vehicle for developing effective organizers who go to the people and work with them to build strong organizational stuctures.

Hannibal

CHAPTER TWELVE

ORGANIZING STRATEGIES

The tools of the organizer resemble the tools of a builder. When the organizer's tools are mastered, and applied, an organizational structure can be erected that stands like a well-built building. A sound organizational foundation rests on solid organizational techniques, just as a well-built building rests on the skills of the builder. In building an organization, the organizer needs to shape a recruitment campaign that defines the type of member the organization needs to carry out its objectives. Once a recruitment campaign is established, arguments should be developed that appeal to the groups you want to organize. When you build your internal organization it is important to establish your community organizing program. In carrying out organizational campaigns, timing is very important. Carefully analyze the position of the Black community and the local power elite to determine the best time to launch a particular offensive. An effective organizing campaign takes advantage of every favorable opportunity that arises during a specific campaign. The organizers of such campaigns shape slogans that mobilize the people into action. Effective organizing also requires that the organizer is a part of the community that is being organized. By becoming a part of the community, the organizer is able to feel the community's pulse. As the organizer masters the tools of organizing, it becomes possible to build strong organizational power in the Black community.

LEARN FROM THE WORLD'S ORGANIZING EXPERIENCES

Good organizers understand that the world is a gigantic classroom. Lessons in effective organizing not only arise from the experience of African people in America, but they also arise from liberation movements in other parts of the world.

The Vietnamese beat the Americans, French, Mongols, and Chinese because they organized a whole people against the common enemy. The people of Guinea Bissau used a similar technique. National liberation struggles have not succeeded because one organization had the power to liberate a whole people; these struggles succeeded because a whole people were organized to liberate themselves.

As a people, we need the vision to see beyond the borders of our own particular group to the broader questions of how we can liberate the race. Organizing our whole people is only possible if our various local and national organizations are strong. So before we can carry out a program to organize our people, we must strengthen what we have, so that we have the organizers, writers, speakers, teachers, economists, soldiers, strategists, and the money we need to implement a broad based organizing campaign.

DEVELOP A RECRUITMENT CAMPAIGN

It is a shame that most of our organizations do not have a systematic recruitment process for bringing in new members. This is especially tragic when our enemy has a program to recruit us into his system as soldiers, cops, etc., and is working daily to place these new recruits into key parts of our organizations. It will not do for us to continue to treat recruitment in a "get what you can get," shabby, haphazard process.

CARRYING OUT A RECRUITMENT CAMPAIGN

Even worse, we cannot sanction the practice of discouraging new membership because the group feels threatened by new members. Some groups feel that because they have developed a few programs that are financially valuable, new members may take these programs over. Other groups have become businesses or other types of institutions that have no overall political concept of how they fit into the long term struggle to liberate our people.

Our political organizations should not be restricted to a select group of Black people. Our organizations should serve as instruments for Black liberation. For these reasons, a well planned recruitment program is required to draw on the broad range of skills of our people.

WHO DO WE WANT TO REACH?

The programs of your organization require specific objectives. You want to recruit members to carry out those objectives. If you want to expand your school, then your recruitment campaign will be directed toward bringing in teachers and parents. If you want to implement a neighborhood organizing campaign, then your recruitment program will be designed to recruit organizers and other back-up people that have the needed skills to execute a community organizing program.

THE KEY QUESTIONS FOR A
SUCCESSFUL RECRUITMENT CAMPAIGN

Once you know the kind of program or programs you want to recruit new members into, then you have to do research to determine the following:

Who do you want to recruit?
Why do you want to do the recruiting?

Where they can be reached?
When is a good time to reach them?[65]

THE UNIQUENESS OF THE GROUP YOU WANT TO RECRUIT

When you have answered the question of who you want to recruit and why you want to recruit them, then determine what is unique about the group you want to reach. The group's uniqueness tells how you can appeal to them. The group's uniqueness becomes the basis for a promotional campaign, which can involve using the full range of publicity, i.e., leafleting, posters, radio, T.V. , personal friends, one-on-one meetings, etc.

To show how this works, let's say that your organization wants to recruit organizers, and your research shows that the unique thing about this group is that they have a history of political struggle and a high political consciousness. Your appeal to this group will be based on your desire to build an organized movement, which will draw on their special organizing skills and political knowledge.

USE THE ONE-ON-ONE APPROACH

Since we know that the most effective way to recruit people is the person-to-person approach, once you have identified an interested person through your persuasion campaign, arrange, home visits with them.

My experience shows that you will have a better chance of establishing personal rapport, and obtaining a personal commitment when these meetings are face-to-face, rather than group meetings.

HOME VISITS

The people who conduct the home visits should establish a relaxed atmosphere by striking up a conversation and getting to know the person they're trying to recruit. It's good to use slides, films, portable chalk boards, newspaper clippings, video tapes, cassettes, brochures, and sections from books to illustrate the persuasion pitch.

Before the meeting ends, the organizer should try to get a commitment from the candidate. Also ask the candidate to recommend other potential recruits: Let the candidate know when your group meets, and invite him or her to attend. A few days after the meeting, follow up on your visit with a phone call, reminding him or her of the meeting and offering a ride, if the candidate needs one.

PERSUASION PITCH SHOULD BE SUITED TO THE NATURE OF YOUR AUDIENCE

Whether you are recruiting through one-on-one meetings, through rallies, leafletting, or the public media, your success will depend on the content of the persuasion pitch. The content of the persuasion pitch is based on who you want to reach. The group you want to reach has special characteristics that you will discover when you study them. These special needs and desires are spoken through the persuasion pitch.

Malcolm X understood how to address his appeal to the audience he wanted to reach:

> I had learned early one important thing, and that was to always teach in terms that the people could understand. Also, where the nationalists whom we had 'fished' were almost all men, among the storefront Christians, a heavy preponderance were women, and I had the sense to offer something special to them. 'Beautiful Black woman! The Honorable Elijah Muhammed teaches us that the Black man is going around saying he wants respect; well, the Black man never will get anybody's respect until he first learns to respect his own women! The Black man needs today to stand up and throw off the weaknesses imposed upon him by the slave master white

man! The Black man needs
to start today to shelter and
protect and respect his Black
woman![66]

To sisters, Malcolm stressed the things
important to them: the need for the Black
man to respect them, and recognize their
beauty. As he developed, Malcolm linked
up the progress and consciousness of sisters
with the progress and consciousness of the
race. To Black youth, Malcolm spoke about
not being afraid of the odds, and about
being thoroughly fed up with the American
system. To Black Christians, Malcolm spoke,
telling them that they did not catch hell
because they were Christians, reminding
them they caught hell because they were
Black. Wherever he spoke, Malcolm tuned
his message to the audience he was
speaking to. This is the art of persuasion. The
good organizer should know his audience
and should shape his appeal to the needs
and interests of the particular audience.

Defining what is unique about the
people you want to recruit, and developing
a good persuasion pitch are necessary; but it
is also important to determine where they
can be reached, as well as how they can
be reached. Often good techniques are
developed from trial and error methods.
Failure is often the mother of success.
Malcolm X's organizing experiences are very
useful in this regard.

LOCATE YOUR AUDIENCE

In the mid-fifties, Malcolm was trying to organize a Muslim Mosque in Harlem. His efforts were not producing great results. At each Mosque meeting, Malcolm was able to get only a few people to step forward to join the nation. After a while Malcolm began to figure out why he was having such poor results:

> I think I was all the angrier with my own ineffectiveness because I knew the streets. I had to get myself together and think out the problem. And the big trouble, obviously, was that we were only one among the many voices of Black discontent on every busy Harlem corner. The different nationalist groups, the 'Buy Black!' forces, and others like that; dozens of their step-ladder orators were trying to increase their followings. I had nothing against anyone trying to promote independence and unity among Black men, but they still were making it tough for Mr. Muhammed's voice to be heard.[67]

Malcolm's ability to coolly assess the reasons for his failure enabled him to develop a recruitment program that was designed to overcome these weaknesses. Since a large variety of competing nationalist's groups were the problem, Malcolm developed strategies in order to use these groups to his advantage:

> In my first effort to get over this hurdle, I had some little leaflets printed. There wasn't a much-traveled Harlem street corner that five or six good Muslim brothers and I missed. We would step right in front of a walking Black man or woman so that they had to accept our leaflet, and if they hesitated one second, they had to hear us saying some catchy thing such as 'Hear how the white man kidnapped and robbed and raped our Black race --'[68]

With the leaflet and some soulful talk, Malcolm began to zero in on the nationalist's meetings. Malcolm's organizing methods would begin to work because he defined who he wanted to recruit, why he wanted to recruit them, and where they could be reached.

> Next, we went to work 'fishing' on those Harlem corners -- on the fringes of the nationalist meetings. The method today has many refinements, but

then it consisted of working the always shifting edges of the audiences that others had managed to draw. At a nationalist meeting, everyone who was listening was interested in the revolution of the Black race. We began to get visible results almost immediately after we began thrusting handbills in people's hands, 'Come to hear us too, brother. The Honorable Elijah Muhammed teaches us how to cure the Black man's spiritual, mental, moral, economic, and political sicknesses --'69

ZERO IN ON YOUR SYMPATHETIC AUDIENCE

Malcolm's method began to work because he went where a sympathetic audience was, and he appealed to the nationalist beliefs. In time he discovered that religious-minded Black people were the best types to recruit:

I saw the new faces at our Temple Seven meetings. And then we discovered the best 'fishing' audience of all, by far the best conditioned audience for Mr.

Muhammed's teachings: the Christian churches.

Our Sunday services were held at 2 p.m. All over Harlem during the hour or so before the Christian church services were dismissing we by-passed the larger churches with their higher ratio of so-called 'middle class' Negroes who were so full of pretense and 'status' that they wouldn't be caught in our little storefront.

We went 'fishing' fast and furiously when those little Evangelical storefront churches each let out their thirty to fifty people on the sidewalk. 'Come to hear us brother and sister --' 'You haven't heard anything until you have heard the teachings of the Honorable Elijah Muhammed --' These congregations were usually southern migrant people, usually older, who would go anywhere to hear what they called 'good preaching.'[70]

WORKINIG SUPPORTIVE AUDIENCES

Malcolm appealed to what storefront-type Blacks wanted to hear -- some good down home preaching. Since the Nation was a religious organization they could appeal to religious-minded Black people. By drawing on the storefront churches Malcolm was reaching a larger audience, and he was able to bring in Blacks who were usually new to Black Nationalism. The Black person who was religious-minded and new to nationalism would not hold conflicting ideas on nationalism that some of the other Black nationalists held.

As Malcolm noted, the method of going to the sympathetic audience to recruit has "many refinements." Black bookstores, for example, are good recruiting centers because most of the customers are culturally aware and open to political appeal. You can assign organizers to mingle with the people in Black bookstores. They can use the books that customers are interested in to strike up political conversations. When possible, get a good member who reads a lot and has an open personality to work in some of these stores. They can use their position to develop contacts and to spread the word about your organization.

Outdoor rallies and political conferences are also good recruitment centers. You can set up a booth at outdoor rallies, and pass out literature on the organization. When possible, get a speaker from your organization on the program and use the platform to push your group. While your speaker is talking, it is good to have organizers mingling with the audience, passing out leaflets. The same technique works well at political conferences. One word of caution, however, avoid the common practice of disrespecting other organization's functions by just using them to recruit. When you can, help with the planning of the program, or volunteer to assist with the security, and offer to help clean up when the program is over.

A good way to recruit is to create a working relationship with other organizations in the Black community. Make a point of letting speakers from other groups make announcements or speeches at your meetings. Get these groups to allow you to do the same thing.

Today, while Black Studies programs are under attack, they are still an important center of consciousness raising. If some of your members are college students, then encourage them to form Pan African Student Unions or Black Student Unions. Allow the student group to operate independently on the campus, but encourage them to recruit and raise money for the organization. Black student unions on high school campuses are also good areas for recruitment. Black bookstores, rallies, conferences, and other community organizations and Black studies programs are all places where people interested in Black nationalism congregate.

All are excellent places to recruit. A strong recruitment program enables you to build a strong membership that can return to the Black community to organize on a mass level.

COMMUNITY ORGANIZING TECHNIQUES

In developing an organizing campaign or strategy, you should carefully study the enemy's strong and weak points domestically and internationally, so that you can time your organizing campaigns to take advantage of favorable local, national, and international conditions. By taking advantage of favorable conditions you increase the chance of success.

TIMING, THE VIETNAMESE EXPERIENCE

Picking the most favorable time for political campaigns is particularly important to small nations and to people who are fighting an enemy who is numerically and technologically stronger than they are. The Vietnamese have a long fighting tradition that has been shaped in struggles against larger and stronger enemies. To achieve victory against numerically and technologically stronger enemies the Vietnamese have learned to use every element to their advantage. One of the most important weapons the Vietnamese have learned to use is time.

When planning political campaigns, the Vietnamese leadership carefully analyzed the local, national and international situations. Major military and political campaigns were timed for execution during periods when their enemy was weakest internationally, nationally, and locally.

Two examples of their expert use of timing were the Vietnamese offensive against the Japanese toward the end of World War II, and the offensive against the American-backed South Vietnamese army after U.S. ground forces withdrew. In the first case, the National Liberation Front timed their offensive against the Japanese, to start when the Japanese had been defeated internationally by the U.S. The National Liberation Front was assured of victory because they launched their offensive when the Japanese had reached their weakest point internationally, militarily and politically. In the second case, the National Liberation Front's military offensive was timed to follow the peace agreement with the U.S., and the withdrawl of U.S. ground forces. The South Vietnamese puppet government no longer had a large U.S. ground force to do the fighting. They had to stand on their own. Consequently, the National Liberation Front ran over this corrupt military force with lightening speed. In a very short period of time Vietnam was unified, many of us witnessed the televised spectacle of Vietnamese puppets rushing to get out of Vietnam with their American masters.

TIMING, THE ANTI-APARTHEID MOVEMENT

The anti-apartheid movement timed their campaign against the Reagan backed constructive engagement policy at an opportune time, when the United States had openly allied itself with the racist government of South Africa. Under this insulting policy of constructive engagement, the Reagan administration had encouraged South Africa to support reactionary groups in Angola and Mozambique. The MNR (Movement for National Resistance), a South African-created group, received South African and American financial support for its campaign of terror and sabotage directed against the government and people of Mozambique. UNITA (Union for the Total Independence of Angola) received South African financial and military support, while the Reagan administration openly endorsed and financed the movement's campaign of terror, which had often been coordinated with the South African military against the people and government of Angola.

South Africa, following America's lead, insisted that Cuban soldiers be withdrawn from Angola as a condition for Namibian independence. Famine in Mozambique combined with pressure from terrorists (MNR) supported by South Africa, led the government of Mozambique to sign the Nkomati accords. The Nkomati accords required that the South African freedom fighters be expelled from Mozambique. In exchange, South Africa promised to withdraw support for the MNR. South Africa also promised economic assistance to Mozambique in exchange for compliance with this accord. Mozambique quickly moved to comply with the agreement by expelling African National Congress officials and members. Nevertheless, the South African government continues to support the MNR against the Mozambique government and people. Angola on the other hand, along with Cuba has negotiated an agreement with the South African government that calls for withdrawal of South African forces from Angolan and the independence of Namibia.

Constructive engagement, military attacks on the governments of Angola and Mozambique, and the Nkomati agreements are all part of an American-orchestrated policy that is designed to give South Africa time to clean up its international image and to shore up its military defenses by depriving South African freedom fighters of military and political support areas in Mozambique and Angola.

Inside South Africa the apartheid government has attempted to divide Blacks, coloreds, and Asians, and gain recognition for the regime, by allowing coloreds and Asians to participate in a white-controlled government. Blacks in South Africa have been excluded from government participation on the dubious premise that Blacks are a part of separate tribal homelands that just happen to be located in arid regions of South Africa.

Black South African workers and students, over a million strong, carried out a general strike on November 5-6, 1984. The apartheid government came down heavy on the movement by arresting 21 trade union leaders, and executing military raids on Black townships, where many Blacks were killed, and thousands arrested.

The Reagan administration closed its eyes to this terrible repression, hypocritically claiming that the white apartheid regime was making progress. Reagan's re-election gave new assurances to the apartheid regime of continued American support.

It is within this international and domestic background that a revived anti-apartheid movement arose out of the Black movement in the United States. Sit-ins, arrests, and mass demonstrations swept the country, occurring in Washington, D.C., New York, Boston, Chicago, Los Angeles, Houston, and Seattle. In San Francisco and Oakland, Black dock workers, members of the ILWU (International Longshoremens Union), refused to unload goods shipped from South Africa.

THE IMPACT OF A WELL TIME ANTI-APARTHEID CAMPAIGN ON REAGAN

These demonstrations were time to coincide with the re-election of Ronald Reagan, and with the anti-apartheid resistance in South Africa. The timing and scope of these demonstrations were so effective that they forced the Reagan administration to voice criticism of the apartheid policies. The South Africa government, feeling the heat of international criticism, was forced to release some of the South African brothers and sisters. These demonstrations validated the Pan African solidarity that existed between Africans 'at home and abroad.' They also showed that electoral struggles must not be the sole arena of struggle. Struggles in the streets, around domestic and international issues, must be tied to electoral struggles that enable us to use reformist programs to build an independent base of power.

THE ECONOMIC CLIMATE OF CONTRACTION

Domestically, the contracting economy has brought the "new right" out of every crack and corner. The gains of the sixties have been largely wiped out, and the American economy is undergoing the most serious crisis since the Great Depression. A number of major corporations, are on the verge of collapse, and unemployment among Blacks is at depression levels.

The major weakness of the U.S. government at this stage, is that it has created major opposition to its policies among large sections of Blacks, other Third World groups, and some sections of the white population. For the first time since the Great Depression, the American power structure has cut out or reduced a larger number of pacifiers that control political struggles. CETA, poverty programs, part of the food stamp program, Medicare, and social programs have either been destroyed or gutted. Large sectors of the Black community have been seriously hurt by Reaganomics. General hardships create conditions that we can organize around, locally and nationally.

TIMING, THE 1984 JESSE JACKSON PRESIDENTIAL BID

The 1984 Jesse Jackson presidential bid, and the Rainbow Coalition were also well-timed campaigns designed to organize the discontent of Blacks and the poor into a powerful mass movement. Black people rallied to the Jackson campaign precisely because it provided an alternative to the right wing repression of Reagan, and the racist policies of the Democratic party.

The Jesse Jackson campaign raised important issues, including voting rights enforcement, full employment, peace and disarmament, issues concerning a foreign policy that opposes the racist regime of

South Africa, and calls for a policy that supports the people of Africa, the Middle East, Central and South America. Jackson has opposed U.S. intervention in Grenada, El Salvador, Nicaragua, and Lebanon. He has proposed a shift in spending away from defense to social programs, and he has favored the Equal Rights Amendment. In massive numbers, Blacks at the grass roots level backed Jesse Jackson's independent bid. Many Black people, who were too young to take part in the struggles of the sixties, joined this struggle. Others, who had withdrawn from struggle, reentered the arena of political struggle. The struggle around the ballot box has become the way to involve millions of Black people in a new wave of political struggle. In some instances, this campaign succeeded in bringing into the campaign other Third World groups and whites.

The Jackson campaign was being used by many organizers from progressive and revolutionary groups to raise the level of consciousness of our people, preparing the groundwork for another more militant phase of political struggle. The discontent created by the Reagan administration, and the hard times caused by the contracting economy, and continuing racism, has paved the way for a new phase of political struggle. As good organizers, you have to take timely advantage of campaigns such as this to increase your allies, deepen your political experience, and gain new resources (larger mailing lists, and more permanent precinct structures).

TAKE ADVANTAGE OF YOUR CONDITIONS TO TIME YOUR ORGANIZING CAMPAIGNS

As organizers, you have to be creative, taking advantage of the present conditions to broaden your base among our people. There are numerous issues, internationally, nationally, and locally, but you have to be creative enough to build on these issues, and exploit them. Timing your campaign to take advantage of important international, national, and local issues can be the key to success.

THE STEP-BY-STEP METHOD OF ORGANIZING

During the present period, as during every period of struggle, use the step-by-step method of organizing to achieve every objective you possibly can out of every struggle or campaign. Plan ahead and try to anticipate and exploit every conceivable opportunity. The Vietnamese mastered the step-by-step method of organizing, and took advantage of many favorable economic, political, and military conditions to defeat the French and the Americans. Le Duan describes how the Vietnamese applied the "step by step" process:

While keeping firmly in mind the revolutionary goal, the art of revolutionary leadership lies in knowing how to win judiciously step by step.

Throughout the long road leading to the final goal, one should never fail to consider the concrete conditions of the struggle in each period. When and in what circumstances are the masses going into action? How are the various social forces aligned? What are the enemy's strong and weak points? How is he maneuvering and what are his aims? Lenin used to demand that the Communists carefully study and view with the greatest objectivity not only the situation at home but also all elements of international economics and politics, and the relation between all class forces within their country and throughout the world. Without taking full notice of all these factors of changing concrete reality a revolutionary may at best perceive the ultimate objective of the struggle, but he will have no command over the means to achieve it. He will not find the ways, methods, and practical means to reach that goal and may commit serious errors in his strategic and tactical guidance of the revolution.

Knowing how to win step by step in a judicious manner means that in various situations one sets the most appropriate concrete laws, directs the fight in such a way as to achieve the maximum success. This approach paves the way for further revolutionary advances and opens up certain prospects for ultimate victory. These steps have been taken in our revolution.[71]

APPLYING THE STEP-BY-STEP METHOD TO THE 1984 JESSE JACKSON PRESIDENTIAL CAMPAIGN

The Jackson campaign provides a good case study for determining how the masses are going into action; how the various social forces are aligned; what the enemy's strong and weak points are, and how he is moving; as well as the economic and political situation internationally and domestically.

In the first 1984 Jesse Jackson campaign, a split occurred within the national Black establishment leadership.   the National Baptist Convention, the largest Black church structure in America, stood solidly behind Jackson, a Baptist minister. Black churches across the country, especially in the south, provided a powerful base of political, moral, and financial support for Jesse. You can say a whole lot when the most influential leaders on the local level, Black ministers, say, "God is on our side." On the other side, a number of big city Black mayors declared their support for Walter Mondale. These included Wilson Goode of Philadelphia, Andrew Young of Atlanta, Coleman Young of Detroit, Tom Bradley of Los Angeles, Arrington of Birmingham, and Lionel Wilson of Oakland. Many within this group were close friends of Jesse Jackson, but they felt bound to support the candidacy of the likely Democratic presidential nominee. Added to this split against Jackson among Black politicians, were a number of opponents within the national Black civil rights leadership, including Benjamin Hooks of the NAACP, Coretta Scott King, and taking a more neutral stance, the Southern Christian Leadership Conference.

It is because of this split that the involvement of the militant forces within the Black community were particularly important. Groups such as the National Black United Front, the Nation of Islam, and others were able to carve out significant roles in the campaign because of this split within the national Black establishment leadership. The Black masses supported the Jackson challenge against the Democratic party, the Reagan administration, and the Black establishment. On the local and national levels, the Black establishment felt the heat of mass Black anger when the people demanded that their leadership get behind the Jackson campaign. In Chicago, when Mayor Harold Washington first took a neutral position on the Jackson campaign, and later said he had a preference for Jackson, the masses started asking "Why isn't the Mayor supporting Jesse?" This mass pressure and local political realities (the mayor's effort to oust white control of the Democratic machine), forced him to support Jackson.

What we shouldn't forget is that the 1984 split between Jackson and the national Black establishment was only temporary. When the democratic presidential nominee was selected, Jesse's national opponents joined with him in a campaign to elect Mondale. Ultimately, after this election was over, we had to prepare for the old business as usual game, where the national Black establishment attempts to lock the militant leadership out of major leadership positions.

THE ELECTORAL STRATEGY'S NECESSARY BUT NOT SUFFICIENT

The problem facing the Black establishment leadership is that the defeat of

Mondale discredits a purely electoral politics strategy. Such a strategy is discredited because both the Democratic and the Republican party have embraced a conservative patriotic platform which does not speak to opposition to apartheid or to poverty in the U.S. This stance of both parties dictates that all of the organizing eggs not be placed in the electoral basket. Instead, campaigns launched from the streets against poverty, Black urban removal, run-down housing, unemployment, miseducation, police violence, etc., must be tied to electoral campaigns. We must organize outside the electoral arena, and within the political arena in order to revive our movement, and to develop a revolutionary power base for the masses of Black people.

Unlike the late 1960s, when the system used electoral politics as a way to replace the militant Black leadership with moderates, today the electoral arena has become an area of struggle, which is helping to revive a spirit of mass struggle. As Pan African Nationalist's we have to use this arena to gain new supporters and needed resources, while not placing our primary emphasis there. Through applying the step-by-step process, we have to develop transitional programs that enable us to use the electoral arena and street action to radicalize the Black population, while getting them to see that fundamental changes will not be achieved through the system. Such a consciousness will only arise through experience with the electoral system. The step-by-step system can be applied to every phase of organizing.

GETTING EVERYTHING OUT OF A CAMPAIGN

For example, if you are carrying out an economic boycott, get everything out of the campaign possible. Get as many jobs as possible, increase your allies, and broaden your base among the people by providing jobs. More important, be alert and take advantage of every favorable opportunity that presents itself at a particular moment.

ORGANIZE ON ALL LEVELS

In assessing the enemy's strengths and weaknesses, we must put ourselves in positions so that we know his plans and intentions. This means that our organizers or supporters should be everywhere the enemy is. They should be in all areas of the government, in the court system, on every level of the university, in the hospitals, in the factories, in the construction sites , in the welfare department, the juvenile system, the prisons, etc. By being in all of these places, we are able to assess the enemy's plans, and we can also use our positions to provide valuable resources and assistance to the struggle.

DEFINE A ROLE FOR EVERYONE

Unfortunately, your limited number of organizers may not be experienced enough to use the skills of Blacks that are located in all of these various strategic positions. As an organizer, you are prone to expect every supporter to be a dyed-in-the-wool revolutionary, who either gives all to the struggle, or becomes a suspect. You have to reach a level of sophistication where you see that there must be specialization in the movement. You need people in the movement who do only one thing. That one thing may involve keeping you informed of the policies of the welfare department, pushing information about our movement among students, or letting you know when a job is available. As an organizer, you have to develop the skill to follow up on the minute detail of people's work. You also have to use arguments, slogans and propaganda, to prepare the people for organizing campaigns.

PROPAGANDA SLOGANS AND ACTION SLOGANS

Slogans are very important because they educate the people and give them strategic and day-to-day guidance. Slogans fall into two categories, propaganda slogans and action slogans.

Propaganda slogans arouse consciousness, but they do not call for a specific campaign or program of action. The slogans "Black Power," "Black is

Beautiful," or "We are an African people," are all examples of propaganda slogans. They were not designed to launch a specific campaign for specific demands; instead they helped to create a positive "Black" and "Pan African" consciousness, which encouraged Black self-help and Black nationalist efforts. A campaign like the San Francisco State Strike, or an organization like the Black Panther Party, could take advantage of the positive atmosphere created by such powerful propaganda slogans.

ACTION SLOGANS

Action slogans, on the other hand, point to some specific action. We have to be careful not use action slogans that we can't back up. "Pick up the Gun," and "Off the Pig," were two action slogans that a lot of young Blacks took very seriously. The problem was that these two action slogans were adventuristic and set up a lot of young Blacks for the police kill. The Black liberation movement was not prepared to carry such action slogans out. These slogans were also unwise examples of "fat mouthing," that exposed a lot of Blacks to unnecessary attacks. Action slogans should be carefully chosen, and they should help to clarify the goals of the movement by helping to actively push the struggle forward.

TALK FACTS AND ISSUES NOT IDEOLOGY

Propaganda slogans, short or long articles, leaflets, word of mouth conversations, all help to mobilize thoughts. Organizers should link up as many issues as possible to show how a single issue i.e., police brutality, ties into how a brutal colonial system uses the police to keep us in our place with force and violence while it protects the property of the "white power structure." Good propaganda should be stripped of all the old sterile cliches and should, in plain simple language, show that the system is not designed to produce freedom, as Malcolm said, "no more then a chicken is designed to produce a duck egg." Good propaganda should also put forward positive alternatives.

THE SPOKEN WORD

The spoken word is the most important weapon in the organizer's possession. Personal communication is more influential than impersonal leaflets, posters, radio, or TV interviews. Through talking and exchanging ideas, we can get people to think. Argument is a way to mobilize thought and to get people to question the slyness and viciousness of the system.

The organizer's words cannot be separated from the organizer's actions. A good organizer should have a good character, (be principled and honest in action, and moral in behavior) and should be skilled in arousing the people. If an organizer has a good tongue, but a shady reputation, then the people will not respect him/her.

Organizing requires patience. People do not change their ideas overnight. Transformation of thought and behavior patterns is gradual. As an organizer, you should patiently follow up on each person, and repeat the message you are pushing over and over again. The power of persuasion lies in repetition and in giving new, soulful examples of your ideas.

To be persuasive, you have to feel deeply about the condition of the people in much the same way that a mother feels for her child. Like a good mother, a good organizer feels the pain and suffering, the joys and hopes of the people. Malcolm was an excellent organizer because he experienced the pain of the people and his words were filled with our people's anger and hope.

ARGUMENTS

Malcolm combined emotion with sharp logic. This is the strength of new African culture, which combines emotion with reason, leaving the listener with a soulful message.

TUNE YOUR ARGUMENTS TO YOUR AUDIENCE

To have effect, the arguments should be tuned to each audience. Like Malcolm, a good organizer should be able to tune his or her arguments into a specific group, showing them how the struggle benefits them. The message of self-help should be broken down so that it is understood by each group. To Black Christians, one favorite argument is "God helps those who help themselves," so the Bible says. God is tired of hearing Negroes beg him for help, when they are doing nothing to help themselves.

To the middle class Blacks you can say: most of our educated people have been educated to look up to the Greeks and Romans and to look down on the African. This kind of education has led most among this group to turn their backs on the race. We are working to unite all classes of Black people, because as long as the mass of Blacks are on the bottom there is a good chance that your children will be on the bottom.

To brothers and sisters, who work for a living, and in large numbers make up the working poor, you can say: for too long we have been taught that only the Black person with a degree is somebody. What we have to realize is that the heroes of our community are those who feed their families and raise their children. Most of the great movements of our race have been pushed forward, usually led by Black farmers, Black carpenters, Pullman porters, janitors, and working, or out of work, members of our community who wanted a better life for their families. Of course, these are only a few examples, but you can use your creativity to shape your arguments to suit the person or group you are talking to.

ORGANIZE EVERYWHERE

A good organizer organizes everywhere. You organize on the bus, in the bar, poolroom, on the streets, in the church, in the school, at a party, in jail, in the military, or while you are getting your hair cut. While you are riding on the bus sit next to a brother or sister and without identifying yourself as a member of an organization, start a discussion about a newspaper article or a television program. The article or television program may be about a drug-related killing in the Black community. Use this article to discuss the relationship between the Mafia, the police and the government as a whole. Talk about how drugs are used all over the world to destroy revolutionary consciousness. Point out how drugs were shot into the Black community after the rebellions of the sixties, to kill the consciousness of Black youth.

As you circulate in the bars or at a party, get a lively discussion going around a particular issue. Black people are thirsty for conversation and friendship, and such discussions help to arouse consciousness. Barber shops and beauty parlors are two central communication centers in the Black community. Develop good relationships with the barber shop and beauty parlor owners, so that you can distribute information and put some ideas into people's minds while they are getting their hair done.

SURVEYS

A number of religious groups effectively use the door-to-door technique to survey community thinking. Surveys are good for indentifying key issues, that you can organize around. Through door-to-door work, you can let people know what your group is doing and what kind of services you can provide to them. Door-to-door work is good for identifying potential support and skills in the neighborhood.

FIT INTO YOUR COMMUNITY

As a good organizer you should learn from nature. Everything in nature fits into its environment. The deer fits in the forest and uses the trees and grass for camouflage. The fish fits into the sea and uses the natural environment of the water. Even a roach know how to fit into the cracks and corners of your kitchen. If the deer, the fish, and even the roach knows how to fit into their environment, then you and I should know how to fit into our environment. Our community is our living environment; where we work is our working environment.

As a good organizer you should fit into your community like a deer fits into a forest, or a fish fits into the sea. Black people are our forest and our ocean, and yes the cracks and corners where we may have to hide.

JOIN OTHER COMMUNITY GROUPS

If you want to last as an organizer, and have influence within your community, then you must have your community's support. You get community support by being consistent, honest, supportive of community struggles, flexible, able to form alliances and coalitions with other organizations, and through joining other community groups.

You should determine which organizations are the most significant in your community, and which can serve to support your work. Depending upon your resources, join some of these organizations and support the positive things that they are doing. Let other groups see that you value their contribution.   Create the kind of dependence where the community sees an attack on you or your organization as an attack on them.

IMPROVISE

Above all, you should follow the example of the so-called jazz (New African) musician. Improvise, be flexible, and creative. Learn to use what you've got to get what you need; and above all develop an overall organizing plan, which can be modified as you put it into practice. Use you base area as a laboratory to test and refine strategies before they are applied to the entire Black community.

DON'T OVEREXTEND YOURSELF

Community organizations should beware of the danger of overextending their organizing efforts, and accomplishing little or nothing. Carefully evaluate your organization's capacity, and try not to take on more than you can handle. Most small organizations overwork their small memberships, creating morale problems, and high membership turnovers.

SELECT A MANAGEABLE
GEOGRAPHICAL AREA

Most national groups target specific cities for chapter building, but they usually don't target a specific geographic area within these cities.

Community organizations, on the other hand, usually operate out of specific neighborhoods, but most do not develop a systematic campaign to organize the neighborhood they are based in. Our organizations must have a base of support. In building a base, select a geographical area that is large enough for your members to handle. The area you select may be close to your headquarters, or it may be where a number of your members live. The criteria you use for selecting a specific area will have a lot to do with the objectives you want to achieve.

CIRCULATE IN YOUR NEIGHBORHOOD

When a neighborhood or larger geographical area is selected, your members should circulate, identifying and making contact with every community group, church, Black business, etc., in the area. Through door-to-door work, and mingling with the people in the bars, pool halls, barber shops, beauty parlors, and community businesses, your organizers should get a feel for the pulse of the neighborhood. By living and mingling with the people, you can determine burning issues of the neighborhood.

SELECT MASS ISSUES

Out of all the issues that the people talk about, your group should select an issue that you can win. If the issue is jobs, you may want to select an employer you can beat; or you want to organize a cooperative business that the community will support.

A campaign around a popular winning issue is a good way to establish a visible, developing, organizational base in a specific geographical location.

Your base is a laboratory to test strategies that can later be used in the larger Black community. For the test to be meaningful, you need to develop an overall organizing plan that can be modified as you put it into practice.

BLOCK ORGANIZING STRUCTURE

Successful national liberation movements that have been organized in different parts of the world, teach us that the block or cell is the structure for organizing a "whole people." Wherever the block organizing structure has been used on a national level, it has been impossible for the West to defeat these movements. Defeat has proven impossible because the West has had to fight a whole people who have drowned the best-equipped Western armies in a sea of "people's power."

ADAPT THE BLOCK STRUCTURE TO YOUR SITUATION

Those liberation movements that have failed (and there very few, i.e., the Mau Mau in Kenya, and the Malaysian movement) failed because they were attacked by the British before they could organize a cell structure and a political party on a national level. For us, it should be clear that a well organized city is not enough. Our cities and rural areas must be linked up on a national basis. If not, the national government will move on us separately and rip our structures apart.

The kind of block structure that is being proposed here is the legal type, which uses a wide range of legal tactics to organize our people against racist oppression. In initiating a block structure, study your base area to see how workable the approach is. If you live in a rural area, where Black people live far apart, you may want to establish road committees. If some areas have housing projects arranged in a large number of blocks, you may want to establish project organizers. Where there are a number of existing block organizations in your area, it might be practical for a few of your members to join some of the block committees to develop working relationships that will help you to organize the unorganized blocks. Each situation will require a creative approach. The suggestions offered here are an approach that has to be creatively applied to each individual situation. When starting to organize block committees, you can use your experience to shape an overall block organizing plan, or you can develop an overall plan before you start organizing. In either case, the plan will undergo many revisions as you put it into practice. At some point you will need an overall plan that ties individual blocks into a larger system. Your organizers should be trained to follow a unified system, but they should also be encouraged to put forward ideas to improve the system. An overall, coherent system prevents block committees from becoming a series of separate, and at times conflicting, systems. A series of disconnected blocks frustrates the very purpose of the block-by-block system, which is to provide organizational power for Black people at the grass roots level, so that the people can strike out against the local, national, and international power structure.

THE ORGANIZATIONAL LEVELS OF THE BLOCK STRUCTURE

A comprehensive block structure should have a number of levels. On the city level, there is the central committee of the local organization or Black United Front organizing the block committees. Below the central committee level, there is a district or ward level. Below this level is the neighborhood level. Last is the block committee.

THE CENTRAL COMMITTEE

The central committee is the body that develops the overall block organizing plan. It trains the initial body of organizers that initiate the plan, and it provides training and coordination for district organizers. For the committee structure of the central committee, see STRATEGIES AND TACTICS FOR BUILDING A MASS BASED BLACK UNITED FRONT.

The central committee serves as the policy making body for the city-wide block structure. For this block structure to be effective, a balance has to be struck between those decisions that have to be finalized on a higher level, and those that can be made on the block. One important consideration is whether the program or issue requires neighborhood or district wide cooperation to carry out. If it does, then neighborhood or district committees should have the final say-so. Where the action affects only a particular block, then the block committee should have the power to carry out those decisions without higher approval. It is important to make this distinction because the greatest amount of democracy should be encouraged. This is the best way to unleash the people's creative initiative.

ESTABLISHING DISTRICT AND NEIGHBORHOOD BOUNDARIES

In establishing the boundaries for districts, neighborhoods, and blocks, develop practical criteria. Practical criteria should include but not be limited to:

> The workable size of the area for organizers.

> Natural ethnic and social groupings in the area.

> Income level within the geographical areas.

Transportation routes which help to create a sense of community.

Location of churches, schools, businesses, and local community groups.

Business and shopping centers within the neighborhoods.

Political precinct boundaries.

Redevelopment agency plans for your area.[72]

THE TOP-DOWN AND BOTTOM-UP APPROACH

There are two basic approaches for setting up a block organizing structure. One is from the top-down, and the other is from the bottom up. In the top-down approach you can organize neighborhood conferences where residents discuss problems and identify people and organizations who are interested in organizing neighborhood, district, and block structures.

The other way is to start from the bottom, organizing on a block by block basis. A block committee could be established in your base area. Once you have organized a block, you could use some activist from your block to establish other block committees. Once a sufficient number of blocks are organized, you can set up a neighborhood council.

THE TOP-DOWN APPROACH

The top-down approach works when you have enough money to hire a staff to carry out a large scale organizing effort, or when you have a hot national or local issue that can be used to bring a lot of different Black folks together. Sometimes the top-down and the bottom-up approaches can run together. The first Jesse Jackson presidential campaign can be seen as an example of these approaches running side-by-side. In many areas of the country the grassroots have cried out "Run Jesse Run." At the same time, some of the progressive local and statewide Black leadership has attempted to impose a structure and leadership on the grassroots.

The danger of the top-down approach is that it discourages the people from using their creativity by making them dependent on direction from the top. Whether the people's creativity and power is unleashed also depends on whether the top leadership wants to build a base of power for the people or for themselves.

THE BOTTOM-UP APPROACH

The bottom-up approach is a slower approach and is the one easiest to use if you lack money and a sizable body of organizers. This approach also has the greatest potential for encouraging the people to rely on their own ideas and power.

QUALITIES OF BLOCK COMMITTEE MEMBERS

In STRATEGIES AND TACTICS, I suggest that members of the block committee should be selected on the basis of their activist orientation. Ideally, members of the block committee should be representative of the people who live on the block. Where possible, you should have an activist mother, father, youth, and elder. If this is not possible, build the block on the committed people on the block, irrespective of their social background.

THE ROLE OF ACTIVISTS ON THE BLOCK AND DECISION MAKING

Everyone who lives on a block will not belong to the block committee. The activists on the block, who will be few in number, will make up the block committee. There committees are broken down into various subcommittees that are necessary for the block to operate. Once the block committee meets and comes up with ideas for action, they should call a meeting of the block to discuss the proposal. If the people on the block go along with the decision, then the proposal should be put into motion. If they do not, then through give and take, an agreement should be reached based on consensus. Where a consensus cannot be reached, either work to reshape your proposal to meet the objections that have been made, or if the majority agree that the issue is an urgent one that requires immediate action, then push for a majority vote.

Once a consensus is reached or the block is bound by that decision, the block committee should be strict in seeing that block decisions are enforced.

The block committee is the base of the struggle. Institutions will be able to build a mass base when a block structure exists. The block structure is the unit that can mobilize a whole people around specific campaigns. The block committee is the collective wisdom of the people. "It sees all" and "knows all." Build solid block structures and you have the best intelligence system in the world.

Once you have established a sufficient number of blocks, you are ready to organize your neighborhood council. Your block plan should spell out how many delegates will be allowed to vote in neighborhood elections. Delegates will be allowed to vote in neighborhood elections. Delegates to the neighborhood conference elect neighborhood council representatives.

Neighborhood councils are responsible for maintaining communication with the blocks in its jurisdiction. Neighborhood newsletters, that carry block news are a good way. of maintaining communication with the blocks. Neighborhood-wide issues or programs are decided by the neighborhood council after they are discussed by the various block clubs.

ORGANIZING DISTRICT COUNCILS

When enough neighborhood councils are formed, you can form a district council. The district can be organized the same way that the neighborhood council is organized. In your plan you should determine how many votes the neighborhood councils have in the district council.

ORGANIZING THE CENTRAL COMMITTEE

Once this structure is fully developed, the district councils should be able to elect some of its members to the central committee. This procedure, of course, violates the left concept of democratic centralism. The violation arises from there being more centralism than democracy. By making it possible for the most serious, politically aware organizer to rise from the bottom to the top, you reduce elitism and factionalism.

THE BLOCK STRUCTURE AS THE BASIS FOR DEVELOPING COLLECTIVE LEADERSHIP

This type of structure should be a part of a national plan, which is structured along local, state, regional, and national lines. When this kind of structure exists, you will have true collective leadership. You will also have a well-organized movement that can resist any attack and develop a winning plan for national liberation.

PROBLEMS IN ESTABLISHING A BLOCK STRUCTURE

However, establishing such a structure will be extremely difficult. Most, if not all, of the organizers will be volunteers; therefore, consistency will be a problem. Without great determination and high consciousness, the problems that organizers will face will be extremely great. It will be easy for an organizer to call it quits. Constant political education and organizing training will have to take place to remind people of the goals of the movement and to refine their organizing skills. This kind of structure will grow if it recognizes talent, and does everything it can to develop skills by giving people progressively more difficult assignments, and promoting people who show outstanding leadership skills.

BUILDING MASS INSTITUTIONS

The professional organizer not only becomes an expert at recruiting, persuasion, an expert timing campaigns, using the step-by-step method, and fitting into the community, but above all else, the professional organizer develops the ability to organize mass institutions, mass issue campaigns, and mass organizations. The professional organizer knows that it is not enough to spend ten years organizing one school, one business, or one small community organization.

Mass organizing requires that we have the vision and skill to see that the organizer who uses the dynamics involved in setting up one school can set up a chain of schools that will serve the needs of a large number of Black youth. The skill that it takes to operate one school can be transferred to the operation of many schools if we have the vision to plan the organization of mass based institutions. There are hundreds of Black churches in most Black communities that could provide a site for independent Black schools or independent after-school programs. The same principle applies to economic institutions. Why plan to set up one store, one restaurant, or one grocery store, when you can plan to establish a chain of businesses that will provide jobs and services to a large number of Black people. The professional organizer thinks in terms of mass institutions because he/she understands that the goal of organizing is organizing a whole people for total liberation.

The largest mass based institution in the Black community is the Black church. As an organizer you must know the history of the Black church and the role it plays in the lives of our people.

Nat Turner

CHAPTER THIRTEEN

THE BLACK CHURCH AND BLACK THEOLOGY
IT'S AFRICAN ROOTS

Leaders in the African-American community, and leaders of African communities throughout the world, cannot be effective organizers if they do not have a knowledge of, and ties with, the Black church. This is simply because African people have strong spiritual and religious traditions that are rooted in the belief in a supreme being. Side by side with this deep religious spiritual tradition, is another tradition, a product of the slave experience. This tradition, which Lerone Bennett chooses to call the "devil experience," involves a large number of Blacks who refuse to accept a belief in God.

LINKING THE SACRED AND THE SECULAR

As leaders and organizers you must recognize these two realities when you prepare to organize African people. The history and theology of the Black church is an important part of the history of the African community. A good leader and organizer understands that spirituality and politics, spirituality and economics, and spirituality and education are two sides of the same coin. In African and African-American communities effective organizing requires that we not separate the spiritual question of creating good people, who aspire to be reflections of the goodness of God, from the effort to improve our people's economic, political, and educational condition. In fact it's hard to be a good person when your pockets are empty, your stomach, hurts and you have no roof over your head. Strong Black churches administer to the soul, the head and the stomach. Weak Black churches are strong on soulful preaching and short on programed direction.

Today, Black preachers as well as members of the Black community, need to understand the history of the Black church, Black liberation theology, and the dynamics of organizations, so they can administer churches that are both spiritual institutions dedicated to creating better human beings, and dynamic community organizations committed to social change for African people. Leaders of community and social organizations, and educational and economic institutions, must also have knowledge of the history of the Black church if they are to shape working relationships that promote social change for the larger Black community.

THE AFRICAN ROOTS OF THE BLACK CHURCH

The distinguished African-American scholar, W.E.B. Du Bois observed that the Black church in America is the product of an African background. According to Du Bois:

"The Negro Priest, therefore, early became an important figure on the plantation, and found his function as the interpreter of the supernatural, the comforter of the sorrowing, and as the one who expressed, rudely, but picturesquely, the longing and disappointment and resentment of a stolen people. From such beginnings arose and spread with marvelous rapidity the Negro Church, the first distinctly Negro American social institution. It was not at first by any means a Christian church, but a mere adaptation of those heathen rites, which we roughly designated by the term OBE worship or Voodooism." [73]

The African torn from Mother Africa, carried to the United States and the Caribbean as well as South America a rich culture that reached back to the beginning of human history. For African people are the mothers and fathers of humanity. Over 5 million years ago Africans lived in Africa. A 5 million year old jaw has been discovered in Africa to prove this. This jaw is older than any human remains discovered in Asia, Europe, or America. Four million years ago Africans lived along the headwaters of the Nile at a place called Lake Nyanza. Over 3.7 million years ago an African female, who has been named Lucy, gained the distinction of being the mother of humanity. Lucy and her brothers and sisters as well as her husband were members of the TWA people, a little people who are today improperly called pigmies. Little Black people laid the spiritual foundation for the rest of Africa and the world, they were the mothers and fathers of humanity.

With this long spiritual, political, economic, social, scientific, and educational tradition, Africans arriving in America did not, upon entering the slave ships, loose their culture. E. Franklin Frazier, the famous Black sociologist was wrong when he asserted that slavery destroyed the culture of Blacks in the United States. With the destruction of African culture, Frazier asserts that Blacks were a broken people without a sense of community, and that it was Christianity that provided the basis for 'social cohesion' among Blacks in bondage.

AFRICAN CULTURAL BELIEFS

As Du Bois states, in the beginning the Black church was African. The African who came to America from Africa, carried a language, a complex view of the universe where the sacred and the secular were one, a family system where the extended family was central, a matrilineal tradition that preceded patrilineal societies, where women played a central not dominating role, and a communal economic tradition, where the wealth was collectively shared by the people. Far from the African giving up these and other cultural views that grew out of millions of years of social practice, the African in America, faced with a slave-master who did not understand African culture but was intent upon destroying it, carried out a war to hold onto as much of his view of the universe as humanly possible. Enslaved on a majority of small southern plantations, Africans in America found it far harder to resist the cultural destruction process than did their brothers and sisters in the Caribbean and South America who were enslaved on large plantations and islands where Blacks outnumbered whites. As a result, Africans in the Caribbean and South America held onto more of the pure forms of African culture the drum, the African music, the African religion (Voodum), and more of the Africanisms in the language. Africans in America, enslaved on smaller plantations were subjected to a harsher cultural attack, which outlawed the drum. They had a greater influence on African-American musical forms than the whites in the Caribbean and South America, and made greater intrusions into the religious life of Africans in the United States.

FROM AFRICAN TO AFRICAN-AMERICAN

The cultural war waged against African culture in the United States led to more complex transformations.   The African in America, deprived of his drum, invented new musical forms such as the work song which was African because of its strong rhythm base.   Out of the work song, a carryover of the African practice of singing while working, grew the spirituals and the blues.   All of these musical forms were the result of the interaction between European and African cultural elements.   As any African-American musicologist will confirm, in this cultural war, the African side won. On the musical level, a new synthesis was worked out between European and African elements, with the Africanisms predominating.   In the case of the work songs, the spirituals and the blues, the African rhythm elements of the music predominated over the European harmonic elements. Out of this great musical legacy would arise the classical music of the 20th century, jazz. Far from Africans loosing the cultural war on the musical level, Africans gave to the world in the form of spirituals, blues and Jazz a soul music of great power, symbolic richness, and emotional and intellectual brilliance that sets the souls of billions of people on fire all over the world.

AFRICAN RELIGIOUS CARRYOVERS INTO CHRISTIANITY

On the spiritual level the African-American spiritual reality was in the beginning an African spiritual reality. Christianity, as it began to make inroads into the African spiritual legacy, changed into something very different from its European form. As Cayraud S. Wilmore notes, in *Black religion and Black Radicalism*, Blacks who embraced Christianity brought into it many of their African religious beliefs. Like African priests and African spiritual practitioners before them, the new African-American convert to Christianity placed great importance on "dreams, visions, trances and voices." [74]

These early converts to Christianity came out of cultural tradition where the spirit was everywhere, therefore the spirit within "was considered superior to the bible as a guide for their religious knowledge."[75] Blacks who became Christians posed some of the same problems for their white Christian teachers that Muslim and Christian missionaries faced in Africa. Africans who converted to Islam and Christianity carried many of their magical systems of divination and other spiritual beliefs into Christianity and Islam. Many of the Yorubas in Africa who converted to Islam continued to practice the powerful Orisha system of divination, under a new name, Islam. The Orisha's are powerful spirits that reflect qualities of the creator. Many an African Christian continued to pay respect to his ancestors and rely upon magical systems. The same was true of the African-

American Christian. Contrary to white Christian teachings and practices, many African-American Christians continued practicing the African divinatory system of conjuring. Many also continued the practice of using protective objects to stave off beatings. Frederick Douglass in his *Narrative of the Life of Frederick Douglass* describes how a slave named Sandy Jenkins drew on the African powers to protect him from a cruel slave breaker by the name of Covey:

"He (Jenkins) told me, with great solemnity, I must go back to Covey; but that before I went, I must go with him into another part of the woods, where there was a certain root, which, if I would take some of it with me, carrying it always on my right side, would render it impossible for Mr. Covey, or any other white man, to whip me. He said he had carried it for years; and since he had done so, he had never received a blow, and never expected to while he carried it."[76]

Interestingly enough, Frederick Douglass was never beaten by a slave master again. When Covey attempted to beat Douglass, as he had done countless times before, Douglass fought back beating Covey. Even more significant was the fact that Covey did not report the beating to Douglass's master. While Douglass was suspicious about whether the root could help him, the fact that he wore the root shows that even Blacks who had been taught to distrust

such magical systems retained some belief
in them. The root, a part of his African culture,
may well have given Douglass the courage
to fight Covey.

There were a lot of Sandy Jenkins on
the southern plantations. These brothers and
sisters didn't worry about what whites thought
about magical powers, they drew on the
spiritual legacy, of Africa to protect
themselves, their children and their people.

AFRICAN VODOUM THE SPIRITUAL BASE OF BLACK CHRISTIANITY

The Voudoun practiced by the early
African priest in the United States, was worked
into Christianity over a period of time.
Voudoun is the title for the religion practiced
by Africans in the Western hemisphere. This
religion represents a mixture of many African
religions, which were synthesized by Africans
brought to the Western hemisphere from
many parts of Africa, though principally from
West Africa. Maya Deren in her book entitled
<u>Divine Horsemen, the Living Gods of Haiti</u>
defines Voudoun in the following way:

> Like all religions, Voudoun is
> built on certain basic
> premises. Briefly, it proposes
> that man has a material
> body, animated by an espirit
> or gros-bonange--the soul,
> spirit, psyche or self--which,
> being non-material, does not

share the death of the body. This soul may achieve (by stages elaborated in the discussion immediately following) the status of a loa, a divinity, and become the archetypal representative of some natural or moral principle. As such it has the power to displace temporarily the gros-bon-age of a living person and become the animating force of his physical body. This psychic phenomenon is known as "possession." The actions and utterances of the possessed person are not the expression of the individual, but are the readily identifiable manifestations of the particular loa or archetypal principle. Since it is by such manifestations that the divinities of the pantheon make known their instructions and desires and exercise their authority, this phenomenon is basic to Voudoun, occurs frequently, and is normal both to the religion and to the Haitians. In fact, the Haitain would find it abnormal if it should suddenly cease to occur. [77]

Africans in Haiti and other parts of the Caribbean and South America were able to hold onto this rich African religion by camouflaging it behind the saints of Catholicism. In the United States even as Blacks began to adopt Christianity, a distinct group of African-Americans continued to practice the religion of Vodum. Zora Neale Hurston, in her important work on African-American culture, <u>Mules and Men Negro Folktales and Voodoo Practices in the South</u>, documents the persistence of Voudoun practices in the rural South.

BLACK CHRISTIAN SPIRIT POSSESSION A FORM OF VODUM

For the majority of Blacks who adopted Christianity, Voudoun was worked into the religious practices of Black Christians. Dr. Yosef ben-Jochannan, a noted expert on Kemetic (Egyptian) history and African religion, in his important work entitled <u>African Origins of the Major Western Religions</u>, makes some very important observations about the persistence of Voudoun in Black Christian religious experiences:

"God-or Voudoun, Jehovah, Oledamare, Jesus Christ, Allah and Baba Loas, neither one is less the divinity that enters and seizes the righteous in a Pentecostal, Baptist, or Voodoo ceremony because He or She is called by either one of these names mentioned. In any of the fundamentally so-called "Save Soul Churches" of African-American and European-American sponsorship, one can easily note that Voodoo and Ju Ju have been co-opted in many of their forms into the Judaeo-Christian setting that is common to Christians and Jews in the United States of America." [78]

The spirit possession seen in the Pentecostal or Baptist Church is a direct carryover from Voudoun, and it clearly reflects the fact that the African in America practices the belief that God is within. The possession state of Vodum is a trance state where the initiate is possessed by a spirit that can speak in a different language (speaking in tongues) and can see into the past or the future. Spirit possession places the possessed in a higher mind state where the past and the future are one. While Vodum priests used their powers to bring the spirits down, in the African-American Pentecostal and Baptist Church, the believer brings the spirit down when they are truly possessed while the preacher preaches. In both cases the believer is "doing it when the spirit says do it." The primary difference between Vodum and Black Christian possession is that the African priest in Vodum is trained in the sacred science of bringing the spirit down, as well as raising the spirit out of the possessed initiate. In fact, many a jazz improvisation has also been a spirit possession where the jazz musician literally goes into a trance and draws his music from the spirit. Many a Black musician has drawn the sound of his music from a dream or a vision. All of this is the Vodum in the African-American spirituality, whether it is Christian spirituality, or musical spirituality.

The Black musician is drawing straight out of the spiritual musical legacy of Africa. Blues and jazz have roots in the spirituals. Spirituals, the most beautiful music this side of heaven, are African in their foundation. Again Dr. Yosef ben-Jochannan notes:

..."Within this phenomenal development, the so-called "Negro Spiritual" is the most common and acceptable "paganistic incantation" to European-American Jews and Christians. Why? Because they see such African-American incantations ("Negro Spirituals") as religious entertainment." Are the Negro Spirituals" in any way a developmental outgrowth of European-American style Christianity? Or, are they not an extension of indigenous African traditional religious chants that underwent European and European-American - style Jewish and Christian influences? The latter is definitely the case"... [79]

The African-American spirituals could not have been created out of a purely or primarily Anglo-Saxon Protestant cultural base, because that base lacked the deep emotionalism, and the deep sense of spirit possession of the African transplanted in America. This music, in its original form, was sacred music with hidden symbolic political meanings of freedom and escape from bondage. "Steal Away" meant steal away from slavery and oppression. "You can have this world but give me Jesus," meant you can have this world of slavery, and give me the Good Ship Jesus. The Good Ship Jesus was the ship that took us from Africa to America. By giving the slave, Jesus, (the Good Ship Jesus) the slave meant return him home to Mother Africa. The spirituals talked to the soul, they healed. They were psychologists before the word had been invented. They were comforters when most people would have given up all hope. They were inspirers when the world of the slavemaster's whip tried to strike every inspiration out of the souls of Black folks. This beautiful African-American music, is Black folks gift to God, Jehovah, and Oludamare, and it has fundamental African rhythmic roots with European harmonic influences.

But to understand the Black church, Black theology, and Black spirituality in all of its dimensions-from Islam to Christianity we must understand the theological roots of Christianity as a whole. The Africanisms that Black slaves worked into Christianity, had a history which preceded the West African and South African civilizations of Ghana, Mali, Songhay, and Monomopata, as well as Zimbabwe. The spiritual foundations of these African civilizations and many more that Africans carried to the Americas had their roots in ancient Ethiopia (Kush, Nubia or Ta-

Seti) and ancient Kemet (Egypt) Ethiopia's greatest and oldest daughter.

THE KEMETIC ROOTS OF ANCIENT CHRISTIANITY

The foundations of Christianity as a whole, not just   Black Christianity, are to be found in the spiritual philosophy of ancient Kemet. Like all religions before and after Christianity, Christian theology was heavily influenced by the religion that preceded it, the Sacred Science mystery system of ancient Kemet. Robertson Smith, the author of "Religion Of The Semites," discusses the impact that earlier religions have on religions that develop at a later time:

> "No positive religion   that   has moved man has been able to start with a tabula rasa, and express itself as if religion were beginning for the first time, in form, if not in substance. The new system must be in contact all along the line with the older ideas and practices which it finds in possession. A new scheme of faith can find a hearing only by appealing to religious instincts and susceptibilities that already exist; and it cannot reach these without taking account of the traditional forms in which all religious feeling is embodied, and without speaking a language which men accustomed to these old forms can understand...."[80]

Christianity draws its roots from Judaism, which rests upon a Kemetic (Egyptian) spiritual foundation. The Jews were inhabitants in Kemet, and it is there that the foundation of their spiritual system was developed. The Kemetic religion was to have a formative impact upon the teachers of what came to be known as Judaism. Dr. Yosef ben-Jochannan states that,

> It is extremely important to note that there are no records that the Jews, prior to any mention of Moses, brought into Sais (which they called "Egypt" in their mythology about the sons of Jacob and Issac) any scrolls or books whatsoever. There are no records that they had any homeland where they had established a government, institutions of higher learning or an organized religion before they entered Sais (Egypt) from their nomadic life in the Asian desert. The first record of them in Egypt speaks of their small settlement around the Nile Delta on the Mediterranean Sea, near the cities where there was a flourishing boat building industry approximately 1640 to 1630 B.C.E. (Before the Christian Era) [81]

These Jews entered a land that the Greek historian Herodotus tells us was populated by Black people who, like the Colchins had black skin and wooly hair.

Herodotus was a reliable eyewitness who reported the color of the Egyptians and Ethiopians in a matter of fact way, since this was common knowledge in the ancient world. Similarly, the Jews who entered Egypt around l640 B.C.E., were also nomadic Africans, who were seeking refuge in Kemet from the harsh life of the desert.

MONOTHEISM, THE GIFT OF KEMET TO JUDAISM, CHRISTIANITY, AND ISLAM

The story of Moses being raised in the house of the Pharoah is well known. Moses was an initiate of the Kemetic Mystery system, then the most advanced system of higher education in the ancient world, a training ground for priests. Moses was educated in Mystery teachings during the reign of the Pharoah Akhnaton. The Pharoah Akhnaton taught the doctrine of monotheism, the idea that there is only one God. Judaism, Islam, and Christianity would all draw their notion of one God, from the teachings of this great Pharoah Akhnaton who was also known in the ancient world as the father of non-violence.

THE KEMETIC FORTY-TWO CONFESSIONS OF INNOCENCE THE BASIC TEN COMMANDMENTS

The foundation of Judaism rests upon the Ten Commandments in the Five Books of Moses (Torah)." These Ten Commandments were supposedly given to Moses by Jehovah, and are the core of Christian teachings. Yet Moses, the Mystery student and Kemetic priest, drew the Ten Commandments from the earlier Kemetic teachings called the Forty-two Confessions of Innocence. These Forty-two moral edicts were requirements for the purification of the soul, so that man and woman could become God-like, and therefore entitled to a union with the one God Creator of all. As was true of Vodoun, an offshoot of this great African mystery system, the goal of life was to free yourself of the impurities of dishonesty, violence, impulsiveness, laziness, gossiping, anger Forty-two and other human weaknesses. When you compare the Forty-two Confessions of Innocence with the Ten Commandments, which came much later, we see the origin of the Ten Commandments. The Forty-two Confessions of Innocence proclaimed:

1. I am not a doer of wrong.
2. I am not a man of violence.
3. I am not evil minded.
4. I am not rapacious.
5. I am not a slayer of men.
6. I am not fraudulent in measures.
7. I commit no fraud.
8. I am not a robber of sacred property.
9. I am not a teller of lies.
10. I am not a robber of food.
11. I am not sluggish.
12. I am not a transgressor.
13. I have not slaughtered the sacred
14. I deal not fraudulently.
15. I am not a land grabber.
16. I am not an eaves-dropper.
17. I am not one of pratting tongue.
18. I trouble myself only with my own affairs.
19. I commit not adultery with one.
20. I am not unchaste with any another's wife.
21. I do not cause terrors.
22. I am not a transgressor.
23. I am not hot of speech.
24. I lend not a deaf ear to the words of Righteousness.
25. I am not a slayer of men.
26. I am not the cause to weeping to any.
27. I am not given to un-natural lust.
28. I indulge not in anger.
29. I am ot given to cursing hand.
30. I am not of aggressive hand.
31. I am not one of <u>inconstant</u> mind.
32. I do not steal the skins of sacred animals.
33. I am not noisy in my speech.
34. I am neither a liar nor a animals.
35. I am not one who curseth the King.
36. I put no check upon the water in its flow.
37. I am not one loud voice.
38. I curse not God.
39. I am not swollen with pride.
40. I have no unjust preferences.
41. I have no strong desire except for my own property.
42. I do not that which offendeth the God of my domain.[82]

Everyone of the TEN Commandments can be found in the Forty-two Confessions of Innocence. What is particularly important is that these high moral requirements speak not only to not <u>doing</u> wrong, but they speak to not <u>thinking</u> or <u>feeling</u> wrong. One is warned against being "evil minded," as well as not being "of inconstant mind" or a mind that shifts from one thing to another, and not having "unjust preferences," or "having a strong desire for the property of another." This goes beyond the ten commandments that stress refraining from doing wrong; the Fourty-two Confessions of Innocence are far more demanding in the wrongs prohibited, but they go much further by requiring a good mind, a consistent mind, one that loves justice and is satisfied with caring for their own affairs without unjustly sticking ones nose into the affairs of another.

The Forty-two Confessions of Innocence, out of which the 10 Commandments came, place an emphasis on the quality of the invisible mind and spirit. Their goal was inner spiritual excellence and purity, which would lead to outer spiritual behavior that was in harmony with the Creator, who represented Maat, (harmony, truth, justice and right order). When the person passed from the physical life into the spiritual life, his/her passage to the next world was determined by being able to affirmatively state that they had not violated any of these virtues.

THE KEMETIC PYRAMID TEXTS AND COFFIN TEXTS FOUNDATION FOR THE CHRISTIAN BIBLE

When a comparison is made between parts of the Christian Bible, the Torah, the Kemetic Pyramid, and Coffin Texts, we find more than similarity. Remembering that the Kemetic texts precede the Christian or Judaic texts, their near identical content is more than coincidental. Dr. Yosef ben-Jochannan provides a comparison between the Proverbs of King Solomon, 976-936 A.D. and the Teachings of Amen-em-ope written much earlier in 1405-1370 B.C.E.

THE COMPARATIVE WORKS

The Teachings of A Amen-em-ope Pharoah of Egypt (1405-1370)	The Proverbs of King Solomon of Israel (976-936)
Give thine ear and hear what I say, And apply thine heart to apprehend;	Incline thine ear, and hear my words, And apply thine heart to apprehend;
It is good for thee to place them in thine heart, Let the rest in casket of the belly. That they may act as a peg upon thy tongue.	For it is pleasant if thou keep them in thine belly, hat thou may be fixed upon thy lips.

Consider these thirty chapters;

Have I not written for thee

They delight, they instruct.
Knowledge how to answer him
that speaketh, And how to
carry back a report to one that
sent it.

thirty sayings,

of counsels and know-

ledge! That thou may-

est make known truth

to him that speaketh.

Beware of robbing the poor,
And oppressing the afflicted.

Rob not the poor for he
is poor, Neither

oppress the lowly in
the gate.

Associate not with a passionate man, Nor approach him
conversations; Leap not
to cleave to such a one,
That the terror carry thee
not away.

Associate not with a
passionate man, Nor
go with wrathful man,
Lest thou learn his
ways,And get a snare
to thy soul.

A scribe who is skillful in his
business Findeth himself
worthy to be a courtier.

A man who is skillful in
his business Shall
stand before Kings.[83]

A comparison of these two texts reveals not only that the Kemetic Mystery system influenced Judaism and Christianity, but that some of the Judaic writings were nothing more than plagiarized copies of Kemetic sacred texts.

THE KEMETIC BASIS FOR THE CHRISTIAN VIRGIN BIRTH

According to the Christian Bible, Jesus was born to a virgin called Mary. His birth occurred through what was described as the Immaculate Conception. Long before the birth of Christianity, the story of the Virgin Birth was known in ancient Kemet. Osiris, who in Kemetic Sacred Science became the neter (principle) of life, death and rebirth, was killed by his brother Set, who cut his body into pieces and spread the parts throughout Kemet. Osiris' wife, Isis went throughout Kemet discovering every part of Osiris' body. When Isis put Osiris' body back together he became ruler of the after-life, and with Isis conceived Horus through immaculate conception.   The Greek writer Plutarch "tells us that the virgin mother Isis was delivered of Harpocrates (i.e. to Horus, considered as the child of the mother alone) [84]

Until the painters Michaelangelo, was directed by Pope Julius II during the 6th century A.D., to paint Jesus white and his parents Asian, the Madonna had been portrayed as Black, along with her son Jesus. Shrines to the Black Madonna exist in Paris, Poland and Spain and they simply portray Jesus and his mother the way the Hebrews, looked during the time of Jesus

THE PARALLELS BETWEEN HORUS AND JESUS

Gerald Massey, in the important book <u>The Historical Jesus and The Mythical Christ</u>, shows some striking parallels between Jesus Christ and Horus, the bringer of iron technology to Kemet, the son of Osiris, and the symbol of divine Pharoahship. The characteristics of Horus and Jesus are very similar. According to Gerald Massey:

> "The Christ is the good Shepherd. So was Horus.
> Christ is the Lamb of God. So was Horus.
> Christ is the Bread of Life. So was Horus.
> Christ is the Truth and the Life. So was Horus.
> Christ is the Fan-bearer.So was Horus.
> Christ is the Door of Life.Horus was the Path
> by which the dead travel out of the sepulchre;

he is the god whose name is
written as the
Road." [85]

The similarities between Jesus and Horus
don't end there. There is a very interesting
parallel between the age of twelve and the
age of thirty for both Horus and Jesus. Again
Gerald Massey notes:

"The first Horus was the child, who always
remained a child. In Egypt the boy or girl wore
the Horus-lock of childhood until twelve years of
age. Thus childhood ended about the twelfth
year. But although adultship was then entered
upon by the Sherau, and the transformation of
the boy into manhood began, the full adultship
was not attained until thirty years of age. The
man of thirty years was the typical adult. As with
the man so it is with the god, and the second
Horus, the same god in his second character is
the Khemt or Khem-Horus, the typical adult of
thirty years. The god up to twelve years was
Horus the son of Isis, the mother's child. The virile
Horus,   the adult of thirty years, was
representative of the Fatherhood and this Horus
is anointed son of Osiris. These two characters
of Horus the child and Horus the adult of thirty-
years are reproduced in the two phases to
which the life of Jesus is limited in the gospels.
Luke tells us that the child of twelve years was
the wonderful youth, and that he increased in
wisdom and stature. This is the length of years

assigned to Horus the child; and this phase of the child-Christ life is followed by the baptism and anointing, the descent of the pubescent Spirit with the consecration of the Messiah in Jordan when Jesus "began to be about thirty years of age." 86

What Massey demonstrates is that there were two distinct phases for Horus and Jesus, both marked by the same ages, the age of childhood represented by age twelve, and the age of adulthood characterized by the age thirty. Adulthood is synomous with wisdom, and the baptism or anointment by the father, God. IN KEMETIC SACRED SCIENCE the knowledge gained through mystery teachings leads to the wisdom of adulthood that is the basis for initiation into the mysteries of spiritual knowledge.

THE WORD AS THE CREATIVE FORCE

In Kemetic sacred science the spoken word is powerful. In the Book of Coming Forth by Day the great God Neb-er-tcher creates all things, including the earth, with the power of the spoken word and creation comes out of the "primeval matter (water)." In the book of Genesis God creates the earth and the universe through the Word, and creation occurs out of the stuff of water. The Word as a creative power, is not only a theme of Kemetic Sacred Science, but it is a theme repeated throughout other African spiritual systems. The Dogon's, a people who reside in Mali, also describe how the Word

(Nommo) is used to maintain order on earth. For the Dogon's water is the source of life.

All of these examples clearly show that the theology of Western Christianity, including Black Christianity, Islam and Judaism have a Kemetic, African spiritual base. Much of Christianity remains a mystery without an understanding of its African theological connection. Monotheism was not a doctrine revealed by Jehovah to Moses, monotheism was a concept that Moses learned in the Kemetic Mystery system. The Ten Commandments grew out of the earlier Forty-two Confessions of Innocence. Many passages in the Bible were directly drawn from the Kemetic Pyramid Texts and Coffin Texts. The immaculate conception in Christianity has its roots in the world's first immaculate conception story in ancient Kemet, when Isis conceived of Horus through her dead husbands spiritual immaculate conception. The story of Jesus cannot be fully understood without understanding the story of Horus, and the creation story of Christianity gains deeper meaning when it is connected to the earlier parallel creation story of ancient Kemet.

All of this is only a short summary of some of the Kemetic Christian connections. Our Black theologians need to do systematic work on connecting Kemetic theology with Christian theology so that a truly accurate Bible can be written. For clearly, Christianity's theological and biological, as well as historical, roots lie largely in Africa, with Kemet providing a rich theological/ philosophical foundation.

But Western Christianity, and Black Christianity cannot be understood without understanding the African basis for the creation of the Christian church as an institution.

THE AFRICAN ORGIN OF THE CHRISTIAN CHURCH AS AN INSTITUTION

Before the Romans embraced Christianity, the African Christian church flourished in Kemet. Christianity had its beginning "on an institutional basis in Egypt this being 200 years before Emperor Constantine (the Great) of the Roman Empire made Rome a Christian Nation. 87

Early African Christians were former JEWS practitioners of Judaism who became converts to what was later called Christianity. They were then called Nazarenes and they lived along the banks of the Nile in Kemet. Nazarenes, like their ancestor Moses, were Black Africans.

In the early period of the Christian Church there were two branches. The oldest branch were Africans from Egypt, "who spoke a local African language and also a mixed African-European (Egyptian Greek) language called "Coptic." 88

The second group of Christians were Greeks, born in Kemet, who were descended from the invaders of Alexander the Great. These people spoke Greek and lived along the Mediterranean Sea near the Delta. Among this group were "Greek speaking Hebrews." These Greek speaking Christians introduced Greek philosophical ideals from Plato into the "Hebrew Sacred Scriptures."

Christianity was once again, through a Greek passageway, being introduced to the ideas of Kemet. Plato was a student of the Kemetic mystery system. The core of his philosophy is based on the Kemetic idea of man and woman purifying themselves and becoming a reflection of God, or the good (the soul).

During this foundation period for the Christian Church, it was the African church leaders, who produced the deepest, most profound center of Christian scholarship in the history of Christianity. These founding African church fathers were deeply influenced by the Kemetic religion of Ra, Osiris and Horus. This is why so much of the Bible draws from Kemetic Sacred Science concepts.

AFRICAN CHURCH FATHERS

Many of the leading African Christian Church fathers were scholars of great brilliance. St. Cyprian was an African, who had been a professor of philosophy, before his conversion to Christianity. After his conversion he became Bishop of Carthage. St. Cyprian, lived during the period prior to Rome's adoption of Christianity. Carthage was a province of Rome, in North Africa, and St. Cyprian facing Roman persecution, went underground where he continued to teach the faith. Eventually, St. Cyprian was captured by the Romans and he was beheaded. St. Cyprian was recognized as one of the early Christian martyrs. He demonstrated great courage as he faced death.

Another great African church father was Tertullian, who was born in Carthage in 155 C.E. (during the Christian Era). Tertullian, like St. Cyprian before him, was an outstanding scholar of "rhetoric, Latin, and Greek."[89] Tertullian made Latin "the official language of the Holy Roman CatholicChurch (an outgrowth of the North African Church) and Christendom in general." [90]

These African scholars and other African evangelists introduced Christianity into Rome by way of North Africa. Before Rome officially adopted Christianity as the state religion, many of Rome's most distinguished leaders, including many of her best generals, adopted Christianity.

ST. AUGUSTINE THE GREATEST INTELLECTUAL LUMINARY IN THE HISTORY OF CHRISTIANITY

St. Augustine was born in Numidia (Algeria and Libya) in 354 C.E. and died in 430 C.E. He was a genius, and he "was one of the greatest thinkers and philosophers of all times." [91]

St. Augustine was well educated in Greek and Latin, Rhetoric and advanced studies. During his early life, prior to adopting Christianity, St. Augustine enjoyed a passionate life, even frequenting houses of prostitution. His greatest strength as a religious teacher after his conversion, was his ability to confront openly his earlier life. Augustine's writings are a living example of the Kemetic principle of rising from the lower to the higher self. St. Augustine taught that people are "citizens of two cities, the city of birth, the city of lower passions and the other city of God. "The struggle of history," says St. Augustine," is between these two societies, and "the ultimate mastery which must fall to the city of God." [92]

St. Augustine's mother was a Christian, however, his father practiced traditional African religion. Augustine's writings reflected an understanding of Platonic thought, which he modified by linking it to "indigenous, African mythological and ancestral spirit worship (veneration)."[93] Part of the African religious tradition that Augustine drew from was the practice of "libations and oracles." [94] St. Augustine's African spiritual orientation was the result of adopting Kemetic religious ideas to Numidia and Carthage, which was the place of birth of a number of "African Christian Fathers of the Church."[95] St. Augustine and other African church fathers "adapted much of its Egyptian format to suit Numidian and Carthagenian culture and religious customs."[96]

Augustine is especially noted for his influence on Christian theology. He took the Kemetic idea that God dwells within each of us and taught that,

> The love of God, destroys all vices; when to the love of one's neighbor puts an end to all crimes. For no one is willing to defile his own dwelling, he ought not, therefore, to defile the dwelling of God, that is himself. [97]

This is saying more than"love thy neighbor." For God is in all of us. To defile my neighbors house is to defile mine, because God is in the house (body) of my neighbor just as he is in my house (body). The purification of the body (dwelling) of God, is the central teaching of the Kemetic Mystery system. Augustine was introducing into Christian theology a notion of self-purification and self-mastery which he had practiced, and which has been largely lost in modern Western Christianity which decided to place more importance on the external material adornments of the world through religious wars, persecutions, and the sanctioning of the slave trade, colonialism and imperialism. By defiling the house (body) of their African, Native American, South American and Asian neighbors, Western Christianity has defiled it's own house (body) thereby departing from this noble path of self-purification and goodness.

The roots of Western Christianity, and the Black Church in America grew out of this Kemetic background, and out of the theological foundation laid by the founding African church.

It is out of this spiritual vision and background, the vision growing out of Africa, out of Kemet, that the Black church in America grows. These great African church fathers were the forerunners of Black giants that rose up out of the bowels of slavery and out of the yearnings of Free Men and Women of Color who looked for a just God who would stand on the side of the oppressed.

THE BLACK CHURCH IN AMERICA

The African-American slave and Free Men and Women of Color while not largely conscious of this African foundation of Christianity, nevertheless carried spiritual beliefs to America that were rooted in the Vodoum tradition, a tradition that grew out of the Kemetic spiritual legacy. The attitudes of African slaves towards the white masters version of Christianity were partly the result of African spiritual beliefs carried over into America, and they were partially good, commonsense opinions that enabled the slave to separate the master's propaganda from Christian teachings.   An ex-slave, Richard Carruthers, told of how preachers used Christianity to control the slave:

> When the white preacher come he preach and pick up his Bible and claim he gettin' the text right out from the good Book and he preach: "The Lord say, don't you niggers steal chickens from your missus. Don't you steal your master's hogs."   That would be all he preach. [98]

From Richard Carruther's account it's clear that he knew the difference between what the white preacher "claimed he was gettin...out of the good book," and the real thing. In fact, this simplistic preaching was ignored. As Mr. Carruthers goes on to note:

> If they didn't provision you' nough, you just had to slip round and get a chicken. That easy 'nough, but grabbin' a pig sure ' nough problem. You have to catch him by the

> snoot so he wont squeal, and
> clomp him tight while you knife
> him. That ain't stealin', is it? You
> has to keep right on workin' in
> the field, if you ain't
> allowanced nough, and no
> (Black) like to work with his
> belly groanin'. 99

Slaves knew the difference between liberating food from a slavemaster who attempted to work them to death, and pure theft. No effort to define survival as theft through references to Christianity could convince the slave that God intended the slave to starve to death, in the name of Christianity.

THE TRANSITION BETWEEN VODOUN AND CHRISTIANITY

African religious beliefs existed side by side with Christianity. Many Black slaves who professed not to believe in Voodoo, revealed in their statements that they continued to hold onto African spiritual beliefs. Anthony Dawson, who was 105 when he was interviewed said,

> "We didn't have no voodoo
> women nor conjure folks at
> our twenty acres. We all
> knowed about the Word and
> the un- seen Son of God and
> we didn't put no stock in

conjure. "Course we had luck charms and good and bad signs, but everybody god dem things, even nowadays..." [100]

A few things are interesting about Anthony Dawson's observation. First, his statement indicates that voodoo women and conjure people were common enough in, Greenville North Carolina. While he professed a belief in the "Son of God", Jesus Christ, he continued to believe in the unseen spirit powers contained in "luck charms and signs". More important, this ex-slave had an identity problem, revealed in the statement "our twenty acres."

In fact, Voodoo and Christianity not only existed side by side, but there were believers and others who taught that Voodoo was contrary to Christian beliefs. But even when these teachings were accepted, African spirit beliefs persisted. Martha Colquitt, an ex-slave reveals this mixed attitude when she states,

Us all de time heard folkses talkin' about voodoo, but my grandma was powerful religious, and her and Ma told us chillen voodoo was a no 'count doin' of de devil, Christians was never to pay it no attention. Us was to be

happy in de Lord, and let
voodoo and de devil alone.
None of us   liked to hear
screech owls holler, cause
everybody thought it means
somebody in dat house was
goin' to die if a screech owl lit
on your chimney and holler,'
cause everybody thought it
means somebody in   dat
house was goin' to die if a
screech owl lit on your
chimney and hollered, so us
would stir up de fire to make
the smoke drive him away.
101

Again we see a similar theme.
Voodoo is strong enough that it has to be
preached against. While Colquitt professes
faith in Christianity, she reveals that she
believed in signs and omens, a part of the
African cosmological view, where every
physical action has a spiritual
correspondence and meaning. Many
Blacks down to this day hold onto some of
these beliefs, outgrowths of the idea that
spirits and people coexist.

The Slave Revolts: Black Liberation Theology

The African-American slave placed a
greater value in his own interpretation of
Christianity. Slaves who adopted Christianity

took an Old Testament interpretation of Christianity and Jesus. Intrinsic in the African-American slave's view of the world was the notion that the Creator of the Universe was a just God. Most slaves believed that the slavemaster would pay in hell for his injustice to the slave. The Jesus that most slaves believed in, was not the meek-turn-the-other-check Jesus of the New Testament. Black slaves affirmed a belief in a fighting, manly, warrior Jesus who fought the wicked. As Lawrence W. Levine, notes in *Black Culture and Black Consciousness*,

> Although Jesus was ubiquitous in the spirituals, it was not invariably the Jesus of the New Testament of whom the slaves sang, but frequently a Jesus transformed into an Old Testament warrior whose victories were temporal as well as spiritual: "Mass Jesus" who engaged in personal combat with the Devil; "King Jesus" seated on a milk-white horse with sword and shield in hand. "Ride on, King Jesus," "Ride on conquering King," "The God I serve is a man of war," the slaves sang. This transformation of Jesus is symptomatic of the slaves' selectivity in choosing those parts of the Bible which were

to serve as the basis of their
religion. [102]

The African-American slave and Free Men
and Women of Color drew from the Old
Testament, because the Old Testament beliefs
practiced an "eye for an eye," and "tooth for a
tooth," philosophy. The images of the Old
Testament were full of warriors, Joshua in the
Battle of Jericho, Moses leading his people to
freedom. The slave and Free Men and
Women of Color alike did not accept the
slavemasters version of the religion. Coming
from a creative, improvising people, the slave
and Free Men and Women of Color preferred
a liberating interpretation of the Bible. Howard
Thurman, an outstanding Black theologian,
spoke of the slaves interpretation of the Bible,
one that differed from the master. Thurman
asked his grandmother why she never read
from the Epistles of Paul.

> When at length I asked the
> reason, she told me that during
> the days of slavery, the minister
> (white) on the plantation was
> alway preaching from the
> Pauline letters--"Slaves, be
> obedient to your masters," etc.
> "I vowed to myself," she said,
> "that if freedom ever came
> and I learned to read, I

would never read that part of
the Bible." [103]

DAVID WALKER'S APPEAL

This attitude was not only held by slaves
but by most Free Men and Women of color.
David Walker, a free man of color, and the
author of the important "David Walker's
Appeal," drew on the same Old Testament
righteousness that most of his slave brothers and
sisters drew from when he aimed his finger of
justice at whites and said,

> But I tell you Americans that
> unless you speedily alter your
> course, you and your country
> are gone! For God almighty will
> tear up the very face of the
> earth. [104]

ETHIOPIANISM

David Walker called on the slaves to
rise up and use violence to free themselves
from slavery. "David Walker's Appeal" has
strong Old Testament overtones, and it also has
a powerful Ethiopian orientation. Africans on the
African continent, and Africans abroad placed
a special pride and faith in Ethiopia. Ethiopia
stood as a symbol of African independence,
during the period of the European slave trade
and after the division of Africa at the Berlin
Conference. During both periods, Ethiopia
remained

independent from European control. As such, Ethiopia stood as a symbol of Africa and her son's and daughter's future freedom and independence.

Ethiopia also had biblical significance. Africans the world over drew inspiration from the Biblical passage that says,

> Princes shall come out of Egypt and Ethiopia shall soon stretch forth her hand unto God.[105]

This passage was taken to be a passage of deliverance. For soon God would free his son's and daughter's descendants of Ethiopia. Ethiopia was not only a symbol of political independence, but Ethiopia was a symbol of divine providence on the side of her Black sable sons and daughters. All Africans were viewed to be descendents of Ethiopia, the Mother of Civilization. David Walker, in his appeal refers to this Ethiopian belief when he says,

> It is expected that all coloured men women and children of every nation, language and tongue under heaven, will try to procure a copy of this Appeal and read it, or get some one to read it to them. Let them remember that though our cruel

oppressors and murderers, may (if possible) treat us more cruel, as Pharaoh did the children of Israel, yet the God of the Ethiopians, has been pleased to hear our moans in consequence of oppression and the day our redemption from abject wretchedness draweth near, when we shall be enabled in the most extended sense of the word, to stretch our hands to the Lord our God.... [106]

"David Walker's Appeal," drawing from the spirit of Ethiopianism, is addressed to Africans throughout the world. The blow that encourages African-Americans to strike for freedom, isn't just a blow for their own freedom, it is a blow for Africans everywhere. The God of the Ethiopians hears the oppressed Africans cry and stands on their side, all that oppressed Africans have to do is strike the first blow.

St. Clair Drake notes that Ethiopianism was a powerful myth that gave Africans the world over, a sense of unity and divine support.

"This Biblical myth is the core of a thought-style that might be called "Ethiopianism," and which became more complex and secularized as it developed during the 19th and 20th centuries. It emerged as a counter-myth to that of Southern white Christians (and many Northern ones). It functioned on a fantasy level giving feelings of worth and self-esteem to the individual, but also as a sanction for varied types of group action. It generated concern for the "redemption" of Black men in the Motherland as well as the Diaspora, so that the ancient state of power and prestige could be restored.[107]

It would be a mistake to think that because Ethiopianism was a myth, that it was an escapist fantasy. African symbols have been incorrectly interpreted as European type myths or stories. African mythology is based on fundamental truths that are revealed through symbols. Ethiopianism rested upon the historical fact that Ethiopia was the mother of world civilization. Ethiopianism as a belief system stood on the independence of Ethiopia during the 18th and 19th century. The Biblical passage that Ethiopia shall stretch forth its hands unto God, rests upon the historical truth of the "just Ethiopians", who the classical Greek historians described as the favorites of God.

Ethiopianism provided a solid foundation of hope and global vision for an oppressed African people.

In the twentieth century, Ethiopianism would provide the foundation for the secular philosophy of Pan Africanism, the ideal that Africans throughout the world are one. Du Bois, Slyvester Williams, Garvey, Nkrumah, Malcolm X, George Padmore, and many other Africans around the world, would draw from this Ethiopian legacy.

THE MAROON TRADITION

Slaves as well as Free Men and Women of Color, drew from another cultural strand, the Maroon tradition. Maroons were Blacks who resisted slavery in the Caribbean, South America, and the United States under the guidance of an African vision. Dr. Jacob Carruthers states in his book <u>The Irritated Genie of Haiti</u>,

> These rebellions seem to have started as plantation up-risings which resulted in slaves razing and abandoning the plantations and establishing free communities organized along the lines of traditional African societies. At this very early date the rallying cry of the rebellions was kill all the whites which was the

emerging spirit of race
vindication.[108]

Africans in the United States were inspired
by this tradition of resistance to slavery. Haiti
became a symbol of the Maroon spirit. In Haiti,
Blacks under the leadership of Vodum priests
launched a scared earth policy, freeing the
Blacks from slavery. Haiti stood as a symbol of
African power for Blacks throughout the world,
and in the United States being the only slaves in
the world who liberated themselves from
slavery. David Walker was inspired by the
Haitian revolution as were many African-
American slaves.

GABRIEL PROSSER

As African-American life on the plantation
and in the North took on a more of a Christian
direction, the Maroon tradition drew from
Biblical sources as well as a desire for
independence. Gabriel Prosser was inspired
by the Biblical story of Sampson. He wore his
hair long to keep his strength, as Sampson did.
Again Blacks were drawing upon manly Old
Testament symbols of power and strength.
Prosser saw himself as a Sampson who would
bring the house of slavery down on the heads
of white slavemasters.

Prosser was also inspired by the Haitian
revolution, and following the Maroon tradition,
he organized his men along military lines and
planned to fight a Maroon guerilla war in the
mountains. While Gabriel Prosser's rebellion
was betrayed, he laid an important foundation

in Black liberation theology, by using Old Testament sources and the Maroon tradition to forge a fighting spirit, and a set of revolutionary strategies and tactics.

DENMARK VESEY

Denmark Vesey organized the most elaborate slave revolt recorded in the history of U.S. slavery. Vesey was a Free Man of Color and a member of the African Methodist Church. He planned his rebellion using African Methodist Episcopal Church meetings as a cover, in 1822.

Vesey, like other Blacks, drew heavily upon the Old Testament for inspiration. He also drew from the Maroon tradition, the example of Haiti and the belief of many slaves in African religion.

In the spirit of the Old Testament "eye for an eye and tooth for a tooth," and the Maroon tradition of "free the slaves and kill all of the whites," Vesey planned to kill all of the whites, except the ship captains. Vesey proposed to save the ship's captains in the event that the insurrectionists had to leave the South for Haiti. The Biblical justification used for killing all whites, was the Old Testament narrative where Joshua destroyed the Canaanite city. Vesey quoted from Joshua 6:2l:

> And they utterly destroyed all
> that was in the city,both man
> and woman, young and old,
> and ox and sheep, and ass,
> with the edge of the sword.[109]

John Olliver Killens, in his
introduction to the *Trial Record of
Denmark Vesey*, shows that Vesey
used other Biblical passages to give
strength and courage to the weak of
heart. He drew from Zechariah l4:l-3:

> Behold the day of the Lord
> cometh, and thy spoil, shall be
> divided in the midst of thee. For
> I will gather all nations against
> Jerusalem to battle; and the city
> shall be taken, and the houses
> rifled, and women ravished.[110]

This was harsh Old Testament history,
that had special meaning to Blacks who
were oppressed by white men and white
women alike, who beat them, starved them,
and worked them to death. Harsh conditions
bred a harsh philosophy. Vesey's
interpretation was far different from the
slavemaster, who quoted from Paul a

philosophy of submission to the slavemaster.
Vesey and most other Blacks interpreted
Christianity in Old Testament, liberation terms.

GULLAH JACK

Vesey also used the power of African
religion. One of his most important lieutenants,
was a man known as Gullah Jack. Gullah Jack
was an African priest, who had the ability to
convert house negroes, into fearless
revolutionaries. He was a conjurer, and he
convinced the slaves that he was too powerful
to be killed by the slavemaster.

VESEY'S POLITICAL APPEAL

Vessey's appeals encouraging revolt
were not only religious. He reminded his
followers that the Declaration of
Independence and the Constitution were
documents that favored freedom.

Like Prosser before him, Vesey was
inspired by the brave example of the Haitian
revolution. As a younger man, Vesey lived in
Haiti. John Olliver Killens tells us that,

> He was profoundly influenced
> by the Haitian Revolution and
> held it before his followers as a
> great example. Once they
> struck a blow for freedom, he
> told them, Africa and Haiti

would come to their assistance. [111]

The Vesey rebellion demonstrated a fearless spirit, that gave whites many sleepless nights. This rebellion was betrayed by a house negro, who accepted the masters version of Christianity. While there were house negroes who joined the slave rebellions, poisoned their masters, and resisted their attacks, too many took on the mentality of the master. These house negroes believed that the white man was God, and to rebel against him was to doom themselves to eternal hell. House negroes who betrayed slave rebellions were either sent to another plantation to prevent reprisals from the slaves, or they were left on the plantation and sooner or later killed by Blacks.

GENERAL NAT TURNER

Nat Turner grew out of the African-American spiritual tradition. He was born with"certain birthmarks that according to African customs indicated the unusual mental abilities associated with a witcheh man" and a conjurer. [112]

Nat Turner was recognized by many Blacks as a spirit man, who had a liberation mission. Turner came out of the African tradition that saw signs and spirits everywhere. While Nat Turner was exposed to Christianity through religious services held by his master, he drew his inspiration from visions, and his own interpretation of Christianity. Nat Turner stands as a model for Black preachers. Cayraud Wilmore observes that,

> The most important thing to know about Turner is that he was a representative of an important group of slave preachers who discovered something white Christians had attempted to conceal from the slaves for more than two hundred years. Nat Turner, like others whose names are buried under the debris of the citadel of American slavery, discovered that the God of the Bible demanded justice, and to know him and his Son Jesus Christ was to be set free from every power that dehumanizes and oppresses. Turner discovered his manhood in the conception of the Christian God as one who liberates. His fanatcal attempt to authenticate that manhood in blood was the inevitable consequence of the fanatical attempt of whites to deny it." [113]

It would be wrong to cast Black preachers from Turner's time to the present, in the mold of Nat Turner. Most Black preachers and most Black people did not, and do not have the courage that Turner had, but Turner stands as a model of the spiritually inspired minister, and the courageous freedom fighter. Turner grew out of a tradition where the spiritual and the political co-existed in harmony.

Nat Turner's interpretation of the Bible was from a liberation perspective. Turners vision of Jesus was not a passive one. The Jesus that Turner believed in, was a fighting Jesus who came armed with the sword of justice. Heaven, Nat Turner believed, was to be experienced by Blacks on this earth.

THE YORUBA VISION OF ORI

Turner, like many other Blacks, believed that God dwelled within each of us. Turner had visions that inspired him to lead the great South Hampton Slave revolt. Cayraud S. Wilmore describes one of his most important visions.

> Shortly after Nat returned to the plantation, he had a remarkable vision in which white and black spirits were engaged in a great battle with blood flowing in streams. The voice that spoke out of that vision reminded him that

the lot had fallen to him to
suffer what had to be suffered
in obedience to his calling
Such is your luck, said the
voice, such you are called to
see, and let it come rough or
smooth, you must surely bear
it. [114]

This call of destiny through the spirits is
African, and many Blacks during Turner's time
and since have relied upon it for purpose
and direction. Among the Yoruba a West
African people, it is believed that each
person carries his or her destiny (Ori) in his or
her head. Ori, also means luck. The Yoruba's
teach that each soul chooses its own destiny
or Ori before birth. Each person has the
choice in life to either fulfil his or her Ori or
betray it. Turner, through his vision, faced his
destiny, a destiny full of blood. His decision
was not an easy one.

Turner decided to follow the voice of
his inner spirit, his destiny. He followed the Old
Testament, Maroon path, deciding to kill all
whites for the freedom of Blacks. To his
followers, Nat Turner, the revolutionary
preacher, became "General Nat." On May
12, 1838, General Nat had a great vision that
told him to wait no longer. Turner gives us this
remarkable vision:

and on the appearance of
the sign (the eclipse of the sun

> in February 1831) I should arise
> and prepare myself and slay
> my enemies with their own
> weapons. And immediately
> on the sign appearing in the
> heavens, the seal was
> removed from my lips, and I
> communicated the great
> work laid out for me to do, to
> four in whom I had the
> greatest confidence (Henry
> Porter, Hark Travis, Nelson
> Williams, and Sam Francis are
> referred to here). It was
> intended by us to have
> begun the work of death on
> the 4th of July last [115]

These were clear signs that the time to
share his plan with those he trusted had
come. The time had also come to launch
the Nat Turner rebellion. In battle, Nat Turner
was recognized by his followers as General
Nat; General Nat was true to his vision. The
South Hampton revolt was bloody. Turner
and his men killed white men, women, and
children. They used the masters weapons to
carryout the work of liberation. Eventually,
Turner and his lieutenants were captured and
hung. But they went to the grave without cries
for mercy. Instead, their example warned
whites that Blacks had a liberation vision of
their own. Men from the bowels of slavery
had risen up who would make the Old

Testament warriors and the great warriors of Africa stand up and take note.

The slave revolts had strong religious overtones, and their leaders were men of vision, who fashioned a Black liberation theology, that encouraged them to fight the slave system. Most importantly, these creative freedom fighters drew on their inner spiritual powers and fashioned a theology that reflected the interests of African people. Black preachers and lay people alike can draw from this creative, courageous spiritual tradition fashion a fighting no-compromise, spiritual political religion based on backbone rather than fishbone, and resistance rather than submission.

THE ORGANIZATION OF THE BLACK CHURCH

While Black spiritual political freedom fighters were drawing from within a vision and spirit to crush slavery on southern plantations, Black men and women who lived in the limbo realm of slavery and freedom, described as Free Men and Free Women of Color, were beginning to build the first Black religious institutions in the United States.

The first Black Church in America was formed in Williamsburg, Virginia, in 1776. The founders of this church and others to follow recognized that they were Africans, and they named their church the African Baptist Church. The beginning of a movement to form a national institutional Black church structure, grew out of the forces of white racism, and the desire of Blacks to create their own forms of religious and political expression. Richard Allen, the leader of this movement describes the forces that led Blacks to leave the white church.

> A number of us usually attended St. George's church in Fourth street; and when the colored people began to get numerous in attending the church, they moved us from the seats we usually sat on, and placed us around the wall, and on Sabbath morning we went to church and the sexton stood at the door, and told us to go in the gallery...We expected to take the seats over the ones we formerly occupied below, not knowing any better... Meeting had begun and they were nearly done singing and just as we got to the seats, the elder said 'Let us pray.' We had not been long upon our knees before I heard considerable scuffling and low talking. I raised my head up and saw one of the trustees having hold of the Rev. Absalom Jones, pulling him up off his knees, and

saying, 'You must get up--you must not kneel here.' Mr. Jones replied, 'Wait until the prayer is over.' (The trustee) said, 'No you must get up now, or I will call for aid and force you away.' Mr. Jones replied, 'Wait until the prayer is over, and I will get up and trouble you no more.' With that (the trustee) beckoned to one of the other trustees to come to his assistance. He came and went to William White to pull him up. By this time prayer was over, and we all went out of the church as a body, and they were no more plagued with us in the church. [116]

This decision by African-Americans to turn their backs on a racist white church, sparked spontaneous walkouts by Blacks from white churches across northern Black communities. These walkouts were the beginning of the development of a national Black institutional structure. Black churchgoers left these white churches not only because of white racism, they were also motivated by a desire to worship in their own way and under their own leadership.

FORMATION OF THE FREE AFRICAN SOCIETY

Richard Allen and Absalom Jones organized the Free African Society in Philadelphia on April 12, 1787. The Free African Society demonstrated the organizational traditions of Africans in America. The founders of the Free African Society came out of African societies that placed a great value on organization, especially spiritual and economic organization. While members of the society differed on religious beliefs, they drew on the African communal tradition, and developed support networks in times of sickness and death. The Black insurance organization would grow out of this collective tradition and reverence for the dead. The Free African Society served as the organizational base for launching the national Black church as an institution.

FORMATION OF THE AFRICAN METHODIST CHURCH

On July 17, 1794, Absolom Jones formed the African Episcopal Church of St. Thomas. A short time later, Richard Allen organized the Bethel AME Church of Philadelphia which would serve as the platform for launching the African Methodist Episcopal Church. Many Black Methodists who withdrew from white Methodist churches affiliated with Richard Allen's church. In 1816, the national African Methodist Episcopal Church was formed with Richard Allen as it's head. Richard Allen promoted an African-American form of worship that favored emotional expression, soulful preaching, and expressive praying. In 1821, the African Methodist Episcopal Zion Church was organized. True to African democratic traditions, Africans in America were beginning the process of creating a diverse national Black church structure.

The Black church formed during the period of slavery had as it's central concern the abolition of slavery. Black churches served as underground railways, and provided aid and support for the abolitionists cause. Richard Allen, who became Bishop of the African Methodist Episcopal Church, was the central leader of Blacks in the North during the 1820's. Lerone Bennett describes Allen's contribution to African-American history:

> Richard Allen was in some respects the prototypical figure in this group. Born a slave, he helped convert his master, bought his freedom, and played a pivotal role in defining the Black posture in America. In fact, he was so closely identified with the birth of Black America that author Vernon Logain called him the Father of the Negro. John W. Cromwell was of a like mind, saying Allen "had greater influence upon the colored people of the North than any other man of his times. " An artisan and believer in

sobriety, hard work, and thrift, Allen was a pioneer Black abolitionist, the founder of one of the first Black churches, and the organizer and first president of the first national Negro convention in the Western world. In these different roles he came to personify the dominant values of the Black Pioneer movement: (1) the assertion, backed up by practical work, that Black people would not accept a subordinate role in any white institution; (2) the importance of sustained assertion; (3) the importance of collective action. Allen's fundamental thesis--and it is still relevant-- was a thesis of power. As I have said elsewhere (Confrontation Black and White) he demanded not only the right to participate in American institutions but also the right to share in the governing of those institutions. [117]

While Bishop Allen was not as militant as General Nat Turner, or David Walker, he was a defender of African people's rights, a promoter of African-American spiritual and cultural self-determination, and he was a strong advocate for Black freedom.

THE FORMATION OF THE BLACK CONVENTION MOVEMENT

Africans in America fought in the war of independence expecting that a war fought for liberty and equality would lead to the abolition of slavery. Instead of gaining liberation, Blacks faced an American government that sanctioned slavery. The formation of the Black Church, the Free African Society and subsequently, the Black Convention Movement all reflected a desire on the part of Black people for power and self-determination.

The Black Convention Movement was organized by Blacks as a political voice for Blacks in America. Denied fundamental human rights, the Black Convention Movement became a quasi Congress, where so-called free Africans of color could exchange ideas, promote programs for self-help and advance the cause for freedom from slavery.

While many of the leaders of the Black Convention Movement were political leaders, rather than church leaders, Black ministers played an important role in the movement. One of the great debates in the Black Conventions was the one over whether slaves should use violence in freeing themselves. In Buffalo, New York, in the year

1843, Henry Highland Garnett, a Black Presbyterian minister, addressed the Black Convention. He addressed his message "to the slaves of the United States," calling on them to use arms to free themselves from slavery. Garnett attempted to get his call adopted by the convention, but his resolution lost by one vote. At this convention, Frederick Douglass, then a follower of William Lloyd Garrision, urged the convention to try non-violence a little longer.

ETHIOPIANISM AND BLACK NATIONALISM IN THE BLACK CHURCH

Ethiopianism was an ideological influence on African slaves and African Freemen and women of color. For many Freemen and Women of color, Ethiopianism provided the intellectual thrust for a Black Nationalists philosophy that called for a return to Mother Africa, and African political independence.   Martin R. Delany, a medical doctor, was one of the most original thinkers that Africans have produced in America. He called upon Blacks to form a nation of their own in mother Africa. Delany believed that Black liberation depended upon our own efforts.   In his own words Delany said:

> Our policy must be--and I hazard nothing in promulgating it; nay, without this design and feeling, there

would be a great deficiency of self-respect, pride of race and love of country, and we might never expect to challenge the respect of nations--Africa for the African race, and Black men rule them. By Black men I mean, men of African descent who claim an identity with the race. 118

Delany called on Blacks to found their own government, to have pride in Africa's great past, and to demonstrate a self-reliant spirit. Although Delany was not a minister, he was a Christian, and he was a critic of Black preachers and lay members alike who expected a spiritual force to solve a political problem. Delany called upon Blacks to liberate themselves by founding a government of their own in Africa.

EDWARD WILMONT BLYDEN

Edward Wilmont Blyden and Delany shared a common vision of African independence under Black rule. Blyden was born in the Virgin Islands. He "became President of Liberia College, Liberian Minister to the Court of St. James," was self educated, an author, linguist, and a minister. Blyden believed that Blacks needed to found a nation of their own in Africa. He was a pioneer in researching African life and customs.

BISHOP HENRY MCNEAL TURNER

Another great Black nationalist and church leader, was Bishop Henry McNeal Turner. Turner rose to be a bishop of the African Methodist Episcopal Church. He was in every sense the forerunner of Marcus Garvey. Turner was denied a seat as a Reconstruction legislator because he was Black. He became convinced that Blacks had no future in the United States. He was a forceful, outspoken voice for grassroot Blacks, especially those in the South, whose sentiments he expressed. In Turner's own words:

> Can't the fool Negro see that there is no future in this country for him? If he cannot, then he should return to slavery. We would be better off as slaves than as freemen. We have worked, enriched the country and helped give it a standing among the powers of the earth, and when we are denied our civil and political rights the fool Negro who has no more sense than a jackass, yet he wants to be a leader, ridicules the idea of asking for a hundred million dollars to go home, for Africa is our home and is the one

place that offers us manhood
and freedom, though we are
the subjects of nations that
have claimed a part of Africa
by conquest.[119]

Turner used his prestige and power as
bishop of the African Methodist Episcopal
Church to call for Black Nationalism and
emigration to Africa. Turner had an original
mind like Delany, Garnett, and General Nat
Turner. He applied his Black nationalism to
Black theology, portraying Jesus as Black. As
a strong Black man, he boldly proclaimed his
pride in being African, and in the face of
Southern segregationists he refused to
assume a servile role. Bishop Turner fought
hard to instill a Black Nationalist philosophy
into the Black Christian church.

W.E.B. Du Bois correctly described
Turner as the last of the strong Black leaders
who, "were the spiritual progeny of ancient
African chieftains and they built the African
church in America." [120]

THE BLACK CHURCH AND POST-RECONSTRUCTION

Turners death was a loss to African
people. It was especially a loss to the Black
church, which lost its foremost Black Nationalist
spokesperson. In a presidential election, the
House of Representatives had the task of
choosing Rutherford B. Hayes or Samuel J.

Tilden for the presidency. The Southerners in Congress, agreed to support Hayes on condition that federal troops withdraw from the South, leaving the South was left to handle Blacks without northern interference.

One of the consequences of the withdrawal of federal troops from the South was the repression of militant Black political leaders, who played a prominent role in organizing rural Blacks during the Reconstruction period. Men like Henry Adams, a Black political leader, were driven into the urban areas of the South away from their Southern rural base, or they were assassinated. The repression of militant secular Black leadership created a leadership vacuum that was filed largely by conservative Black ministers.

Most of these Black ministers operated in a climate where Blacks were being forcefully removed from the ballot box, and a segregated Jim Crow system was being erected. By the turn of the century, Booker T. Washington emerged as a national spokesperson for Black people. While many writers on Washington have misunderstood his significance, treating him as a Uncle Tom, his contribution has been far reaching and significant. He founded a major Black educational institution, Tuskekee, encouraged the organization of Black businesses, and attempted to provide a program for Black economic development. Still, he pursued an accommodationists approach to white Southerners, which was similar to the approach being pursued by the majority of Black Ministers.

While General Nat Turner, living under the violent system of slavery had along with many other slaves viewed Christianity through their own eyes. Black ministers began to adopt a religious interpretation of Christianity which was in line with the conservative white evangelicals. Drawing from the Old Testament and Maroon Ethiopianists Voudom traditions, these Southern Black preachers, as Cayraud S. Wilmore notes in his book *Black Religion and Black Radicalism*.

> a nonviolent, self-effacing, patiently-suffering white Jesus held up by the conservative evangelicals and revivalists at the turn of the century became for many Black preachers the authoritative image of what it is like to be a Christian.[121]

At a time when Black people in the South needed a creative leadership, too many Black ministers were coming under the theological control of their white oppressors. To paraphrase Fanon, 'when Blacks came to worship Christ as white, they were really worshipping the white man as God.' When they came to derive their conception of Christianity from white theologians, their minds were shackled by the psychological chains of slavery. The Nat Turners did not draw on white images of Jesus, or white theology, they went inside themselves and communed with a just God who would not sanction slavery.

The Black church in the South had come a long way from ancient Kemet, to the African Church Fathers of the Christian Church, to General Nat Turner and Bishop Henry McNeal Turner. Too many southern Black ministers, by their own ignorance of the African roots of Christian theology, became imprisoned in the theological framework of the oppressor.

THE AMERICAN DREAM

Part of the reason for the shift of the dominant wing of the Black church away from a radical theological posture was that with emancipation, growing urbanization and education, Blacks in America were coming under the influence of American values. One of the first significant value shifts among Blacks after slavery, occurred among the "representative men of color." These were Blacks who achieved some degree of Western education and took on the values of whites. Many of them took on the language of the oppressor, abandoning their southern dialects. Along with the imitation of the oppressors language came an acceptance of the oppressors viewpoint. With migration from rural to urban areas this process of acculturation increased. According to Cayraud S. Wilmore,

> To the contrary, the leaders and many of the constituents of these primary representatives of organizational life in the Black community were members of the new bourgeoisie, or at least lower-class strivers who were rapidly gaining sufficient economic security to permit them to begin participation in social reform if an appropriate leader had been presented.. [122]

The first wave of migrants from the South to the North, at the turn of the 20th century, were skilled Blacks many of whom were descendents of house negroes. These Blacks made up the base of the Black church and Black social organizations. They had been acculturated into white values during the period of plantation slavery, and the institutions they supported reflected those values.

The majority of Black Churches were made up of leaders and members who were "lower-class strivers", who desired middle class respectability. The direction of the Black church toward middle class values, was compounded by the formation of the

Black Establishment, a grouping (noted in Volume I of the Art of Leadership) made up of civil rights, business, educational, social, publishing, and church groups. This formation, created after the death of Booker T. Washington, by his representatives and W.E.B. Du Bois, would serve as a national leadership that would pursue on a national and local level an accommodationists approach towards the white Power structure. The Black establishment formed a nexus of power with the Black church. The NAACP used and continued to use the Black church as an organizational base for recruitment and meetings. The moderation of the Black establishment, and its middle class integrationist values, served to further moderation and integration in the Black Church. The reverse was also true. The Black church would serve as a moderating force on the Black establishment.

The mass migration of Blacks to the urban areas of the North during World War I and World War II would bring in grassroots Blacks, who had come out of areas of the rural South, where Ethiopianism, Black Nationalism, extended families and a communal self-help approach to life prevailed. These new migrants were viewed with contempt by many of the light skinned Blacks, who viewed Black folk culture as uncouth.

MARCUS GARVEY

It was from the ranks of rural Blacks who had migrated north, and were in transition from rural to urban life, that the support base for the Garvey movement came. The Blacks who made up the membership of the Garvey movement north and south, were not only looking for a political movement that provided power for Black people, but they were also looking for a spiritual outlook that wasn't bleached white as snow.

Marcus Garvey's Universal Negro Improvement Association formed the African Orthodox Church, which portrayed Jesus as Black, and propagated a Christianity that encouraged Blacks to stand up and fight for their liberation. Unfortunately, the African Orthodox Church had little impact on the mainstream Black churches in America.

CIVIL RIGHTS AND THE BLACK CHURCH

A wing of the Black Church, during the fifties and sixties, assumed an activist role, under the leadership of Martin Luther King. King pulled together a group of activist Black ministers who formed the Southern Christian Leadership Conference. These ministers led boycotts, sit-ins and other voter registration campaigns in the South, and by the mid-sixties attempted to carry their campaign to the North.

Unlike the Nat Turners and Henry Highland Garnetts, who drew from an Old Testament, aggressive "eye for an eye" and "tooth for a tooth" self defense and insurrectionists strategy, Martin Luther King drew from the New Testament, loving turn the other cheek philosophy. While Bishop Henry Turner tried to inject Black Nationalism into Christianity, King, while rooted in the soulful preaching tradition of the Black ministry, was committed to integration.

King's great strength was that he linked the spiritual role of the ministry with the political role of agitation and education for social justice. In this sense, King came out of the radical ministerial tradition, and he was opposed or not supported by a majority of Black ministers, who were preaching a "pie in the sky, get yours when you die" philosophy.

For many mainstream Black churches that were seeking middle class respectability, the Civil Rights Movement provided an opportunity for them to form stronger ties with the white power structure.

BLACK POWER AND THE BLACK CHURCH

By 1966, many members of the Civil Rights Movement, mainly those coming out of SNCC (Student Nonviolent Coordinating Committee) and CORE (Congress of Racial Equality) moved to a Black Power position. A combination of experiences including a continuous struggle with the racist federal, state, and local governments, along with the nationalists teachings of Malcolm X and the

Nation of Islam helped to transform the movement from one for Civil Rights to one for Black Power and Black nationalism.

Some Black ministers attempted to respond to the Black Power Movement by calling for the development of a Black theology.

TOWARDS A LIBERATION THEOLOGY

As leaders and organizers it is important to understand the spiritual legacy of African people. Christianity has a Kemetic spiritual foundation based on high ethical principles. The Kemetic spiritual legacy provides a path for Blacks to save themselves through cultivating their characters. The chapter on political education provides step by step approaches for accomplishing this important task.

Whether we, as African people, believe in Islam, Christianity, traditional African religion, Eastern religions or no religion, we have the responsibility to fill the spiritual void that exists in our communities. Too many of our people feel that their lives lack value or meaning. Far too many African people do not know who they are. As the ancient spiritual teachers of Kemet taught, "self-knowledge is the basis for all knowledge." As leaders, and organizers both lay and ministerial, we have to encourage our religious leaders to develop an African based theology of liberation that links the political needs of our people with their spiritual needs. This does not mean that Blacks if they are Christian have to leave the church, it just means that we have to make Christianity relevant to our people.

In our University Black Studies Departments, and our community organizations and churches we need to establish Afro-centric leadership academies that train our ministerial leaders in African and African-American history and culture. Our ministers need to know the history from which their religion springs. Many Black churches are small and poorly administered. Many don't become large because the minister is afraid that he will loose control. Black ministers, through leadership academies, need training in the Art of Leadership, which includes the art of managing Black institutions.

PROGRESSIVE BLACK CHURCHES

On the positive side, in virtually every Black community there are a few significant Black churches that are efficiently run, administering to the needs of the Black community. Some teach a Black liberation theology, provide housing, education, and other social programs to the Black community. These progressive Black churches are models for revitalizing the Black church and the Black community. Ideally, the Black church should be both a spiritual center that encourages our people to be the best human beings possible, by becoming one with the God within, as well as a dynamic, militant, no-compromise community organization dedicated to African liberation worldwide. As leaders and organizers it is your responsibility to establish links with the Black church as you go about organizing the Black community.

Toussaint L'Ouveture

CHAPTER FOURTEEN

ALLIANCES AND COALITIONS

BROADENING YOUR BASE

An alliance is a formal union between organizations, while a coalition is a temporary union of organizations. Examples of alliances on the international level are NATO (North Atlantic Treaty Organization), the United Nations, and the Organization of African Unity. These formations are considered to be alliances because they are formal unions, that are relatively permanent.

COALITIONS

Examples of coalition formations are the March on Washington and the Free South Africa Coalition. Both of these were temporary formations where groups came together to fight around a specific issue and once the issue was settled the members of the coalition went their separate ways.

You may choose to form a coalition with other groups for a variety of reasons. If your organization is too weak to function alone, a coalition may enable you to carry out certain programs that your group could not carry out by itself. Generally when groups enter into coalitions because of their own weaknesses, you can expect them to move away from coalition building when they become organizationally strong. Coalitions may arise spontaneously when a burning issue such as a police killing or some other racist attack on the Black community creates an atmosphere for coalition building. Whether or not a coalition emerges out of such a "crisis" will depend upon the flexibility and creativity of the leadership. Black people are crisis oriented, so we respond to crisis issues. Coalitions around a crisis issue can bring new people into the struggle and raise their consciousness. Coalitions built in this fashion often help to break down suspicions and divisions that exist between different community groups. Coalitions can also be organized to carry out a specific campaign, such as a struggle for jobs or an electoral campaign.

BUILDING A COALITION

Regardless of the particular issue or campaign that ties it together a coalition is usually the product of years of organizing. A specific coalition, such as one organized to fight for a civilian review board, is often the product of previous struggles and relationships where support has been exchanged between different groups. So while coalitions often form suddenly, the groundwork that makes it possible for different people and groups to work together is part of a long term process. Over the years you build up credibility and obligations based on the support that is exchanged. By being able to consistently work with other groups, you help to break down petty jealousies and negative perceptions.

THE UNITED FREEDOM MOVEMENT COALITION

Between 1960 and 1963 the San Francisco Chapter of the Congress of Racial Equality organized a number of campaigns for open housing, quality education, support for low income housing, and most importantly, demonstrations and boycotts for jobs. Over a period of three years, our struggles began to grow from small to large ones, and in the process we developed ties with different community organizations. When the Bayview Hunter's Point Citizen's Committee, under the leadership of Ardath Nichols, called for a halt to redevelopment until a plan for low income housing could be provided, San Francisco CORE, and the NAACP supported their demand. When CORE demanded jobs for Blacks from the downtown department stores, and the stores refused to meet our demands, a coalition was formed with the Baptist Minister's Union to carry out boycotts against Penneys. As the struggle developed, various ties were formed with community groups. Eventually, after three years of struggle, we were able to formalize our ties through the organization of the United Freedom Movement. The United Freedom Movement took years to build. It was organized to carry out three job campaigns, against the Sheraton Palace Hotel, Auto Row, and the Bank of America. An article in the San Francisco Examiner dated July 24, 1963, explains the purpose of this coalition:

> A broad-front alliance of civil rights organizations spurred by 'the growing anger of San Francisco Blacks' publicly girded itself yesterday for an all-out campaign to wipe out what they considered to be widespread racial inequality in the city. The strategy was clear: unified action to eliminate discrimination in employment,   housing, education, politics, and law enforcement.   But tactics which   will   be   used deliberately were left vague. However, there was little doubt   that   mass demonstrations -- sit-ins, boycotts, picket lines -- will be employed   if   necessary. Announcement of the alliance came at a conference of top people in the following civil

rights groups -- Dr. Thomas N. Burbridge, president of the National Association for the Advancement of Colored People; Bill Bradley, Chairman of the Congress of Racial Equality; Mrs. Ardath D. Nichols, President of the Bayview Hunters Point Neighborhood Citizen's Committee, and Harold Brooks, Jr., Field Secretary of the Negro American Labor Council.

Doctor Burbridge and Mrs. Nichols were announced as co-chairmen of the ad hoc committee which will direct the campaign. They said that at least eight other civil rights groups are represented on the ad hoc committee and that more groups are expected to join the alliance shortly....

Bradley told the reporters that "mass protests will arise if the power structure of the city is unwilling to deal reasonably with the (Black) community" in its demands for full equality....Mrs. Nichols summed up the feelings of the new San Francisco

Alliance like this: "We've been second class citizens for a long, long time -- 1963 is the time for complete fulfillment of the United States Constitution. That's what we're here for."

Bradley said that future action -- presumably mass demonstrations -- depends on the reaction of San Francisco's power structure to the ad hoc committee's program.[123]

THE POWER OF UNITY

The initiation of the United Freedom Movement created an example of unity for the Black community. This broad based organizational unity encouraged Blacks and other groupings to move together on a mass level. Before the formation of the United Freedom Movement, civil rights demonstrations were small. After the formation of the UFM, demonstrations increased from 10,000 at the Sheraton Palace, to 15,000 at Auto Row and the Bank of America. Years of building relationships paid off in a broad-based coalition that became the spark that lit the flame of mass struggle in San Francisco.

USING BIG ISSUES TO TIE A MASS BASED COALITION TOGETHER

Major issues have the power to bring together forces which previously had no desire to work together. Such issues, when properly used, can bring together people and groups that you have not been able to reach through years of patient organizing. Such groupings may consist of opportunists who are looking for publicity and power, or they may include sincere elements that have ideological differences. In any case, the issue has to be strong enough to temporarily override the differences.

IDENTIFYING COMMON INTERESTS

In order for groups with personal and political differences to work together, they have to see that working together is in all of their better interests. For some, their "interests" may be defined by ego needs. Some may need the glory of publicity. Where this is the case, then the coalition should feed this need while utilizing the strengths of the particular group. In other cases, particular groups may want to establish their legitimacy through working with established groups. Others may have a sincere desire to improve the conditions of the people. The sincere elements should lead the coalition formally if a formal leadership exists, or informally if no formal leadership exists.

ASSESSING COALITION MEMBERS

Before entering a coalition you should be able to assess the motives and interests of the various groups participating. Because interests differ in coalitions, your job is to see that the progressive, selfless forces control the coalition, while meeting the needs of the participants.

Control means that you have to work the hardest, and anticipate the turning points, so that you can put forward timely ideas for direction.

Coalition and alliance work means that your organizational representatives have to be flexible in working with different groups, and you have to maintain a majority consensus for progressive action. Organizational representatives should learn not to push ideologies, because ideologies will only clash in a coalition made up of different ideological outlooks. Your representatives should be issue-oriented and should build the issue that the coalition was formed to fight.

LEADERS OF COALITIONS

If the coalition decides to select a leader, or a collective leadership, then the person or persons selected should have a progressive or revolutionary history, and they should have the widest appeal possible. In some cases, your group representatives will head up the coalition. In other situations, the leadership will be assumed by other organizational representatives. Whoever is chosen, the selection should be based on who will serve the best interests of the coalition.

In coalition work, you should place consistent workers in key organizational positions, which include committee heads and representatives on the executive committee. Your representatives should work hard, respect the opinions of others, and use their common sense in arriving at decisions.

Integrity in coalition work, and in organizing work in general, is very important. Don't try to rip off members from other coalition organizations. Too many so-called revolutionary organizations use the Communist Party bore-within-tactic, trying to feed off other progressive and revolutionary organizations. There are plenty of potential recruits in the Black community. Why should you have to pick the fruit off someone else's tree? Why not pick fruit that does not belong to someone else? Raids on membership only create antagonisms between organizations.

Coalitions, when properly handled, work for everyone's benefit. They show the community a level of unity that encourages larger numbers of Black people to take up the political struggle.

ALLIANCES

Alliances are more permanent arrangements than coalitions; therefore, the issues or interests that tie them together have to be more permanent. The Organization of African Unity is a more permanent body than was the March on Washington, because the development of continental African unity is more long-term than a single march organized to demand a faster pace in the enactment and enforcement of civil rights legislation.

DECISION-MAKING STRUCTURES

Alliances, because they are long term, have to develop formal processes for making decisions, defining leadership, and developing programs. The formation of the National Black United Front is an example of how alliance's are formed. Local BUF's created the motion that encouraged others to join in. Because the Front was a more permanent arrangement, it took a year to spell out a constitution and elect a permanent leadership. People from different parts of the country, with different ideologies, personalities, and interests could not be expected to build a formal alliance without a clear structure and a definable leadership. The July 9, 1980, issue of the *Black American*, a Black newspaper, described the founding convention of the National Black United Front:

The immensity of our task and the desperation of our situation make it imperative for all Black men and women to assume responsibility for all thirty million Black people in everything they say and do. For if Blackness is worth talking about, if it is worth meeting about and shouting about, it is worth living.   And the challenge we face now is to internalize the Black imperative and to live in the spirit of the United Black community to come.

I think that this statement by the Reverend Herbert Daughtry, could best sum up the Founding Convention for National Black United Front organizing for victory in the 1980s.

I was at the convention on Saturday and when I arrived Reverend Daughtry was on the floor accepting nominations for representatives from the 33 states present.   After the nominations were closed, Jitu Weusi, also one of the founding members called the convention to order and opened the portion of the convention where proposals are put to the floor to be voted upon. The first to present their resolutions were the women. They stopped the floor about one half hour. The women were dissatisfied with their position in the convention and let it be known by not accepting the reading of the resolution. Thus the floor was opened to the women, who attempted to organize resolution and present it to the convention in a comprehensive form. This was accomplished and the convention was able to go forward. I could not help but feel I was witnessing history in the making as I watched the events unfold before me. The magnitude and the immensity of this convention rivaled only by that of the Philadelphia convention when our founding fathers had their Continental Convention. History indeed, for this is the beginning of the National Black United Front, where the voice of the Black people will be heard in force.

They came from far and near, high and low, professionals and amateurs alike with one purpose firmly embedded in their hearts. Unity and recognition for Black men and women. And in one voice from this day on they shall be heard as a united people that must be reckoned with....I feel that Black people have reached a new stage of self-awareness and that this awareness will continue to grow until you hear every voice lifted in unity declaring and proclaiming their unity, one for all and all for one. In Reverend Daughtry's words, "Our stand must be the stand of the winner. We must walk with the majestic steps of the victor. We must struggle not with heavy hearts and sad faces, tearful eyes and whining lips. Nay, but however difficult the days, we must struggle with the glad assurance that freedom is ours. Let us then sieze the future and live triumphantly in the present.[124]

The fighting spirit of the founding NBUF convention fueled the organization of over 20 Black United Fronts throughout the United

States. An alliance consisting of Black Christians, Muslims, Nationalists, Marxists, progressives, and many formerly unorganized Blacks came together around the needs for unified resistance against racist capitalists. To this date NBUF has succeeded in building a cohesive national collective leadership; it has internationalized the struggles gaining allies for the Black liberation movement in Africa, Cuba, and other areas of the world, and it is laying the foundation for building a mass-based movement for Black liberation in the United States.

With all of its achievements, NBUF is still a small organization struggling to organize Black people for liberation. We have much work to do before the organization is truly representative of our people. Financially we are weak. Our administrative structures, locally and nationally, need strengthening, and we need to refine our strategies and tactics. Still NBUF offers great promise in spite of the great difficulties that face it, because it has a deep and sincere commitment to carry out a noncompromising struggle for liberation. NBUF has also been able to avoid divisive struggles over who is the blackest, or the most revolutionary. We have been able to work in the areas of agreement, while avoiding conflicts around our differences.

Still, the more broad-based the alliance the more differences that will exist within the alliance. Alliances usually work as long as people see an overriding issue that the alliance can address. Alliances can fall apart when attempts are made to impose an ideology on the alliance, or when narrow forces within the alliance attempt to restrict the alliance's purpose to issues that do not cut across a broad spectrum.

LEADERSHIP

Within every alliance there is a center, that represents the leadership of the alliance. The center may be the strongest group in the alliance, such as the U.S. in NATO or Al Fatah within the Palestine Liberation Organization. Or other criteria may be used to select the leadership including selecting a group that is least threatening to the majority of organizations. Whatever formula is used for determining the leadership of the alliance, you should protect the interest of your group by securing a leadership role in the alliance. Leadership may involve leading the alliance, chairing a committee, holding another major office, and membership on the alliance executive committee. Regardless of the leadership position that your group occupies within the alliance, the groups participation in the leadership is essential for guaranteeing that you have influence on the direction of the alliance.

Alliance work, like coalition work, includes being able to form alliances with member organizations based on common interests. Ties will often change within an alliance when organizational interests change. As an organizational representative to an alliance, you must represent the interests of your group, the best interests of the race and the interests of the alliance as a whole.

Within the Black United Front alliance, group representatives will have to distinguish between their organization's position on a question, and what is in the best interest of NBUF as a whole. At this time many organizations within NBUF have many different positions on the land question, and most think their position is the correct one. A large section of NBUF members have no land position whatsoever. At this time it would be a strategic mistake for any member organization of NBUF to attempt to impose their land objective on NBUF because if such an imposition did succeed it would probably split the Front. Those that disagreed with the position would probably leave, and those who have no position at all would either end up confused, become supporters, or remain neutral. The land question is one in which individual organizational representatives must see that while they adhere to a particular organizational position, they must be flexible enough to weigh other positions and be disciplined enough not to try to impose a single position on the Front.

THE SHIFTING NATURE OF ALLIANCES AND COALITIONS

Both alliances and coalitions are shaky formations, and keeping them together is like balancing eggs. Why are alliances and coalitions such tenuous formations?

In an analysis by Melvin Small and J. David Singer of fifty interstate wars and forty-three colonial and imperial conflicts between 1816 and 1965 (in which more than a thousand battle fatalities occurred), a fifth of the 209 pairs of opposing enemies had previously been allies. Of the 136 nations with more than one experience in war, four-fifths of the ninety-five pairs with some experience as enemies had been allies at least once. Citing hundreds of treaties between 1535 and 1968, Laurence Bellesen showed that political treaties will be broken if it is in the national interest to do so. He concluded that no reliance should be placed on the long-term honoring of treaties by any nation. [125]

ALLIANCE AND THE HAITIAN REVOLUTION

The history of the Black liberation movement, and trends in the international revolutionary movement support Bellesen's conclusion. In the Haitian revolution, an ally at one point quickly became an enemy at another. C.L.R. James describes this process:

> The French Revolution, being still in the hands of liberals and 'moderates,' was clearly bent on driving the Blacks back to the old slavery. Thus when the Spaniards in San Domingo offered the Blacks an alliance against the French government, naturally they accepted. Here were white men offering them guns and ammunition and supplies, recognizing them as soldiers, treating them as equals and asking them to shoot other whites. All trooped over to join the Spanish forces and Jean Francois and Biassou were appointed lieutenants-general of the armies of the King of Spain. Toussaint went also, but he made his terms with the Spaniards as an independent leader, and not as a subordinate of Biassou. He had 600 men, well-trained and absolutely devoted to him, and he received an official title of colonel. Like all the other Blacks, Toussaint attacked the godless kingless

republic and fought in the name of royalty, both Spanish and French. But for him, already, these slogans were merely politics, not conviction.[126]

Toussaint used the coalition with the Spanish to strengthen his own position. He continued to rally Blacks to the cause of liberty, while attacking the French. When the French promised the Blacks freedom, Toussaint broke his alliance with Spain and formed an alliance with France. Unfortunately, Toussaint's French mentality blinded him to the fact that the French were also only temporary allies who would turn on the Blacks and return them to slavery when the chance arose.

BLACK RECONSTRUCTION COALITIONS

In the United States, Blacks have experienced the thesis that your so-called friends today can become your enemies tomorrow. During the reconstruction period Blacks formed a coalition with northern capitalists, white abolitionists, and a minority of whites (scallywags) who participated in the reconstruction government. Northern capitalists formed a temporary coalition with Blacks to prevent the white South from nationalizing the banks, lowering the tariff on foreign goods, repudiating the national debt, and forming an electoral coalition with farmers in the West, which would have taken the presidency away from the party of big business (Republicans) and placed it in the hands of Democrats. Blacks were allowed to vote in order to protect the interests of big business, and its mouthpiece, the Republican party, joined with the Democrats in "bulldozing Blacks" when the Northern capitalist Black coalition ceased to serve the interest of big business. White Republicans and white Democrats alike, tightened the noose around the necks of Blacks.

POPULIST CIVIL RIGHTS AND PAN AFRICAN ALLIANCES

In the 1890s Blacks and whites in the South formed a coalition that was known as the Populist movement. Not long there after white populists, who had professed friendship for Blacks, joined the Ku Klux Klan. So called allies had become staunch enemies.

During the 1960s a coalition of Blacks, labor, churches, liberals, and Jewish groups, was formed around the Civil Rights movement. By the 1970s former Jewish allies were pressing the courts to oppose affirmative action for Blacks; labor became a bastion of support for Nixon and Reagan, and liberalism became a joke.

In the 1970s two promising Pan African Coalitions, the Congress of African People, and the African Liberation Support

Committee had split apart, with former allies becoming bitter enemies.

PROTECTING YOURSELF IN AN ALLIANCE OR COALITION

So with this bitter experience, how can you protect yourself in alliances and coalitions? First, only enter alliances and coalitions when your objectives can be achieved in no other way. If you can achieve your objectives without entering into such arrrangements, then avoid doing so.

MAINTAIN AN INDEPENDENT ORGANIZATIONAL BASE OUTSIDE THE ALLIANCE OR COALITION

Second, when entering an alliance or coalition, maintain an independent organizational base that has an independent life outside the alliance or coalitions. It is a serious blunder to put all of your organizational eggs into an alliance or coalition. The Chinese Communist Party made this mistake in the 1920s. They subordinated themselves to the United Front, even failing to adequately arm their members. The Kuomintang an ally in the United Front, turned on them, and killed over a million communists.

Toussaint didn't make this mistake. When he allied with the Spanish he maintained an independent organizational base that was loyal to him. Avoid alliances or coalitions where you are only an appendage, or a weak link in the alliance. If you join as a weak link, the chances are good that you will be used by the strong members of the alliance. It's better to be the head of a mouse organizationaly, than to be the tail of the larger elephant.

Third, before joining an alliance or coalition, spell out what you expect to get out of the arrangement. Don't allow yourself to become the virtuous fool who expects to get nothing out of the relationship. Your allies have specific objectives. If you have none, you can expect to get skinned alive.

Fourth, monitor the relationship to see if the agreements reached in the beginning are carried out. You can protect yourself in alliances and coalitions by forging personal and political ties, that protect you from flanking movements from opponents.

Fifth, above all, during the alliance and coalition work, maintain a balance between continuing the independent work of your organization and working with the coalition or alliance. Whatever type of organizing you are doing it's important that you attempt to win the minds of our people.

CHAPTER FIFTEEN

PROPAGANDA, PUBLICITY AND

PUBLIC THINKING CAMPAIGNS

PROPAGANDA, PUBLICITY,
AND PERSUASION

Your mind is your seat of power. White propaganda systems are mind-controlling systems. They are so effectively organized that they can take control of your mind without you knowing it.

Marcus Garvey provided a very vivid description of the white system of propaganda when he said:

We are living in a civilization that is highly developed. We are living in a world that is scientifically arranged in which everything done by those who control is done through system; proper arrangement,proper organization, and among some of the organized

methods used to control the
world, is the thing
known and called
'PROPAGANDA.'

Propaganda has done more
to defeat the good intentions
of races and nations than
even open warfare.

Propaganda is a method or
medium used by organized
peoples to convert others
against their will.

We, the Black race, are
suffering more than any other
race in the world from
propaganda -- propaganda
to destroy our hopes, our
ambitions and our
confidence in self.[127]

MIND CONTROL

Through the scientific arrangement of
ideas, through the medium of the printed
word, religion, the school and university,
television, the newspapers, radio, movies
and magazines (to name only a few), the
modern european nation state manipulates
thought and in so doing controls the behavior
of so-called modern man (men and
women). The rulers of the modern nation-
state seek to control the minds of all their

subjects, both Black and white.   Hans J. Morgenthau in his book, *Politics Among Nations*, describes the system of mind control:

> When we speak of power, we mean man's control over the minds and actions of other men...Political power is the psychological relation between those who exercise it and those over whom it is exercised. It gives the former, control over certain actions of the latter, through the influence which the former exerts over the latter's minds.[128]

THE HISTORY OF WHITE PROPAGANDA

J.A.C. Brown in his book, *Techniques of Persuasion from Propaganda to Brainwashing*, states:

> The Oxford Dictionary defines propaganda as 'an association or scheme for propagating a doctrine or practice, and the word takes its origin from the Latin propagare which means the gardener's practice of pinning the fresh shoots of a

plant into the earth in order to reproduce new plants which will later take on a life of their own.　　Therefore　one implication of the term, when it was used in the sociological sense by the Roman Catholic Church, was that the spread of ideas brought about in this way is not one that would take place itself, but rather a cultivated　or　artificial generation. In the year 1633, Pope Urban VIII established the　Congregation　de Propaganda Fide, otherwise known as "The Congregation of Propaganda" or simply "The　Propaganda,"　a committee of cardinals which had, and still has charge if the foreign missions of the Church. Naturally this was regarded as a beneficient process, which by preaching and example, attempted to lead the heathen from darkness into light and it was an artificial or cultivated one only　in the sense that, without outside intervention, these peoples would never have learned about Christianity....[129]

THE CATHOLIC CHURCH AND PROPAGANDA

The Catholic Church organized "the Propaganda" to turn African people and other people of color away from their traditional religions which were labeled as "heathen" "dark" and "savage." African religions that were labeled in these distorted terms were the source of original Christianity. Egyptian religion is the source of Christian mythology and religion. Traditional African religions provided a connection between the living and the dead, and were the source of science, medicine, and other systems of knowledge. But because they were not Catholic, they were attacked. The implantation of Western religion (a religion changed from its original African origins) was the way the West went about controlling the minds of African people. Christianity was a foreign plant sunk into the earth in order to create a passive mentality, willing to allow the European to grab the land while the African waited for heaven in the next life.

THE PRINTED WORD

The propaganda units of the Catholic Church were very crude and unsophisticated compared to the propaganda systems that would follow. The invention of printing worked to spread ideas through the printed word, and this made it easier for the state to control ideas. It was a difficult matter to control the spoken word, but it became relatively easy for the state to control the written word. Powerful money interests gained control of the press, and the printed word became a tool for manipulating public thought.

In England during the 15th century, the pamphlet and the newsletter were journals for English cities. Both of these organs were gossip journals that pandered to ignorance and kept the people's minds off serious matters.

Weekly newspapers were organized and censored by the state. These news sheets printed the news the state wanted printed. By the first quarter of the 19th century, the English press consisted of journals of opinion that only promoted their own narrow viewpoints. Contrary viewpoints were not printed. Such journals also specialized in blackmail. Information that was embarassing to leading citizens was withheld from publication if they paid a handsome bribe.

The gossip tabloids of Britain are the origin of the sensational journalism found in the American press today. Most news in the U.S. does not elevate or educate, it appeals to the public's desire for sensational gossip, and sick behavior (murder, rape, etc.).

SUGGESTION

Modern propaganda systems are the most sophisticated systems of thought control known in the history of mankind. They employ the latest techniques in psychology. According to Leonard W. Dobb, the author of *Public Opinion and Propaganda*, modern propaganda can be defined as:

> a systematic attempt by an interested individual (or individuals) to control the attitudes of groups of individuals through the use of suggestion, and consequently, to control their actions.

Suggestion is defined in the New College Edition of the *American Heritage Dictionary* as:

> The psychological process by which an idea is induced in or adopted by an individual without argument, command or coercion.[130]

Suggestion is used to control attitudes, thoughts, and actions of groups of people without giving any self evident or logical grounds for their acceptance.

BLACK PUBLIC THINKING STRATEGIES

White mass media strategies have been explained so that we could assess their strengths and weaknesses and develop creative "public thinking" strategies. I choose to use the term "public thinking" instead of "public relations" because public relations or propaganda has been used in the West to subvert thought, while public thinking is designed to mobilize creative Black thought.

Black public thinking strategies cannot be limited to cookbook recipes on how to handle the white mass media. We are dealing with a media that uses the latest scientific techniques to capture and demobilize the thinking of races and nations. Black public thinking strategies have the task of organizing creative media strategies that undermine, disrupt, and frustrate nonthinking, suggestive, media techniques.

The central goal of Black public thinking strategies should be to free captured Black minds from the manipulation of propaganda, through encouraging creative, sensitive Black thoughts, Black pride, and self-confidence. Positive Black thought should be encouraged so that positive Black action can take place. The development of creative Black thought patterns will pave the way for creative Black behavior patterns. A conscious, aware, creative people cannot be psychologically controlled.

BALANCED THINKING

Black public thinking needs to encourage Black people to consciously learn how to analyze things from all sides and see that there is a positive and negative aspect in everything. Anyone who suggests that we should accept something on the basis of blind faith, should be automatically rejected as an insult to our intelligence.   Balanced thinking is not easy because it calls for work.   We have to investigate things, go below the surface, and separate appearance from reality. This takes time and is often confusing. It is a lot easier to let the media or someone else do our thinking for us. But like anything that appears to be free, it comes with a high price tag. Without knowing it, we end up placing our minds in hock to someone who doesn't look like us and doesn't have our interests at heart.

In utilizing the media, Black public thinking encourages people to think, by investigating issues of concern to Blacks from all sides and reaching balanced conclusions.   Balanced media coverage requires careful investigation just as balanced thinking does. This kind of media strategy is the opposite of "selective new coverage" and the "big lie" technique, for the goal of balanced coverage is to uncover the truth, or truths, on a specific topic. Our media strategy can never be based on the "big lie" technique, because our greatest strength is in the high principles that we defend and fight for. We maintain our personal dignity and preserve the dignity of our people by standing for the truth of our history, and culture, and over just desire for liberation.

HISTORICAL EDUCATION

Black public thinking is the branch; African identity and Black pride are the roots from which creative thought springs. The Egyptians said "first know thyself"; self-knowledge is the foundation of all knowledge. A knowledge of ourselves gives us an understanding of our unique creative gifts as a race and as individuals. Self-knowledge transforms the thought and behavior patterns of our people, from shameful and dependent slave thought patterns, to proud, loving, independent thought patterns. Self-hate gets transformed into self-love, and the search for white approval is changed into a desire to serve Blacks and gain recognition for our achievements from Black people. The awakened Black person cannot be manipulated to accept the corner reserved for him by whites. The conscious, aware Black person strives to carve out an independent place in the world. African identity elevates the Black person from the level of crawling, where our greatest ambition is to squirm in the shadow of the West -- to the position where we will rest in no one's shadow.

African identity and Black pride arise from two sources - mass struggle and deep, historical study. This book as a whole puts forward ideas for organized activity, but here we will focus on what the media and the individual can do to expand their historical and cultural horizons.

Black public thinking media has to place the highest priority on providing a wide range of information on ancient African history and on the history of Blacks in America. Our history should balance the history of African civilizations and culture with the history of Blacks in America, because this approach gives our people the whole picture of our historical contribution, rather than a selective picture of that contribution. A balanced picture shows our historical strengths and weaknesses. An understanding of these strengths and weaknesses helps us to avoid repeating these mistakes in the future. The strengths are building blocks, that we can draw on in our struggle. A balanced historical coverage minimizes the chance that we will either attempt to restore the past today, or act on the false assumption that we had no history before slavery. An exclusive emphasis on African history and culture can lead those who take this approach to attempt to return to the traditional African past. The exclusive emphasis on Black history in the United States usually leads to a rootless, alienated, American outlook. A balanced historical approach allows us to adapt certain positive elements from our African past into the present, so that we can more effectively organize and plan for the future.

Since white media strategies are organized to destroy Black identity and Black self-confidence, "Black thinking" strategies have to rebuild and reinforce self-confidence and African identity.

A balanced historical understanding not only gives us a knowledge of ourselves, it also opens our eyes so we can see the true enemy. Although the enemy has Black pawns that he uses against us, the true enemy does not look like us. One reason that white propaganda subverts our thinking is to avoid identifying those who run this system, and those who support it, as the true enemy. Winning strategies are only developed when we know ourselves and the enemy. Narrow analysis will lead to narrow action. Narrow action is doomed before it gets off the ground.

The Black person who knows himself and examines things in a critical way is a person who reads and studies everything he or she can get their hands on, about the topic of Black people, the system that oppresses us, economics, political theory, international politics, technical subjects, etc. Black public thinking is by its nature a strategy that encourages our people to read. But reading alone is not enough. We have to read critically with our minds open; we must be observant. Critical reading is necessary because the printed word is monopolized by the owners of the major publishers. These publishers often tell their writers what to write, and censor and edit their final manuscripts. The best books are probably either in the publisher's garbage can, or they are published by small publishers, who are only able to reach a small part of the public. This state of affairs does not mean that we shouldn't read, because there is a lot of good material on the market. What we have to do is learn not to form an opinion of a group or individual solely on what we read in a book or in any other printed medium. Our reading should form only part of our research. In addition, we should carry out independent investigations and find out all we can about a particular subject. We should also research the background of the author and the publisher. Often the writer's background will reveal his/her bias or special outlook. By knowing the type of books that a publisher puts on the market, we know something about the firm's orientation.

CRITICAL READING

To encourage critical thinking and reading, our media should show our people how to find the major premise of a book or article. This is usually found in the article's opening sentence or paragraph. Once the major premise is understood, the reader can subject it to questions and analysis.

Of course, since many Black people can barely read or are not able to read at all, literacy programs should be promoted by our organization.

Just as our people should be encouraged to investigate what they read, they should also be encouraged to investigate what the media says about a group, individual, or an issue. Our media should be a people's media, that has two-way input. The Black audience should not be mere receivers of information, but they should be able to submit articles, be subjects of interviews, and offer criticism on how to improve media content. This approach makes the people feel that their voice is being heard, the feeling of loneliness and powerlessness is reduced. A sense of community is being built through our people's involvement in media production, and the robot information-receiving-system of the white media is undermined.

White propaganda systems recognize the fact that word of mouth communication is the most effective form of communication. Therefore, they spend a lot of time identifying opinion leaders in a community, so that they can manipulate them to push their message. Since Black people rely on television almost totally for news, opinion is often shaped in the Black community through the tube. Often the views of an opinion shaper in the Black community is not a view that he or she has gained through research, but they are opinions based on what some news commentator has said. Since the average news story is only 30 seconds long, it has to be one-sided. What often gets spread in the Black community as news is actually half-truths, outright lies, or trivial information. We usually call this fat mouthing or gossiping.

Repeating what Dan Rather said might be easy, but that doesn't make it accurate or right. As much as possible, our media systems should expose the distortions and lies of the propaganda system. It should evoke feelings of anger, rage, and love.

DEVELOPING SENSITIVITY

Our feelings and sensitivity for each other's condition reflects our humanity. The media programs us to accept the destruction of Black life as a normal thing. Out media should combine reason with emotion, because the two are combined in our culture, and when reason is separated from feeling, it becomes unfeeling and inhuman. Like Aretha Franklin says, "think, think;" let us think about how we can open up the creative powers of our people to gain freedom. In doing this, our creative thoughts cannot be separated from our feelings.

Our public thinking workers should live with the people and feel their pains and sufferings. What we have to say in our newspapers, newsletters, radio and television programs should speak with the fire and emotion, pain, suffering, joy, and hope of our people. Our public thinking campaigns should cut away at the unfeeling robot system of the media, the schools and at every corrupt aspect of the society.

THE ORGANIZATION OF PUBLIC THINKING CAMPAIGNS

A word of mouth system of communication needs to be organized within our various organizations. A good name for describing these committees is Nommo units. Nommo units are word of mouth committees that are composed of brothers and sisters who have a natural speaking ability. People with natural rapping talents should be trained in the art of public speaking, and be given assignments to speak at various public functions. A part of public speaking training should consist of having the participants attend church and other functions where good public speakers are performing. Each trainee should be carefully observed so that you can assess their strengths and weaknesses. If a speaker has a strong emotional delivery, then that speaker should be encouraged to use that strength. If, however, that same speaker is weak on logical analysis, then the training should give special emphasis to combining logic with emotion.

Whatever the speaker's special talents are, training would encourage them to develop their own voice and style. Nothing is worse than having a group of talented speakers who all sound alike. A good Black public speaker is like a good Black New African (so-called ensemble); all musicians are a part of the team, but each has his own creative sound.

In addition to people who have public speaking skills, the Nommo committee should consist of people who are good in one-on-one communication. One-on-one communication training should focus on how to appeal to different groups of Black people, including older Blacks, Black youth, Black workers, Black professionals, and Blacks of varying political ideologies.

All members of your organization should be required to undergo training in how to defend the ideology and program of the organization.

Another communication committee that needs to be formed within all of your organizations is a writer's committee. This committee should be made up of people with natural writing talents. Skilled writers are needed to write our pamphlets, brochures, newspapers, books, etc. Writer's workshops can be held within the organization, and promising writers can be encouraged to attend Black writer's workshops held in the community, as well as take writing courses in school. However, the best training for a future writer is writing. People with writing skills should be given every opportunity to develop their talent through assuming writing assignments.

An effective media program should include training members in television, radio, 16 mm filmmaking, and video operations. You should make full use of the visual image by developing media technicians who can be trained by Blacks with media skills. You may have members with some or all of the necessary skills, but most often, you will have to tap brothers and sisters outside the organization.

CABLE TELEVISION

It is easier than you think to get a cable Television program. Most communities have public access, educational cable stations. These stations are looking for educational programming. Most of them have very little Black programming, and usually they allow you to use their cameras and studios to film your programs, once your people are trained to operate their equipment. The biggest problem that most volunteer organizations face in operating these types of programs is consistency. Cable programming demands that you have your programs ready for airing. If you are taping the program in the studio, then your crew and panelists have to be at the studio and ready to go at the specified time. Getting consistent people is not easy. If your organization has been operating for a long time, then one way to get reliable people is to draw heavily on members who have been committed over the years. People are also more likely to be consistent, if they are interested in the program they are working on. If, after using your creativity, you still have a problem of inconsistency with some of your people, then be prepared to recruit new people to take their places.

Along with cable television, Black radio stations provide another good opportunity for you to get a regular weekly program. Black soul stations have large Black listening audiences because they play Black music. They also have public programming on which topics of interest to the Black community are discussed. Your organizations can develop an appealing programming proposal for presentation to the station management.

The best cable TV and radio program proposals can end up in a wastebasket, if you have not developed personal contact with station management. Have either the head of your organization or the head of your radio and television committee cultivate a relationship with the local station management. Do what you can to help them get good news tips, and use your resources in ways that are helpful to them. Good personal contact will pay off later on.

Getting your own programs is extremely important, because you will be able to shape your own image rather than having the major media shape it for you. But independent media programming is not enough; you also have to be able to handle the major media.

The major mass media is geared to sensational reporting and the use of suggestion techniques to manipulate public attitudes. As we have seen, the media is the most dangerous instrument that the enemy possesses. And precisely because of this danger, it cannot be ignored. By the middle sixties, negative media coverage of the movement led many of us to retreat from the use of the media entirely. This reaction was understandable, but erroneous. The propaganda system is aggressive. Therefore, we cannot afford to be passive when facing it.

Movement experience indicates that new political movements are unpredictable to the media, and therefore, novel and exciting. The novelty and newness make good print or good news coverage. New movements also catch the government and the power structure by surprise and it takes them awhile to develop counter strategies. It is especially difficult for these counter strategies to be developed if the new movement has a broad public appeal.

COINTELPRO MEDIA STRATEGIES

After awhile though, the government and the managers of the public media begin to develop policies for handling these new movements. By the middle sixties the FBI was instructing the media, through plants, etc., (see section on COINTELPRO), on how to present various Black and progressive movements in a negative light. In some cases though, the media was carrying out smear campaigns against the movement from the earliest period of the movement.

Once negative media began to take place, the government had a built-in justification for attacking the groups that were targets of sophisticated propaganda assaults.

In the present period, the mass media has accepted a policy of providing very little national or local coverage of progressive or revolutionary Black political struggles. So whatever media strategies we develop towards the major media, we must develop them with the idea in mind that the overall coverage that we will receive will be influenced by the mass media's general policy toward Black political movements. Our media strategy should creatively maneuver so that we can get the maximum advantage out of the situation that we are in.

MASS MEDIA COVERAGE

Organizational morale can be uplifted through positive media coverage. Members are human and want to see that their organization is recognized. Favorable coverage administers to a psychological need of your membership. Media coverage, whether network or independent, increases your organization's visibility in the community. An organization can be working for years doing outstanding community work, yet because it has not publicized that work it can remain invisible to most of the community. Positive community visibility increases the impact that your group has on the community, and it is extremely helpful in broadening the base of your organization.

A media campaign has a number of targets: your own people, allies, the foreign countries, liberation movements, Third World peoples in the U.S., and the various sectors of the white public. In the past , it has been thought to be wise for Blacks to aim all of their propaganda at Black people. Certainly the main concern is winning the minds of your people; however, if this is your only focus, then you have failed to grasp the purpose of mass media campaigns, and have conceded psychological defeat on many fronts. Your public thinking campaigns should also be used to win as many international allies as possible; it should help to disrupt the "divide and conquer" tactics sown between the Blacks and other Third World peoples in the U.S., and it should at least work to neutralize and, where possible, divide whites against the power structure.

A media committee should be organized to handle the external media. The media committee should talk to members and leaders of various community groups to see which reporters in the external media have a good reputation for accurate reporting on community issues. Your media people should develop a relationship with these people. Personal contacts should also be developed with media members in general.

Once you have developed personal contact with the media, your media committee should develop strategies for maintaining regular contact with them. One technique that is often effective is the informal breakfast or lunch, where you get together with a number of reporters and hold off-the-record discussions.

NEWS CONFERENCE

The press conference is an important media event and should be handled in a professional manner. The first problem with press conferences is one of logistics - getting the press to come. It is not enough to call the press and tell them that there is going to be a news conference. Sometimes a newsworthy topic will have to be dressed up with some catchy adjectives that make the issue more exciting. The more inviting the issue seems to be, the more likely the media will be willing to divert reporters or cameras to your event.

TIMING YOUR PRESS CONFERENCE

A newsworthy issue is not enough. If you have a good issue and you call your press conference at the wrong time, you still will get poor attendance. There are a number of things you can do to pick a good time for the conference. Ask the media people what times are good for press conferences. For the weekly newspapers, such as the Black press, find out their deadline for stories. Base your timing of the press conferences on these factors. As a general rule, it is better to hold a press conference around 11:00 a.m. because that allows for afternoon and evening coverage in the newspapers, television and radio.

THE PRESS CONFERENCE SITE

Select a site for the press conference that is comfortable and large enough for the number of press members you expect. Sometimes you may want to hold a press conference at a particular site in the community to illustrate an issue such as police killing or an eviction. Whatever you decide, the key thing is that the site is appropriate for the particular issue under discussion.

ORGANIZING THE PRESS CONFERENCE

The press conference should be well organized. The people who will represent the organization at the conference should be chosen on the basis of their public speaking skills and political consciousness. The media committee should meet with the people who will do the interview to rehearse the interview. It is very important in the rehearsal, to spell out what the organization wants to project in the press conference. Equally important is your ability to anticipate what questions the press will ask. Answers to the questions you want to answer should be practiced.

An iron rule of press conferences, talk-shows, etc., is that you don't let the media trap you into answering questions that you don't want to answer. A good technique for avoiding answering undesirable questions is to shift your answer to a point you want to make.

When conducting a press conference you should understand that there is a difference between how you answer questions asked by newspaper reporters, and those asked by the television reporters. Responses to television questions should be very concise, never more than thirty seconds. The more concise your statements the greater your chances of not having your words cut to pieces in the editing room.

Responses to newspaper reporters (that are not covered by the camera) can be more extensive. Don't be intimidated by reporter's questions. If you need more time to answer a reporter's question, make it clear that you have a few more points to make.

DEFINE THE OBJECTIVES OF THE PRESS CONFERENCE

In your press conference rehearsal, draw up a list of points that you want to make. During the course of the conference, check your list to see if you have covered all of your points. It is not unusual for inexperienced people to conduct a press conference or interview, and not tell the audience where a particular rally is to be held, or on what date. Pay attention to the details.

BE ACCURATE IN YOUR INFORMATION

Sometimes in the emotional heat of a press conference you may overstate a point, misquote a statement, or erroneously give some information. Do everything you can to avoid these kinds of errors, because they undermine your credibility. Research your topic in advance; make sure that your facts are accurate. Remember the external media is not sympathetic to you, so don't give them any excuse to make you look irresponsible and dishonest.

When holding press conferences there are a number of organizational formats you can choose from. One option is to have the principle spokesperson introduce the topic and the ground rules for the interview. Another is to have a member of your media committee introduce the topic, spokespersons, and the ground rules to the press. It helps to have refreshments and informal conversation with the press before the conference. A friendly atmosphere places both the press and your spokespersons at ease.

WRITING THE PRESS RELEASE

The press release is the vehicle you use to explain the whats and wherefores of your issue. Very often we send in press releases to the media without using the correct format. Press releases that are incorrectly written are often not used by the media.

When writing a press release, type in the top right-hand corner, "For Further Information:" then list the name and contact person, including their business and home phone numbers.

On the left-hand side of the page, under the organization's name, put the release date or "For immediate Release." Under this, write the title of the event.

The opening sentence of the release should explain the who, what, when, where, and why of the particular topic. It is important that you include all of the important information in the first sentence because quite often the public will only skim through the first or second sentence and you want to get the meat of your message over.

As a rule, editors usually cut stories from the bottom, so put the most important news in the beginning paragraph. Paragraphs in a press release should be kept short. Try to keep the press release to one page in length.

If you want to use quotes, give the name of the person you are quoting, enclosing their statements in quotation marks. A sample press release is on the following page.

Check your spelling and grammar to see that it is correct. When it is necessary to go beyond one page, then put ("more") in parenthesis at the bottom right-hand corner. At the bottom of the press release put "30" or "#####."

FEATURE NEWS STORIES

A press conference is a good way to get coverage for the afternoon newspapers and the evening television news. Feature interviews on radio and television give you more time to express your views.

PREPARING FOR THE QUESTIONS AND ANSWERS

Conducting a Feature interview, like a press conference, is an art. The person to be interviewed should be a person who has good speaking skills, and topic depth. That person should be thoroughly familiar with his or her topic, and should rehearse the delivery. The panelists should develop a list of questions that they want the interviewer to ask. Before the interview, give the questions to the interviewer. Often talk show hosts are busy, and appreciate this kind of help. Some may have prepared something special for you, and may choose to disregard your questions. If your questions aren't asked, use the old technique of answering the questions the way you want to.

In talk shows find out as much as you can about the kind of audience that listens to the program, and research the background and style of your hosts. Gear your discussion to the audience. If the audience is young, you should make your comments interesting to that audience; if there are a lot of senior citizens, orient your topic to their interests, etc.

DEBATES

The most challenging talk show format is the debate. Debates arouse interest because there is an exchange of viewpoints that gives the listening audience a choice. Debates require a great deal of preparation. You should be familiar with the outlook of your opponent. Find out how effective his or her delivery is. Determine whether your opponent is quick to respond or slow. Try to predict the line of attack. Develop a position that will overwhelm your opponent. The best strategy for overwhelming an opponent is the technique of surprise. Your ability to find a surprising angle depends upon your creativity and how well you have mastered the topic. When you have depth, you understand the complexities of a question. Combine this with creativity and you should be able to hit your opponent with an angle that is unexpected. Usually when you succeed with a suprising strategy, your opponent will be trying to figure out how to handle you, instead of preparing for counter arguments.

COMMUNICATION AIDS

The use of major media is one form of communication, but there are also a variety of internal and external publications. One type of publication that can be used for the general community and your own membership is the organizational booklet. The organizational booklet gives an overall picture of the organization through a written history, description of the programs and philosophy of the organization, and photographs that depict some of the organization's activities.

THE BOOKLET

The organizational booklet should be done in a professional way, with clear writing, justified paragraphs and photographs. The brochure provides an image of your organization to the public, so make it a document that you will be proud of.

NEWSLETTERS

Most organizations make use of the newsletter as a way to communicate with their membership and with the general community. Newsletters have the advantage that they can be read quickly. Newsletters can be mimeographed, or printed out from a word processor. The more professional the better. Usually it takes awhile before an organization is able to move from a mimeographed, or typed newsletter to a printed one. A group of writers should be asked to write the newsletter and an editor should be appointed. The various committees of the organization can be asked to provide newsworthy information for the newsletter. The newsletter can be mailed to your supporters, and if your membership is large enough, to your membership as well.

Another good media technique is the printed speech or printed position paper. Key organizational documents, including important speeches and position papers should be printed for distribution and sale. These kinds of documents can be used to combat negative media coverage. They are often popular because they are taken from the spoken word and put into the printed form.

If you have an organizational headquarters, then you probably have an organizational bulletin board. The organizational bulletin board is an excellent way to transmit information. Keep your bulletin board updated, so that it doesn't become stale. Do a little art work with the board to make it interesting. Keep the notices short and to the point.

Information racks are not only used in bookstores, but they can be effectively used to hold pamphlets, small booklets, magazines, and other reading material that we are promoting. Informational material can either be free or for sale.

TELEPHONE COMMITTEE

The telephone committee is a must for every Black organization. Word of mouth is the most important type of communication in the Black community. Organizational morale can be uplifted by having a consistent system of positive communication in the Black community.

Positive communication about the organization, programs, breakthroughs, etc. keeps the minds of the members on a positive track. This kind of contact helps to undermine negative communication that can eat an organization up. The telephone tree can be established as a communication system in the Black community at-large. Various organizations in the community can be recruited to pass on information to their members; this kind of grapevine can be used to mobilize Black people for rallies, demonstrations, and other types of community events.

ORGANIZATIONAL NEWSPAPER

The organizational newspaper is a communication organ that is necessary if an organization wants to build a strong mass base in the Black community. Most Black organizations that have built a strong base of power in the Black community have had a newspaper that informed the community, rather than misinformed them with sensational news.

Most organizations have some talented writers. Writers are the backbone of a newspaper. A good newspaper needs writers who are interested in writing different types of articles. Writers of newspaper columns need to develop a number of articles on local issues of interest to the community. Someone needs to focus on religious news that is educational. Most revolutionary Black newspapers disregard this area, because of their negative views toward Christianity. What we have to remember is that most Black people are Christians. If we want our paper to be read by a large section of the Black community, then our news should be oriented to their interests. A Black church section can be used to promote Black nationalism in religion. If you have a strong Black nationalist minister in your community, ask him to write your religion column. This will give you access to his members and other churchgoers who are either interested in what he has to say or support his views. Some of your younger members can be asked to write a youth column. The newspaper should appeal to the various social groupings in your community.

Another team of writers needs to develop files and articles on national and international topics. Most community newspapers only report on local news, which consists largely of gossip, shoot outs, and community social life. The Black community is interested in what is going on outside their local communities. By reporting such news, the movement press is counteracting the selective reporting of the major mass media, which leaves out almost all news on Africa. Along with skilled writers you need to either have some printers and a press, or access to an inexpensive system of printing.

A newspaper budget should be prepared that specifies the cost for operating the paper. In the beginning you will probably only be able to afford volunteer help. But planning should prepare for a paid staff that will give you the consistency you will need to keep a newspaper going on a regular basis.

An editorial system should be established. A senior editor should be responsible for approving all copy. A managing editor should handle the financial operations of the paper, including subscription, sales, advertising, etc. The art editors are responsible for seeing that art illustrations and photographs are ready. The copy editor is responsible for editing all articles for grammatical errors and syntactical accuracy.

An important decision that you will have to make is how often you want the paper to come out. This decision should be based on your financial and physical resources. Commit yourself only to what you are capable of doing. Gradually work to make the paper come out more often.

One of the hardest things for the movement newspapers to do is to develop a good system of distribution. One system that works very well for the major newspapers and some Black papers is the use of delivery boys. There are plenty of Black youth with no jobs, and building up a group of customers and delivering their paper is an excellent way for them to make money. You need to appoint a group of people who will manage the delivery boys, train them, and keep track of their work.

Another distribution system is the newspaper rack system. The best location to set up a rack is near a place of business in the Black community. A percentage of your profit will have to be shared with the store owners. You can use the creativity of your members to make newspaper racks, or you can investigate to find the cheapest readymade racks available. Most important, a good system of distribution has to include sales of your papers by members who have been trained in the technique of selling papers.

Advertising is the heart of the funding system for newspapers. Most Black movement papers don't accept advertising because it usually comes with strings attached. It might be advisable to develop a system of selective advertising. You should consider Black advertisers that are nonexploitative. This type of policy will not make you rich, but will give you a little extra income without compromising your principles.

Ultimately, public thinking campaigns have one central objective, to win the minds of African people. We cannot forget Marcus Garvey's observation that white propaganda systems are used to destroy our people's sense of ambition and self-confidence. Western enslavers and colonizers deliberately took control of the Africans past in order to control the African today and tomorrow. The systematic lies created about Africa, that Africa had no history, that Africans had no great civilizations, that europeans saved Africans from savagery -- all of these lies were dreamed up to justify the white races right to rule the Black race.

We must never forget that the system of slavery and colonialism were designed not only to keep the European in power; slavery and colonialism were designed to make the slave and colonized believe that whites were qualified by white right to rule, while the

Black slave and colonized victim were entitled to follow the masters will.

Modern western propaganda systems are even more sophisticated than during Garvey's days. Today television and the movies use subliminal suggestion to place the Black mind under white control, without the Black victim even realizing that his mind has been placed in the hands of another. Subliminal suggestion is a technique whereby ideas are introduced to the subconscious mind without the victim knowing that the idea has been introduced. These ideas are flashed across the television or movie screen so fast that only the subconscious mind can pick it up.

Creative public thinking strategies seek to restore a sense of pride and self-confidence in African people. The self-confidence we want to create is the kind of self-confidence in which the African has the confidence to wield national power. This was the self confidence that Garvey attempted to instill into the race. We have to be creative if we are to create a sense of national self-confidence.

We will need a sense of national self-confidence to withstand not only European mind control, but also to withstand European systems of counter insurgency.

Shaka

CHAPTER SIXTEEN

SECURITY COUNTER INSURGENCY

Counter insurgency systems are used all over the world, according to brother Olomenji, former co-convenor of the Chicago Black United Front and an authority on counterinsurgency and intelligence. Counter insurgency operations are "A system of war designed to halt, disrupt and crush any mass movement. This system is used all over the world. Counter intelligence is a component of counter-insurgency."

Counter insurgency's four components as Olomenji describes them (1) Programs of Pacification; (2) Psychological Warfare; (3) Relocation; and (4) Counterintelligence.

PACIFICATION PROGAMS

Pacification programs have been used against the Black liberation movement in the United States, the Vietnamese National Liberation movement, and the people of Zimbabwe to name a few. Pacification programs are designed to convince the people who are actual or potential supporters of national liberation movements, that the government is able and willing to reform itself. If the government can convince the people that reform is possible, then they can divert movements of national liberation into the warm embrace of the system.

REFORM AND REPRESSION: THE FORD FOUNDATION

In the U.S., Black movements have usually been hit by the dual hands of repression and reform. The most militant sections of the movement have been repressed, while a sector of the masses and leadership have been offered reform. In the middle 1960s this pacification strategy was carried out by the U.S. government and the Ford Foundation under the leadership of McGeorge Bundy. Bundy had used the same methods on the Vietnamese, when he served as Kennedy's National Security Council advisor. According to Robert Allen in his book, *Black Awakening in Capitalist America*:

> Under the leadership of Bundy, former Special Assistant to the President for National Security Affairs -- and in this capacity one of the chief architects of this country's aggression in Vietnam -- the Ford Foundation in 1966 made an important decision to expand its activities in the Black movement. Prior to that time, the organization had

limited its activities among Black Americans to philanthropic efforts in education and research projects, all aimed at incorporating more Blacks into the middle-class mainstream. The 1966 decision, which was made in response to the Black rebellions was a logical extension of an earlier decision to enter the political arena.

....In remarks to the National Urban League in 1966, Bundy stated:

...."Bundy told the Urban League meeting that in addition to the familiar fields - of jobs, education, and housing, the Foundation thought that the areas of leadership, research, communication, and justice were also important concerns for the Black movement....In other words, as the Civil Rights movement faded away a new breed of Black and white leaders was required to negotiate the road from right to reality."

In the area of research, Bundy threw out several questions which he said needed answers: "What kinds of better schools will help most to turn the tide of hope upward in the ghettos? What patterns of cooperation among whites and Negro-business, labor, and government can bring new levels of investment to both the city center and the southern rural slum?" ....The first two questions are especially significant because Bundy was later to become deeply embroiled in New York City's school decentralization dispute and the Foundation would play a leading role in promoting private business investment in the Ghetto. Anticipating this latter development, Bundy urged in his remarks that "strong minded business leadership can put itself in the forefront of the effort to open doors for the Negro."

Significantly, Bundy also hinted that the political arena was to assume greater importance in the Black struggle. "We know....that political influence brings political results," he told

the group. He did not say,
however, that the Foundation
would soon play a leading
indirect part in electing Carl
Stokes as the first Negro
mayor of Cleveland.[131]

CREATING NEW MODERATE BLACK LEADERSHIP

The Ford Foundation put forward a
pacification program that called for jobs,
education, and housing, and the creation of
a buffer leadership group that would
"negotiate" with whites as a "new breed of
leadership." The "new breed" would pursue
moderate accommodationist's goals that
would help to restore the faith of Blacks in the
American system. This moderate leadership
group would consist of the major civil rights
organizations, CORE, SCLC, NAACP and the
Urban League, as well as Black politicians.
The Ford Foundation supported the mayoral
campaign of Carl Stokes as part of an
overall strategy for creating a group of
moderate Black politicians, who would take
the place of the militant leaders of the Black
Panther Party, SNCC, the militant wing of
CORE, and others.

Bundy was even willing to experiment with Black community control of the public schools as one possible method for restoring Black faith in the system. Black capitalism programs were proposed and later financed by the Ford Foundation, the Nixon administration, and other private businesses.

While this pacification program was being implemented, the progressive and militant wings of the movement were being eliminated. Malcolm, King, and a large number of Panthers, as well as other leaders within the Black community were assassinated, imprisoned, forced into exile, discredited, or driven back into local organizing.

This type of repressive campaign coupled with social reform proved very successful. We will have to develop some sophisticated strategies if we are going to be able to withstand even more sophisticated assaults of this type in the future.

PSYCHOLOGICAL WARFARE

Psychological warfare is the second weapon in the Counter insurgency arsenal. According to brother Olomenji, psychological warfare is designed, "to repress Blacks to death, and to destroy the collective inner fiber and collective will." Once the collective will of the group is broken, the will to resist is destroyed.

ISOLATING THE MILITANTS FROM BLACK MASS SUPPORT

Psychological warfare is structured to isolate conscious Blacks from politically unaware Blacks. This is done by labeling conscious Blacks as crazy, radical, and dangerous. Attitudes of individualism, religious escapism, fads, (health food, jogging, etc.) are encouraged so that the individual will be diverted into activities that are isolated from political struggle. Obviously, Blacks are facing a deadly program of psychological warfare.

RELOCATION

The third part of Counter insurgency warfare is relocation. In Vietnam relocation tactics were used by the Americans and the South Vietnamese puppets to remove villagers from their homes and place them in "strategic hamlets" or concentration camps that were under American control.

This same technique is being used against Blacks with considerably more success. Across the U.S., an "Urban Strategy" of "New Towns in Towns," and "Urban Gentrification" have been carried out to break down the high concentration of Blacks in the Black community to smaller, more manageable levels. The "New Towns in Towns" is part of the "Urban Strategy," and is used in urban areas where there are a million or more Blacks. Blacks in these large communities are moved out to the suburbs to "New Towns in Towns," and they are placed in scattered housing where there are three whites for every Black person.

Gentrification is the process whereby whites are encouraged to move into Black communities, with offers of cheap financing, from the leading institutions and redevelopment agencies. Black communities across the country are being invaded by whites who are displacing Black tenants by raising the rents to extremely high levels and placing a preference on renting to whites.

THE PURPOSE OF RELOCATION PROGRAMS

Relocation programs scatter the Black population, and make resistance difficult if not impossible. R.G.H. Siu, in his book *The Craft of Power*, puts the issue succinctly when he says:

> There comes a time when the only alternative to complete breakdown is to share a small portion of your power with a disgruntled minority. This should be accompanied with a delicate but effective program of assimilation. To ensure that you are not letting the camel's nose into the tent, you should first neutralize or

isolate the most militant, who are trying to foment mass action, then bring the more moderate leaders, one after an assimilated one, into your higher councils, while incorporating his followers into your own constituency at large. If the allegiance of their former constituencies is not transferred, however, the invited leaders will continue to be autonomous of your control with their own power base, resulting in the increased danger of potentially challenging you on your own turf....

Because of the implications of such a strategy, the assimilation of the Black race into the American hybrid would constitute a disconcerting nebulous problem for a Black leader in the U.S.....when viewed strictly from the standpoint of long-term national power, however, continued segregation would be disastrous. The longer the delay, the greater will be the difficulty of assimilating a genetically dominant Black minority, which is increasing at a faster rate in population than the average. Were the Blacks to acquiesce to segregation, they would naturally begin to congregate and, unless liberty is suspended entirely, everyone would migrate into those cities and states with greater tolerance and economic generosity. The 1970 census showed that of the cities over 200,000 in population, Washington, D.C., Atlanta, and Newark consisted of over 50 percent Black. Those with a third to a half include Chicago, Philadelphia, Detroit, Baltimore, Cleveland, New Orleans and St. Louis. If the present differential segregation and differential rates of population increases continue, the U.S. will be confronted with a de facto internal split into two citizenries within several generations.

Regardless of what party platform the president of the U.S. runs for office and regardless of his personal ethical standards, the consideration of national power alone will drive him to push integration as rapidly as his political supporters will permit. He must ensure that the rate of integration will not fall below that necessary to prevent the formation of a stable and expanding solid Black community with its own distinctly Black leaders in the country. Quite apart from constitutional guarantees, private feelings of many of the white segregationists and Black nationalists, and considerations of humanitarian values, he as a president of power will instinctively bow to the inescapable realistic demands of unity and national survival. The Civil Rights movement of the minority Blacks of the 1960s for greater opportunities is now becoming a movement of majority whites of the 1990s for the preservation of their union.[132]

Relocation programs and Black political assimilation pose the greatest threat to Blacks, because if successfully implemented it will mean that the conditions for effective Black resistance will be destroyed.

COUNTERINTELLIGENCE

The purpose of counterintelligence operations is to "disrupt, brutalize and destroy" (Olomenji). Counterintelligence strategies are not new. They have been used against slave revolts, the agrarian land movements of the 19th century, the Garvey movement, and the Black movements of the 50's, 60's, 70's, and 80's.

The Black Liberation movement has a rich history of struggle upon which to base its organizing strategies and tactics. We have put millions of Black people into the streets, organized slave revolts, provided support for movements for African independence, and created a political crisis inside the western political system.

THE COINTELPRO COUNTER INTELLIGENCE PROGRAM

At the same time that our movements have escalated, the repressive knife of the oppressor's attacks have sharpened along with smiling reformist's programs. In the 19th century, we faced the dual force of Reconstruction reform and Ku Klux Klan. In the twentieth century, the sophistication of our movements (the Garvey movement, the mass movements of the sixties, and the movements for self-defense and Black Power) were met with an even more sophisticated campaign of intelligence agencies' disruption. Garvey was deported from the U.S., through a Hoover orchestrated campaign accusing him of using the mails to defraud (Martin, RACE FIRST); the peaceful movements of the fifties and sixties, and the nationalist movements of the sixties and seventies were hit with the dual force of reform (poverty program, expansion of the welfare program, civil rights and voting rights laws, etc.), and naked repression. The repressive campaign used against the Black liberation movement was as hard hitting and sophisticated as the most disruptive campaigns used against revolutionary governments. To quote William C. Sullivan, former Assistant to the FBI director:

> This is a rough, tough, dirty business, and dangerous. It was dangerous at times. No holds were barred....We have used (these techniques) against Soviet agents. They have used them against us. (The same methods were) brought home against any organization which we targeted. We did not differentiate. This is a rough, tough business.[133]

REAGAN'S 1981 EXECUTIVE ORDER

If disrupting Black movements and other radical groups were seen as rough, tough, and dirty, how much more rough, tough, and dirty will the intelligence agencies get, since they have had a long time to perfect their dirty tricks? Ex-president Reagan's Executive Order of 1981, a draft proposal on how the intelligence agencies should be unleashed against domestic protest, should give some indication of how far they are prepared to go.

This draft executive order provides the CIA with domestic powers that violates U.S. law. The CIA is allowed to break into the homes and organizations of U.S. citizens and residents. Intelligence investigations against U.S. citizens and residents are allowed, in spite of legal restrictions to the contrary. The CIA is given access to confidential records, e.g., tax returns. And most importantly, the CIA can do its thing (infiltrate U.S. organizations, disrupt and smear them) even when these groups are legal. Of course, the CIA and FBI have been using these tactics all along. What should concern us is that they have become so bold that they are putting the Black bag, character assassinations, and elimination conspiracies into written orders. When they go this far we know they are actually going much further in real fact.

With the new-right representative in the White House, they have begun to paint a picture of "international terrorism" (mythical Libyan hit men; intelligence agencies, whose hands are tied by restrictive executive orders; and a violent Black liberation movement, which is supported by elements of the white left, e.g., the Brinks armed robbery.) These and other incidents are used to justify a "cowboy" war on the Black liberation movement, the Native American movement, and any other forms of protest, whether they are legal or otherwise.

The repressive machinery is being put into high gear, at a time when a mass movement does not yet exist. It pays for us to understand some of the past strategies and tactics used by these agencies so that we can counter them. For it is a basic law of struggle, that as the oppressor becomes more sophisticated, our level of sophistication must rise to an even higher level.

THE INTELLIGENCE AGENCIES

The book *State Secrets Police Surveillance in America*, describes U.S., intelligence agencies in the following terms:

> The heart, but not the whole, of the domestic political intelligence apparatus consists of three interrelated networks; local police, the FBI, the Military Intelligence.
>
> Local police departments have police intelligence units commonly called red squads. They are loosely affiliated in a national organization, the Law

Enforcement Intelligence Unit (LEIU), and collectively, do the greater share of the spade work of domestic political surveillance. Most of the units are attached to city police departments, the rest to the state police and to local district attorney's offices. The Federal Bureau of Investigation devotes a substantial percentage of the time of its 8,700 Special Agents to squads that do only political work (called security work), but all agents are somewhat involved. The army operates the U.S. Army Intelligence Command (USAINTC). During its heyday (1966-69), many of its 1,200 agents spent part of their time watching anti-war Black activists. The operation is now somewhat curtailed, yet its files are still available to civilian authorities. Overseas, military intelligence appears still to pursue surveillance of civilians, as indicated by disclosures in the summer of 1973 of MI operations in Germany. A crude estimate puts the collective strength of these agencies at a force of 8,500 operatives employed on a

full time basis....Many other
agencies are often listed as
part of the surveillance
apparatus. None, however,
ranks in size with these central
three....Seven of them do
have investigative personnel
in their employ. These are the
IRS, the Navy, the Air Force,
the Coast Guard, Customs,
the Civil Service Commission,
the Postal Services. One unit
of the IRS, the Alcohol and
Tobacco Tax Division, has
been known to check library
records for the users of books
on explosives. It has
participated in investigations
of radical organizing efforts in
at least one place, Fall River,
Massachusetts. The IRS is said
to have a seven person unit
assigned to check left-and
right-wing political
organizations and their
leaders for tax violations. That
the IRS receives requests to
investigate somewhat more
establishment groups is clear
from the Watergate memo
from Charles Colson to John
Dean asking for a check on
Teamster maverick Harold
Gibbons....The investigative
staff of the Civil Service
Commission appears to

consist of seventeen clerks who clip articles from dissenting publications and file the names of people mentioned favorably therein. They have compiled a list of one and a half million names.....The Post Office has been known to 'cover' mail -- to record the return address on mail addressed to a suspect.   John S. Lanf reported for the Associated Press that the Post Office told a Senate Committee several years ago that it had such covers on more than 24,000 Americans....Put together, these seven agencies form only a small part of the surveillance apparatus. The other five agencies cited by Donner do not even have their own investigative staffs. These are Immigration; Justice's Community Relations; Health, Education and Welfare; the Office of Economic Opportunity; and the Passport Division, is known to keep a 'lookout' list including the names of some 14,000-15,000 suspected 'subversives.' Reports on passport applications and movements by designated people are sent to the agency requesting the information. These agencies are all easy sources of information, but they are not parts of the collection, evaluation, or dissemination machinery of the surveillance apparatus. Many non-government organizations are in almost the same position. Credit bureaus, banks, and telephone companies are constant sources of employment and financial information for police and FBI units, as the Media FBI documents prove. The Secret Service, the Bureau of Narcotics and Dangerous Drugs (BNFD), and the CIA are each more important than these twelve, but because of one factor or another, none is as important as the FBI, the police, or military intelligence.[134]

The above excerpt shows that while local police intelligence units, the FBI, and military intelligence agencies are the most important domestic agencies, their effectiveness is determined by the support they receive from various other government agencies. Any government agency that gathers information is an intelligence source.

With computerized systems this information is now centrally stored, and is immediately available to the local cop, the FBI, CIA or military intelligence.

MILITARY INTELLIGENCE

After the FBI and local police intelligence units, Military Intelligence plays the next most important role. According to the "Select Committee to Study Governmental Operations," Military Intelligence aimed at private groups and individuals consists of the following: "(1) The collection of information on the political activities of private citizens and private organizations in the late 1960s; (2) monitoring of domestic radio transmissions; (3) investigations of private organizations which the military considered threats; (4) assistance to other agencies engaged in surveillance of civilian political activities."[135] The army started collecting information on the political activities of private citizens and private organizations in the late sixties, after they were called upon to control civil rights demonstrations, urban rebellions, and anti-war demonstrations. As the urban rebellions, and anti-war demonstrations began to increase, the White House and the Justice Department encouraged the army to develop intelligence information on individuals and groups.

Using approximately 1,200 men working across the U.S., Army Intelligence developed a filing system on over 25 million people. Approximately 80 percent of this information came from the FBI, and local police intelligence. Military Intelligence also developed an early warning system for urban rebellions.[136] They monitored organizations trying to organize within the military. Also, army agents took part in the Chicago demonstrations at the Democratic Convention in 1968, and private organizations were infiltrated by military agents; Army agents posed as newsmen and they used civilian informants.[137]

Section 605 of the Communications Act of 1934, makes it illegal for anyone to intercept and publish the content of private radio broadcasts. Yet despite this prohibition, the army intelligence intercepted U.S. radio transmissions. These illegal interceptions were used by various intelligence agencies to prove that certain Black organizations were engaged in subversive activities.

Military investigations of private organizations considered a threat to the military, were carried out domestically and internationally. Targeted groups were allegedly those considered "threats to its personnel, installations and operations."[138]

Military intelligence assists local intelligence squads in their intelligence activities. In turn military intelligence receives a large part of its information from local intelligence units. Military intelligence is not nearly as important as the FBI in domestic intelligence activities.

COINTELPRO

In 1967, the FBI established the COINTELPRO (Counter Intelligence Program) against Black nationalists groups. This program was designed to smash the massive Black resistance to white oppression. The letter from the FBI that described the purpose of the COINTELPRO scheme in part set out to:

> ....expose, disrupt, misdirect, discredit, or otherwise neutralize the activities of Black nationalist, hate type organizations and groupings, their leadership, spokesmen, membership, and supporters and to counter their propensity for violence and civil disorder....Efforts of the various groups to consolidate their forces or to recruit new or youthful adherents must be frustrated.[139]

Every major Black organization with any kind of progressive leaning was targeted by this program. The Organization of Afro-American Unity, the Southern Christian Leadership Conference, the Student Non-

Violent Coordinating Committee, Revolutionary Action Movement, Deacons for Defense and Justice, Congress of Racial Equality, and the Nation of Islam were targeted initially. Later, other groups were added, including the Black Panther Party, US organization, and the Republic of New Afrika.

GOALS OF COINTELPRO

On March 4, 1968, the FBI outlined five goals for COINTELPRO:

> 1. to prevent the coalition of militant Black nationalist groups, which might be the first step toward a real "Mau Mau" in America;
>
> 2. to prevent the rise of a "messiah" who could "unify, and electrify," the movement, naming specifically Martin Luther King, Stokely Carmichael, and Elijah Muhammed;
>
> 3. to prevent violence on the part of Black nationalist groups by pinpointing "potential trouble makers" and neutralizing them "before they exercise their potential for violence;"

4. to prevent groups and leaders from gaining "respectability" by discrediting them to the "responsible" Negro community, to the white community (both responsible communities and the "Liberals" the distinction is the Bureau's) and to Negro radicals;

5. to prevent the long range growth of these organizations, especially among youth, by developing specific tactics to "prevent these groups from recruiting young people."[140]

ASSASSINATION OF MARTIN LUTHER KING AND MALCOLM X

The COINTELPRO activities disrupted Black organizations, took the lives of Black leaders (Malcolm X, Martin Luther King, Fred Hampton, Mark Clark, Bobby Huggins, George Jackson, Bunchy Carter, etc.), and led to the imprisonment or exile of many more dedicated Black freedom fighters.

For information on the assassination of Malcolm X, read my book entitled *The Political Legacy of Malcolm X*, for information on the assassination of Martin Luther King, read the book *Code Name Zorro*, by Dick Gregory and Mark Lane.

DENY CREDIBILITY TO MOVEMENT ACTIVISTS

Along with assassination techniques, the Bureau launched a campaign to deny credibility to progressive persons. Individuals were attacked through campaigns to prevent them from speaking, teaching, writing, publishing, and holding meetings.

The Bureau often furnished information about the alleged subversive background of prospective public speakers to the news media, and university officials. In some cases University administrators cancelled speaking engagements after receiving Bureau information on the background of particular speakers.

The FBI believed that teachers were in a strategic position to influence the thinking of students, and their status was believed to give teachers public credibility. Therefore, the Bureau manipulated principals, and University presidents to either fire, or put on probation, targeted teachers. State teaching credential boards were given false information on teaching candidates to deny them, teaching credentials.

The FBI tried to prevent targeted individuals from getting their writings published by carrying out a variety of smear campaigns against them as authors. The effectiveness of this campaign can be measured by the fact that today very few

Black writers can get their writings published by major publishers.

Efforts were made to discourage owners of public meeting places from renting their places to targeted groups and individuals.

COINTELPRO objectives were carried out in a variety of other ways, including media manipulation; reprint mailings; encouraging violence between rival groups; disseminating derogatory information to family, friends and associates and agent infiltration, to name only a few.

MEDIA MANIPULATION

A key goal of COINTELPRO was to "prevent groups and leaders from gaining respectability by discrediting them to the responsible Negro community, to the white community (both distinctions, responsible community and liberals, are the Bureau's) and to Negro radicals..."

Every section of the Black community, and supportive groups within the white community, were encouraged not to support the Black liberation movement, through a variety of techniques, the most sophisticated of which was the manipulation of the mass media.

Media manipulation was accomplished through selective leaks from the Bureau to friendly media people who agreed not to reveal the source of their information. The Bureau maintains a list of friendly journalists, and TV commentators who they instruct on how FBI information should be written and presented to the public.

Usually the newspaper editors or television station managers were not aware that the news leaks were supplied by the FBI. The Bureau used the news media to place unfavorable information about targeted groups or targeted individuals. Two examples are listed below:

> A typical example of media propaganda is the headquarter's letter authorizing the Boston Field Office to furnish 'derogatory information about the Nation of Islam (NOI) to established source (name excised)':

> Your suggestion concerning material to furnish (name) are good. Emphasize to him that the NOI (Nation of Islam) predilection for violence, preaching of race hatred, and hypocrisy, should be exposed. Material furnished (name) should be either public source or known to enough people as to protect your sourses. Insure that the

> Bureau's interest in this matter is completely protected (name).[141]

Note that in the above FBI memorandum, the agency instructs their media contact on how to discredit the Nation of Islam and stresses their desire to remain anonymous.

The next example shows how the FBI manipulates the media without the knowledge of the station management.

> In another case, information on the Junta of Militant Organizations ('JOMO,' a Black Nationalist's target) was furnished to a source at a Tampa television station. Ironically, the station manager, who had no knowledge of the Bureau's involvement, invited the Special Agent, his assistant, and other agents to a preview of the half-hour film which resulted. The SAC complimented the station manager on his product, and suggested that it be made available to civic groups.[142]

The film was made available to civic groups so that JOMO could be widely discredited in the Black and liberal white communities. FBI media manipulation is used to make the "victim look like the criminal and criminal look like the victim" (Malcolm). The victims of racism and violence are made to look like "racists" and fanatical advocates of violence. The false image is used to justify government attacks against these groups, which are pictured as a threat to the public. Images are discredited, so that physical attacks and assassinations will be welcomed.

Media manipulation was the most sophisticated method used to discredit targeted groups and individuals, but it was by no means the only method.

REPRINTED MAILINGS

The FBI sent reprints of movement articles, which were insulting to a support group. For example, Jewish supporters of the Black Panther Party received Black Panther articles that attacked Jews. College administrators received articles from major magazines that encouraged them to crack down on campus demonstrators. Anti-war advocates were sent articles that were critical of opposition to the Vietnam War.

Bureau efforts were not limited to influencing the opinions of supporters of issues, but the Bureau also carried out underhanded campaigns designed to "prevent the coalition of militant Black Nationalist's groups," and to ...."Neutralize the activities of Black Nationalists...." A variety of dirty tricks were used to accomplish these objectives, including promoting factionalism within groups and between groups, and encouraging violence between rival groups.[93]

PROMOTING ILL WILL AND FACTIONALISM WITHIN AND BETWEEN GROUPS AND ENCOURAGING VIOLENCE BETWEEN RIVAL GROUPS

Government investigators estimate that approximately "28% of the Bureau's COINTELPRO efforts were designed to weaken groups by setting members against each other, or to separate groups which might otherwise be allies, and convert them into mutual enemies."[143]

Pamphlets and fliers written by the FBI were sent under the name of one group to create ill will and factionalism with another group. Black groups that already had problems relating to each other were encouraged by Bureau-authored mailings, to become actively hostile toward each other. To quote from government sources:

> ....These efforts included anonymously distributing cartoons which pictured the US organization gloating over the corpses of two murdered Panthers and suggested that other Black Panther Party members would be next....

O yes! We are not concerned about Hilliard's threats. Brains will win out over brawn. The way the Panthers have retaliated against US is another indication. The score: US-1; Panthers-0.

Why, I read an article in the Panther paper, where a California Panther sat in his car and watched his friend get shot by Karenga's group and what did he do? He ran back and wrote a full page story about how tough the Panthers are and what they're going to do. Ha Ha B--- S---.

Goodbye (name) baby -- and watch out. Karenga's coming.[144]

These primitive methods were effective because they played on weaknesses that existed within the Black Liberation Movement. US organization and the Panthers were struggling for influence in the Los Angeles area and nationally. Also members of both groups previously belonged to rival gang structures in Los Angeles. The FBI tailored their game to the mentality of the groups. Here, the gang-banging mentality existed and the FBI played on it. Our inability to deal with ego conflicts, and gang mentalities, to name only a few, led to the loss of many lives. Insulting mailings sent by the FBI were designed to do precisely what they did, create factionalism and cause bloodshed between rival groups.

Another way factionalism was created was through anonymous mailings sent by the Bureau. These mailings ranged "from the relatively mild mailing of reprintings of fliers criticizing a group's leaders for living on the high side or being ineffective speakers, to reporting a chapter's infractions to the group's headquarters with the intent of causing censure or disciplinary action.[145]

FBI agents used the interview technique to create suspicion among the membership of a targeted group. This technique consisted of FBI agents interviewing particular members to create suspicion about them or other members. Or, they would interview landlords, encouraging them to throw targeted tenants out. In cases where the interview technique created suspicions that a member was disloyal, the suspected member risked being thrown out of the group, or losing their life.

SNITCH LABEL

Usually the FBI used more direct methods such as labeling a target as an informant. Routinely, the snitch label was placed on targeted individuals, by circulating a rumor that a person was an agent, or by arresting a group of members and then letting all but one go. The rumor would then be circulated that the one not released was cooperating. The snitch jacket method worked in a variety of ways, and it aroused dangerous suspicions about targeted persons.

A standard procedure of the FBI is to use natural political enemies against each other. The American Legion printed under their own name Bureau-written pamphlets attacking SDS (Students for a Democratic Society) and the DuBois Clubs. Recent revelations show that the FBI tried to pit the Mafia against Dick Gregory. The use of the Mafia hit men to try to eliminate Castro is another example of how the intelligence agencies use enemies against each other. What better choice for a Castro hit man than a Mafia figure who wanted to return Cuba to the days when organized crime ran the island's gambling.

DISRUPTING FAMILIES

The Bureau wasn't satisfied with just putting groups against each other. They sought to make activists ineffective by disrupting their families. Wives received letters charging their husbands with adultery, and dishonesty. These letters were written by FBI agents in the language of the particular group. Sometimes when adultery actually occurred, the FBI made sure that the wife or husband found out about it. However, most of these mailings were false. It can be assumed that a number of families were destroyed through these underhanded methods, and resultingly, the effectiveness of many movement activists was destroyed or reduced.

DENYING ACTIVISTS JOBS

Breaking up families was logically linked to making the target totally ineffective. Employers were contacted by the Bureau and encouraged to fire targeted individuals. This approach met with some success. Needless to say, an activist without a family and money was in real trouble.

Targeted individuals and groups were victims of selective law enforcement that made a point of arresting targets on bogus charges, or hitting an organization with health code violations.

District attorneys received anonymous mailings encouraging them to stick it to the movement activists who were being charged with various offenses. The FBI made a point of tying activists up in court so they would not have time to organize on the streets.

SHUT OFF FUNDS TO MILITANT GROUPS

Every effort was made by the Bureau to determine the source of movement funds. Once the Bureau determined who was contributing to a particular group, then every effort was made to encourage contributors not to support that group. Two things that the

Bureau did not want a Black organization to get were a large number of members and a good sized bankroll.

These are only some of the techniques used against our movement, but these techniques cannot be separated from the first line of intelligence work, that of the grimy, seamy agent.

AGENTS

The intelligence units of local police departments are the main gatherers of intelligence, and the agent is the key weapon used against targeted groups. The FBI is spread too thin to rely exclusively on FBI agents for first hand intelligence gathering. They usually rely on the intelligence gathered by local "red squads."

Agents come in many different forms and serve a variety of purposes. Some agents are information gatherers who don't draw attention to themselves while they are developing background information on targeted groups. Some have a deep cover and are expected to stay underground for years, penetrating and rising up the command ladder of targeted groups. This type of agent is popularly known as a mole. Another type of agent is the provocateur, who is sent into groups to incite them to take illegal action. The agent provocateur often participates in illegal action, and may surface to testify later against the group he/she set up.

Whatever the agent's assignment, it is a mistake to think that they can be easily identified. Agents are usually the most hardworking members in the group. Most are intelligent, ruthless, and often the ones you have the least reason to suspect. Agents fit into their environment, and when they are successful, are often confidants of the top leadership in an organization. Lenin was surrounded by agents whom he had the greatest confidence in. Every progressive or revolutionary movement has to deal with the problem of agents.

Brother Simba Imara, a former member of the Pan African People's Organization, and an authority on security, lists a number of basic infiltration methods used by government agents:

> Agents gain the confidence of members through forming personal relationships with them. The agent works through friendships, knowing that people will share confidences with friends, and they will protect friends.
>
> The agent shows empathy or sympathy for the group or the individual. Empathy is shown through being willing to listen

to a person's problems, and offering personal assistance.

The agent fits into the particular group, adopting the local rhetoric and ideology. Oftentimes the agent knows the group's ideology better than do many of its own members.

The agent is a supplier of what people need or want. They may lend money, supply dope, or be a source of comfort.

Agents operate under believable cover. They claim to have, or actually have, occupations which allow them to move around the community without arousing suspicion. The cover will fit the group the agent is penetrating. If the agent is penetrating a campus group, then their cover will usually be that of a student; if the agent is infiltrating a union, their cover will be that of a worker, etc.

The agent uses the weaknesses of the group to promote divisions within the group. The agent is a manipulator who thinks for others, and offers appealing remedies to disgruntled disenchanted members.

Often the agent moves in and out of groups gathering information. If the agent is a provocateur, he will encourage the group to commit illegal actions, to justify government vamps.[146]

Agents are instruments of the government who execute government plans. The entire intelligence system is made up of professionals and non-professionals that are recruited to disrupt or eliminate you or your organization.

LOW INTENSITY OPERATIONS AN IMPROVEMENT ON COINTELPRO

The COINTELPRO strategy was an improvised ad hoc approach that reeked tremendous damage upon the Black movement during the sixties. For all of its damage to Black organizations, COINTELPRO suffered from a serious weakness. COINTELPRO targeted movements for disruption after they developed a national and sometimes international following. Consequently, movements continued long after many of their leaders were assassinated, exiled or imprisoned. In fact, COINTELPRO repression worked like a forest fire, with the winds of repression inflaming Black activists into more radical postures. This weakness of the state's repressive tactics led it to reevaluate its approach in the seventies and eighties. The new strategy of repression certainly draws from the governments past successes; however, the new approach is based on a careful study of national and international liberation movements. Today the intelligence agencies and the military see liberation movements developing through distinct stages of struggle and seek to identify and disrupt liberation movements when they are going through their earliest stages of organization. By taking this approach, the intelligence agencies are seeking to avoid the errors of the sixties, where they took on the Black liberation movement and the Vietnamese liberation movement, when they had reached a stage of strength where they were either difficult or impossible to defeat.

FROM CRISIS REPRESSION TO PLANNED REPRESSION

To defeat national and international wars of liberation, the government has moved from a crisis approach (which waited for the crisis to develop) to a planned systematic policy of continuous repression. The new strategy of repression is going on around us, yet most of us aren't aware of its existence. This new strategy is not as obvious as the old COINTELPRO approach, because it is a deliberately low level strategy that operates continuously against barely visible, small, unknown groups that are perceived by the state to pose a future threat to its security. The essence of this new strategy of counter insurgency is to identify a future political threat *before* it becomes large or a national threat, and then to prevent it from becoming one. This is qualitatively different from the COINTELPRO strategy that zeroed in on political organizations or leadership *after* they had become a threat and *after* they gained national and international support.

GENERAL FRANK KITSON

The author of this strategy, which has gained many refinements since it was developed, is British Brigadier General Frank Kitson. General Kitson, authored the classic text on counter insurgency that is used throughout the western world, especially by the military intelligence and police agencies of the United States. General Kitson's book is entitled, *Low Intensity Operations, Subversions, Insurgency, Peace-Keeping*.

THE MAU MAU, MALAYSIAN, CYPRUS AND IRISH EXPERIENCE

Kitson's theories were developed out of his counter insurgency experiences gained while suppressing the so-called Mau Mau movement in Kenya and the Malaysian liberation movement in Malaysia. His theories were also based on experiences gained while in Cyprus, and when he commanded the 39th Airportable Brigade of the British Army in northern Ireland. Since America is the leading counter-revolutionary force in the world, Kitson drew lessons from the American experience in Vietnam. Judging from the American military's use of Kitson's theories, they have been more than welcome.

Kitson's strategy of "Low Intensity Operations," has application nationally and internationally.   Implicitly, his strategy recognizes the central weakness of America's Vietnam strategy. This strategy was doomed from the start because it sought to defeat a well organized popular national liberation movement.   Similarily, the COINTELPRO strategy, used against the Black liberation movement and other progressive forces, took years and years to finally disrupt these movements because the COINTELPRO strategy was launched after these movements became strong.

The British experience in suppressing the Mau Mau movement in Kenya proved that a liberation movement could be disrupted if it was attacked before it gained national support and national organization. In applying this strategy against the emerging Black liberation forces, the strategy of low intensity operations seeks to disrupt and destroy these developing organizations while they are small, financially weak, and generally unknown to the larger Black population. The government targets groups when they are small because the state recognizes their potential for growing from small local organizations to large national movements with great international support.

ATTACKING MOVEMENTS WHEN THEY ARE SMALL

Today the military and the intelligence agencies have moved to attack political movements before they become strong. This is called a preemptive strategy. The governments preemptive strategy grows out of a careful study of the national liberation movements in Algeria, China, Vietnam. Guinea Bissau, Malaysia, the Mau Mau's in Kenya and the Black liberation movement in the United States during the sixties. The intelligence agencies have learned from Mao and General Giap that national liberation movements around the world go through distinct stages. Counter insurgency strategies deploy measures to prevent similar movements from moving through the lower stages of struggle to the higher stages of national liberation.

THE LOW INTENSITY THEORY OF STAGES OF NATIONAL LIBERATION STRUGGLE

The stages of national liberation struggles that Kitson's strategy attempts to disrupt are: (1) the preparatory phase; (2) the non-violent phase; and (3) the insurgency phase.[147] Advocates of the strategy of low intensity operations conclude that national liberation movements the world over move through these three stages, if they are well organized and are not disrupted by government police or military units.

STAGE ONE, THE PREPARATORY STAGE

The preparatory phase is a subtle phase where, on the surface, it appears that little or nothing is going on of a radical or progressive political nature. Kitson advises the state to assume that militant or radical forces are preparing to challenge the state by building support among the population during this quiet preparatory period. Rather than being inactive, militants are identifying grievances and they are quietly going door-to-door organizing support. As popular support is gained from the population, an organizational structure is put into place. While the preparatory phase may appear to be one where little is going on, it is actually the most important phase in a liberation movement. This is because the militant forces are identifying their support base, as well as their opposition within their population, and they are establishing a national organizational structure. Generally speaking, the more thorough the preparatory phase, the better the chances that the liberation movement will succeed.

IDENTIFICATION OF MEMBERS

Low intensity strategies recognize that the preparatory phase is the most important phase and it seeks to destroy the budding liberation movement before it completes this stage. A number of strategies are used to destroy the emerging movement during this preparatory period. The key strategy used by the state during this stage and every other, is the identification of the opposition forces. Whatever strategy is employed, it cannot work if the opposition groups remain unknown. Identification of the militant forces becomes the central task for the government intelligence agencies.

SELECTIVE ATTACK

Once the groups and leaders are identified then any of a number of measures may be used against them depending upon the political circumstances. Kitson pretends that the least feasible approach is that of destroying the militants because in the preparatory phase they have committed no crime; they have simply talked to the people about the people's grievances against the government. Still, Kitson used the approach of destroying the militants during the preparatory phase in the British Army's campaign against the Mau Mau's in Kenya.

Kitson notes that the army and the police face more restraints when moving against domestic resistance, than they face when they are fighting liberation movements in the Third World. Domestically, the military and police in countries such as the United States, have to deal with democratic institutions including courts, laws, and the alleged right of free speech and free assembly. Kitson suggests that the state has to choose between two approaches when dealing with the question of democratic rights and repression of political groups. One approach is to administer the law fairly something that would be difficult for the West to do anywhere in the world. Another approach is to use the law to selectively dispose of unwanted members of the general public, ie., so-called terrorists. Kitson says he favors the legal route, yet he makes it clear that the legal approach makes the military's job more difficult, because it gives opposition forces time to organize.

SELECTIVE APPLICATION OF THE LAW TO BLACK MILITANTS

Clearly, the U.S. has often opted for the approach that selectively disposes of its opposition. An example would be the new federal conspiracy law that redefines conspiracy so that the law can be used selectively against politically progressive and radical groups. The new federal definition of conspiracy states that simply talking about an illegal act constitutes a conspiracy. The normal definition of a conspiracy requires not only a plan, but an overt act to carry out that plan. Now a person can be tried and convicted for simply exercising their free speech. Clearly, the new federal conspiracy laws are intended to selectively dispose of militant groups and individuals that the state labels as terrorist.

Another example of the selective application of the law to suppress political dissent, was the Washington, D.C. crime bill enacted in the seventies. This bill, authorized by Nixon's attorney general Kleindiest, gave the police authority to stop and frisk suspicious persons, as well as to enter their homes for searches without knocking or warning residents. This kind of legislation was designed to intimidate potential supporters of progressive movements. It also allowed the police to use the pretext of cracking down on crime as a cover for harassing political activists.

Still another example of the selective application of the law to repress militant political groups, was the 1972 U.S. Supreme Court ruling which said that a defendant in a state court could be convicted by a non unanimous jury. This decision was designed to overcome the situation where one or more people on a jury could hang it. During the seventies, a number of political trials ended in hung juries and forced the prosecution to drop the charges. This is a clear example of the selective application of the law by the highest court in the land solely for the purpose of making it easier for the state to convict political activists.

APPLICATION OF SELECTIVE FORCE AGAINST KEY LEADERS AND SUPPORTERS

Another way to dispose of an emerging progressive or militant movement is to use selective force against it. Ideally, selective force is used to destroy key leaders and supporters without enraging potential supporters of the organizations. The U.S. has a long history of using selective force against more progressive and radical leaders, while it promoted more moderate figures as the new Black leaders. The selective assassination of Malcolm, and King, was done when the government was grooming a new moderate leadership to take their place. Reformist poverty programs were designed to pacify many uncommitted Blacks, while the more militant leadership was being repressed to death. By mixing selective violent repression with cooptive reforms, the government sought to remove the militants from the broader Black population without enraging the general Black public. The new moderate Black leaders were given publicity and money, and the masses were encouraged to believe that their demands could be solved by the system.

PUTTING AGENTS INTO GROUPS DURING THE PREPARATORY PHASE

The selective use of the law and selective violence, combined with reformist measures, is certainly part of the strategy used by the state against militant forces during the preparatory period, but these methods are simply icing on the cake of state repression. The heart of the state's repressive strategy consists of identifying the opposition organizational forces while they are small and weak. Emerging militant organizations are identified by placing a small number of agents into these groups while they are going through the preparatory period. Groups are most vulnerable to state penetration during the preparatory period because they often think that they do not pose a sufficient threat to the state to warrant penetration and attack. It is not unusual for organizations to be extremely lax in security during this early organizing phase. Many organizations will not have a system for screening new members, thereby making it very easy for the state to send agents into their ranks. Having joined the organization during the period when it first started to organize, state agents will be in a position to establish bonds of trust with the leadership and with hard core members who are the backbone of the organizations. Very often these agents will be able to rise to positions of leadership and influence in the organization.

Whether state agents rise to leadership or not, they will be in the position to identify the leadership, membership, and support base. The information agents provide to the intelligence agencies will enable the agencies to move on these groups when the intelligence agencies are ready.

During the preparatory phase, the state relies on a small number of quality sources. These agents can be former militants who were secretly turned against the movement; they can be members of the general population who are used to gather information; they can be elements from the underworld who work for an intelligence agency; or they can be professional agents. Whatever their background, agents are the most important source of information for the state agencies. It would be foolish for militant forces to underestimate the damage that these individuals can do. If allowed, they can prevent the most promising political formations from getting off the ground.

CONVINCE THE PEOPLE THAT STRUGGLE IS FUTILE

The state's strategy of repression during the preparatory period is designed to match and outdo the militant's strategy used to win the minds and support of the people. Since opposition organizations will work to educate the people about why they are unemployed, undereducated, underfed and poorly housed, the state will develop psychological operations to try and convince the people that the government is working to improve their lives and that political struggle is futile. During the seventies the state manipulated mass media, carried out a wide ranging campaign to convince different segments of the American population that political opposition to government policies was futile. Black exploitation movies portrayed Black militants as fools and opportunists. Drug pushers were elevated to the status of heroes. Perhaps the movie that best represented the new a/political thrust was Woody Allen's movie the Sleeper. "When asked what he believes in, Allen, having ruled out politics, religion and science declares: 'I belive in sex and death -- two experiences that come once in a lifetime." It is no accident that the seventies was known more for its sexual revolution (to name only one) rather than the political revolution of the previous decade.

CREATING COUNTER ORGANIZATIONS

The state's campaign to divert the minds of the people away from militant political struggle is combined with a serious effort to counter sincere militant organizations with state supported organizations that are dressed up as organizations of the people. Organizing counter organizations is not new the COINTELPRO programs as previously mentioned used right wing groups against militant organizations. What is different is that counter groups are now disguised as legitimate liberation organizations. These techniques have become refined in the international arena, a laboratory that has yielded important lessons for domestic repression.

In Vietnam, CIA and the American military built up a puppet army and government which was used along with the American military to fight the Vietnamese national liberation front. This American experiment ended in failure. The national liberation front quickly established control over all of Vietnam, once the American forces had been forced to withdraw. The U.S. government's sponsorship of the Nicaraguan Contras isn't going any better. The armed forces, fighting for the people of Nicaragua, have been successful in imposing defeat after defeat on the Contras. More important, the Contras are viewed as a wholly U.S.-controlled puppet army that receives its directions from the CIA.

JIM JONE'S PEOPLE'S TEMPLE

In spite of the international blunders there is considerable evidence that U.S. intelligence agencies have been much more successful in building organizations to sow confusion and division inside the United States. While there is no conclusive proof that Jim Jone's People's Temple was either organized or later infiltrated and controlled by the intelligence agencies, there is much that suggest state involvement in the organization. Counter organizations are organized by the government to draw the people's loyalties away from militant movements that are genuinely opposed to the government's policies. Ideally, counter organizations should develop a reputation for helping the people solve day-to-day problems. This is the same method used by sincere groups to win support of the people. In the case of People's Temple, the group offered help to families that were having problems with their children. Temple members worked with youth who were on drugs and the church developed a reputation for being able to handle youth that families found to be unmanageable. On the religious level the Temple preached a religion of liberation and they provided support to a variety of community struggles. By linking religion to political issues the Temple was able to draw a lot of Blacks away from the largest established Black churches in San Francisco, which were viewed to be ignoring the political needs of their members.

In the area of community organizing the Temple used some very advanced methods. Their disciplined members provided the balance of power in the mayoral election, and Jim Jones was rewarded for the Temple's political support, by being appointed Chair of the Housing Authority. He used his position to provide public housing for his members. Jim Jones' wife worked for the social service agency as a case worker. She exploited her position as a case worker to go through the welfare files and identify potential Temple recruits. A key

Temple member was placed in the district attorney's office. This assistant district attorney was able to discourage the DA's office from carrying out any prosecutions against People's - Temple.   Jim Jones also established close relationships with key members of the press who gave the Temple favorable publicity.

In the Black community, Jones made the owner of the community newspaper the Temple's physician: Jones joined the NAACP and was elected to its executive committee. He directed Black and white youth in the People's Temple to join the all Black NAACP Youth Council, forcing it to disband.

As a minister, Jim Jones studied the methods of Father Divine. He became the "father" of the congregation. Often he was able to make himself the center of authority in the family. His influence over his members was so strong that he could mobilize his members to demonstrate, rally, etc., on extremely short notice. Many politicians and community leaders acknowledged him as an important leadership figure and praised his work.

Now the techniques used by Jim Jones were very sophisticated.   They either reflected brilliant leadership, or they were based on counter insurgency techniques. If Jim Jones' organization was an instrument of the intelligence agencies then it demonstrated that the agencies are operating on an organizational level that is higher than the organizations they are moving against. Whether this is true or not, it is mandatory that progressive and revolutionary organizations learn from the opposition, just as they have learned from us.

Overall, the preparatory period is viewed by the state as the most important period in the organization of political movements. The state seeks to destroy the emerging movement before it gains mass support by identifying it, applying the laws selectively against it, selectively repressing it, and by trying to win over the people through attempting to convince them that the state is on their side and struggle against the state is futile. To win the people to its side, the state will create counter organizations and counter leaders. All of these strategies simply support the main objective, which is to find the opposition organizations and leadership, through placing agents inside their ranks. If the state succeeds at this level then the struggle will end until another movement emerges. If the movement forces are able to survive the state's attack or avoid their detection, then, according to Kitson's theory, the movement can be expected to use the technique of non-violent struggle to mobilize larger groups of people into action.

THE SECOND STAGE: THE NON-VIOLENT PHASE

Kitson's theory of low intensity operations views non-violent struggles within a historical context.   Historically, reform can be the mother of revolution. Reformist struggles can teach many of its followers that the system they are trying to reform is not capable of producing freedom for them. For many that learn this lesson, peaceful struggle may be the classroom that educates them to the need for a more serious armed struggle.

THE DUAL NATURE OF NONVIOLENT MOVEMENTS

Therefore, under certain circumstances, non-violent movements can be transformed to movements for self-defense, or movements for armed struggle. Still, not every non-violent movement will become a revolutionary one, and Kitson recognizes this. Yet the potential for the movement's transformation from non-violent to armed struggle makes the practitioners of low intensity operations view the non-violent phase as a threatening phase of struggle.

THE RELATIONSHIP BETWEEN PEACEFUL AND ARMED STRUGGLE

The state has good reason to be concerned about the revolutionary potential of the peaceful stage of struggle. Usually, the peaceful stage of struggle precedes the stage of armed struggle. The armed struggle can arise where the peaceful struggle is repressed. Kitson advises the state agencies to avoid a campaign of wholesale repression because this may drive the peaceful movement into the stage of armed struggle. Massive repression can increase the movements support among the people that the movement is trying to organize. This is precisely what happened when the struggles against the past laws were violently repressed by the South African authorities in the sixties. The peaceful African National Congress and the Pan African Congress realized that liberation would only be achieved through armed struggle.

Peaceful campaigns can be transformed into armed ones when the peaceful struggle fails to produce fundamental changes on behalf of the people. This was true in the case of the Civil Rights movement of the sixties. The non-violent movement forced the federal government to enact civil rights laws that gave Black people the right to vote and access to desegregated public facilities. While these were important achievements, they did not address the most basic needs of Black people for jobs, housing, and education. As a result, when the Civil Rights movement achieved these major victories, Black people realized that their lives had not significantly improved. With this realization, the struggle shifted from a peaceful struggle, to a largely violent one. In the case of the Black liberation movement, the violent struggle could not be characterized as a revolutionary struggle because it had not defined revolutionary objectives. So all violent struggles are not revolutionary, yet low intensity strategy sees the potential for revolutionary organizations to turn urban insurrections into revolutionary struggles.

Kitson recognized that a political party could organize a non-violent campaign alongside a violent struggle. The national liberation front in Vietnam combined peaceful struggle with armed struggle. Peaceful struggles were used to win over Vietnamese who were fighting on the side of the United States. Non-violent struggles were also organized to win over uncommitted sections of the population. These struggles diverted South Vietnamese troops away from military struggle thereby weakening the South Vietnamese military campaign.

Another way that the non-violent campaign can turn into a violent one, is when a political organization progressively organizes the struggle from the stage of non-violence to the stage of revolutionary violence.

EXPLOITING THE NON-VIOLENT MOVEMENTS INTERNAL WEAKNESS

Since the strategy of low intensity operations views non-violent struggle as having a revolutionary potential, Kitson proposes a disruptive strategy that takes advantage of the non-violent movement's internal weaknesses. Kitson treats the revolutionary has only one interest, the overthrow of the government. In Kitson's view, the people on the other hand, are only interested in gaining reforms (jobs, housing, education, etc.)

DIVIDE THE NON-VIOLENT MOVEMENT BY GRANTING REFORMS

Acting on the assumption that the people only want reforms, Kitson proposes that the government grant concessions (reforms) to the movement as a way to separate the moderates from the militant leadership. However, the reforms are not to be granted immediately. Instead the government is encouraged to promise to grant reforms when the mass struggles cease. During this period, when the population is being encouraged to abandon political struggle, selective force is used to whip the people in line by making life uncomfortable, but not unbearable.

ELIMINATING THE MILITANTS

If the government succeeds in creating a state of calm, two strategies are to be put into effect as quickly as possible. First, the government is encouraged to grant the concessions so the militants won't have grounds for again organizing the people against the government. While concessions are being granted, the militant core should be identified and eliminated. Where possible, the government should separate some of the militants from the others by coopting them onto the side of the government.

The strategy of cooptation and repression is taken out of the American government's sixties game plan. Many Blacks moved away from the mass movements of the sixties when they gained jobs, educations, and other creature comforts. Some former leaders of major Civil Rights organizations were recruited onto the government payroll at the local, state and national level. Of course some militants who made their way onto the government payroll used their position to provide money and resources to the mass movement. Government concessions and government repression against the advanced leadership of the movement went hand in hand.

PIT-FALLS IN THE REPRESSIVE STRATEGY

There are circumstances when the government is either unwilling or unable to grant concessions. Under such circumstances, the governments main response will be to repress the movement. The danger of this approach from Kitson's point of view is that the government will destroy the non-violent movement. This is a danger because general repression of the peaceful movement may not only lead to a violent movement, but it may make it extremely difficult for the government to identify the revolutionary leadership and membership, since it will go underground to lead the armed struggle. So for the intelligence agencies, the non-violent movement must not only be surgically sliced up, but it must be used as a laboratory for gathering information on the movement's leadership, membership, and programs. Again, the most important weapon that the state can use against the movement is intelligence that identifies it's leaders and supporters.

The advocates of low intensity operations do not view non-violent struggle the way the FBI COINTELPRO viewed it in the sixties. Then, the intelligence agencies and the government in general were put on the defensive by the non-violent movement. The Southern Civil Rights movement created international and national support for Black rights. The government found itself responding in different ways. The Kennedy administration tried to divert the movement by encouraging it to take up voter registration. Kennedy also tried to discourage mass demonstrations, and when he couldn't prevent mass demonstration such as the March on Washington, he financed it, thereby taking it over. Ultimately, though both the Kennedy and Johnson administration were being forced to grant concessions to the movement in the form of civil rights legislation. In the end, government concessions did not prevent the movement from turning to violence. The Kitson strategy alerts the government to the revolutionary potential of non-violent movements. It proposes that the government use a scientific approach to separate the non-violent movement from its leadership. This approach is designed to prevent the non-violent movement from developing to the stage of armed struggle.

THE THIRD STAGE ARMED STRUGGLE

General Kitson assumes that armed struggle in the urban situation will follow a classic pattern. Under the classic pattern the revolutionary groups have a legal organization that operates in the open and an underground organization that operates secretly. This is the approach used by the revolutionary movement in Algeria.

ORGANIZING CELLS OR BLOCK STRUCTURES

In Algeria, the secret organization developed along the lines of cells. Cells were organized on every block and these cells were coordinated at higher levels. To counteract this structure, Kitson proposes that the police and/or military set up the same kind of cell structure. Police and military forces are warned to expect revolutionaries to infiltrate this system. Kitson thinks that alert authorities can spot these elements and weed them out.

CREATING POLICE CELLS

The strategy of having the government build a parallel block organization is so that the government can organize the uncommitted population that would otherwise support the revolutionaries. A government controlled block system serves as the eyes and ears of the government, because block leaders can get an idea of who makes up the membership of the above ground organization. Once the authorities know this they can begin to keep track of the above ground members as a way to identify members of the underground cell system.

NEIGHBORHOOD WATCH, POLICE CELL IN ACTION

In the United States the police are using a neighborhood watch system to recruit neighborhood residents to serve on block committees. These block committees are supposed to protect neighbors from crime. Actually, they serve to give the police detailed information on the people who live on the block. This system enables the police to identify political elements in the neighborhood.   Often   the   police representatives are skilled in community relations. The police use the fear of crime as a cover for isolating progressive forces within the block. The police officer maintains an active file on political activists on the block.

PLAYING CATCH UP

The problem that this police strategy poses for political activists is that usually the police have developed a sophisticated block structure when political activists have none. This is a serious problem that has to be overcome if the progressive forces in the Black community are to out-organize the state.

RONALD REAGAN'S ROLE IN DEVELOPING LOW INTENSITY STRATEGIES

It is not by accident that low intensity strategies have been adopted by police and military units in the United States. Ronald Reagan, during his term as governor of California, appointed people who adapted low intensity strategies to American realities. Louis Giuffrida was appointed head of the CSTI (California Specialized Training Institute) by Reagan while he (Reagan) was governor of California. The CSTI brought together members of the National Guard, the army, police representatives, members of fire departments, and representatives of big business, for special counter-insurgency training.148

CSTI CALIFORNIA SPECIALIZED TRAINING INSTITUTE

CSTI strategy recognizes that the United States is divided along racial and class lines. Violence is viewed as the way that whites have kept people of color down, and CSTI strategy understands that violence is a weapon for liberating people of color from oppression.

CSTI strategy is therefore based on the assumption that violence is the central part of the government's policy toward people of color. The government's extermination of the American Indians, and the government's use of violence against each other's ethnic group is viewed as being a natural outgrowth of the dominance of whites over people of color.

Peaceful struggles waged by people of color against the government are viewed as the first step toward revolution. Under the Reagan presidency Louis Guiffrida led the Federal Emergency Management Agency that coordinated counter insurgency programs at the federal level.

ORGANIZATIONAL SECURITY

A security system that can fight COINTELPRO and low intensity type operations has to operate on a number of levels at the same time. First your members must be highly conscious and able to defend the ideology of the organization. Ideological security means that your members are grounded in the ideology and program of the organization. Agents and COINTELPRO low intensity type programs attack your weaknesses, which are your weakest members, and weaknesses that we all possess.

DEFENDING THE ORGANIZATIONS SPACE

The second level of security is the defense of the organization's physical space. This includes the organization's headquarters, leaders, and members. Physical security means that you have a disciplined security force that is politically conscious and is trained in various techniques of self defense.

ORGANIZATIONAL MEMBERS SECURITY

The third level of security is organizational security. At this level every member is versed in security techniques and is trained to practice them on a regular basis.

FAMILY AND PERSONAL SECURITY

The fourth level of security is family and individual security. At this level the security of the family is maintained through developing family security systems.[149]

COMMUNITY SECURITY

The fifth level of security is community security. Community security involves establishing grassroot structures on the block level, which serves as the eyes and ears of the movement.

INTERNATIONAL SECURITY

The sixth level is national security, where national security systems are developed on the national level. The seventh level is international security. The basis for a strong international security system is a strong national and local security system.

DEVELOP IMAGINATIVE PLANS TO COUNTERACT THE INTELLIGENCE AGENCIES

Creativity is the basis of any effective counter intelligence plan. Creative planning is also based on careful study and thorough training. Read all of the literature you can get your hands on that deals with intelligence. Some material that is necessary reading includes, *Inside the Company: CIA Diary*, by Philip Agee; *Dirty Work*, by Philip Agee *(I & II)*; *In Search of Enemies: A CIA Story*, John Stockwell; *Code Name 'Zorro'*, by Mark Lane and Dick Gregory; *The CIA and the Cult of Intelligence,* by Victor Marchetti and John D. Marks; *State Secrets Police Surveillance in America,* by Paul Cowan, Nick Egleson and Nat Hentoff; *Final Report, Book II: Supplementary Detailed Staff Report on Intelligence Activities and the Rights of Americans: Riots, Civil and Criminal Disorders - - Part II 1968; Riots, Civil and Criminal Disorders -- Part 17 1969: Riots, Civil and Criminal Disorders -- Part 21 1969; COINTELPRO the FBI's Secret War on Political Freedom,* by Nelson Blackstock, with an introduction by Noam Chomsky; *Top Secret,* by Christy Macy and Susan Kaplan; *The FBI and Martin Luther King, Jr.* by David Garrow; *Shoot-Out in Cleveland Black Militants and the Police: July 23, 1968;* and *The Assassination of Malcolm X,* by George Breitman, Herman Porter and Baxter Smith. There is a lot more out there on the subject of intelligence.

In developing a creative counterintelligence plan, remember that COINTELPRO's low intensity type plans are constantly updated to exploit your weaknesses. Your organizational and personal weaknesses are your biggest enemies; therefore a good security system is one that transforms weaknesses into strengths.

SELF-EVALUATING SESSIONS

Your organization should carry out regular self-evaluation sessions where members analyze the strengths and weaknesses of the organization. Allies and opponents should be talked to on a regular basis to determine their perceptions about your organization. Once you have tallied up your strengths and weaknesses, develop strategies for overcoming the weaknesses. Regular self-criticism sessions should be included in your business agendas and procedures. You should be careful about how you approach criticism and self-criticism. Often, people can be alienated when they are criticized because you have used the wrong approach. You cannot evaluate a person's contribution to the group if you do not know that person. Before you think about offering someone else suggestions for self-improvement, try and see things from that person's standpoint. Often, when you get to know a person and see things from their side, you will have a different view of their behavior.

For example, if a particular member seems unreliable and often forgets or fails to carry out assignments, before launching into a criticism find out why that person fails to carry out your assignments. Let's say that after getting to know the person you find out that the person is the type that likes to do a lot of different things, and in the process of doing a lot, very little is accomplished or completed. Since doing too much is a problem, you can approach this person with suggestions on how to focus another energy. You might suggest that the person continue to do a variety of things because that is how he or she maintains their interests, but you might also suggest cutting their projects down to a manageable number of things. You might encourage the person to experiment to see how much he or she can handle, and still produce results. In encouraging the person to focus on a manageable number of projects, you might want to show them how this change will help him or her in their family relationships, on the job, with friends, and in school. Whether the person resists your suggestions or not, there is a good chance he or she will see them as a positive rather than a negative, because you are looking at things from his or her angle, and your suggestions suit the particular person's personality.

In conducting group evaluations, you should be very sensitive about what should be discussed with the whole group and what should be discussed privately with individual persons. Some personal problems are too sensitive to be discussed in a group setting. Often, you will only know whether the topic is private or public by knowing your members well. Some members can discuss intimate family questions in public, others cannot. The art of constructive criticism involves knowing the person, and offering positive alternatives that provide avenues for self-improvement.

HAVE A RETREAT

The section on program development suggests that a retreat is a good way to get away and look at yourself. Try to have a yearly retreat in a quiet place, where you can relax and look at the group as a whole. Once you have assessed strengths and weaknesses on a collective level, develop a program that is shaped to overcome your outstanding weaknesses. If your organization lacks money, develop a fundraising program based on your members' strengths. No matter what your weaknesses are, deal with them while they are small, so that they don't pile up into big problems. You should do everything to avoid the trap in our movement of not dealing with problems because you are afraid of hurting a person's feelings. By putting problems off you are not only setting the individual or the organization up for a bigger hurt, but you are allowing seeds of self-destruction to grow. Treat organizational problems like housecleaning. It is better to clean the house when a little dirt has piled up than to wait until everything is a mess and the damage done is expensive. We cannot afford the price of expensive organizational cleanups that lead to a loss of members and sometimes destroy the organization itself. It is when the dirt has piled up that our common enemy can be expected to sweep it in our faces. Good organizational cleanings are psychologically good, and they are the first line of defense against external disruption.

POLITICAL EDUCATION YOUR FIRST LINE OF DEFENSE

A strong organization is made up of conscious members who understand the group's line, and can think for themselves. Your organization's political education process is a security process because you are affecting the thought and behavior process of the person, and you are screening new members to determine their backgrounds and personalities. In this regard, it is of great importance to encourage members to think things through, and discuss the various sides of any question. It is a truism that "no one is thinking if everyone is thinking alike."

STRUCTURE YOUR POLITICAL EDUCATION PROGRAM

Your organization should have a well-structured political education process (see POLITICAL EDUCATION section) which, through theory and work, develops dedicated members who place the race first. Dedicated, conscious, thinking members should be able to defend the organizational position, carry themselves in a principled way, and spot suspicious behavior.

Since no political education system is fullproof, there will be members who are not transformed by the political education process. Knowing that your PE process is not perfect, you should work to continually improve it by learning from your mistakes and improving the quality of your new members.

CREATING A COLLECTIVE MISSION

Since we know that intelligence agencies prey on personal weaknesses, we should do our best to create a selfless commitment that transcends pettiness. The members who place the interest of the race first are members that are hard to manipulate, especially if they are dealing with their personal insecurities. A good security system is based on the idea that political, personal, and spiritual development is continuous and never ending. As our members grow and develop, the organization must present them with new challenges to improve themselves even more.

TRANSCENDING THE LIMITED VISION OF AMERICA

As sophisticated as the strategy of low intensity operations is, the complexity of America requires a counter response from progressive and revolutionary forces that defeats the low intensity strategy and raises the Black liberation struggle and the progressive forces in America to a level that transcends basic western assumptions about people, material things, and society.

AN OLD/NEW VISION OF PEOPLE AND SOCIETY

A new vision of people and society is necessary because the capitalist vision of material gain for the few, through rapid economic development, has not only left millions homeless and jobless, but it has created a society that has a vision of individual material gain but not of human growth and perfection. Marxism, on the other hand, proposes that rapid economic development can be used for the majority when the power is placed in the hands of the many (or the workers). The Soviet Union demonstrates quite to the contrary that while their system provides more benefits for the people as a whole, still the vision of the people is not one of being the best person they can be, rather, the vision is to have a better material life.

Under both systems the goal in life is acquisition. In one, the goal is acquisition for a few; in another, it is acquisition for the many. Yet neither places the acquisition of human values first. It is this area, the creation of the new man and the new woman, that is fundamental for change in the world today, and in the United States in particular.

Low intensity strategies cannot be defeated, and the seductive embrace of capitalism cannot be resisted, if a new set of values and a new vision of society are not created. This is so because as long as so-called revolutionaries operate on the same values as the oppressor, they will not have the principles to maintain a non-compromising posture when the enemy butters their bread and puts cream in their coffee. Before the so-called revolutionaries know it, they will find themselves dining at the oppressor's table, and sleeping on their diluted pacifiers. New human and social values provide the only corrective to a corrupt sick society that thinks that money is the supreme power in the world.

The strategic task for organizers is to reach the people in our communities who aren't working who are homeless, without food, or underemployed; or in the universities, being prepared to escape from their communities; or in skilled professions or occupations; or in prison; or in the military -- we have to reach all of our people and begin to exchange ideas on the kind of society and people we want to create. From these exchanges new short range and long range approaches to the people's oppression can be devised through collective methods.

MAKE BEING THE BEST HUMAN BEING THE CENTRAL GOAL OF OUR MOVEMENT

As we talk to the people about how we can improve our political and economic conditions, we have to discuss the central task of the struggle, how we can be the best human beings possible, and create a society centered around human values. It is this vision of creating truthful, spiritually developed people that was at the core of Kemit's (Egypt's) greatness. This was the core of the Dravidian, Chinese, and Native

American cultures during the periods of high culture.

MAKING PEOPLE THE CENTER OF SOCIETY

This vision that places people at the center of society, is the central value that enables the revolutionary organizer to define himself according to the people's needs and interests. For the organizer, the central value is the people, and nothing not money, power, or prestige can be allowed to compromise the peoples struggles and the people's needs. Human principles have a power stronger than money or a bullet. Human principles enable people to conquer the most powerful systems on earth. Those who maintain high human principles in the struggle for human liberation possess an eternal power that no bullet can kill, for the truth embodied in high principles cannot be killed.

TURNING OUR BACKS ON MATERIALISM

Yet it is the western vision of material acquisition that has dulled the higher vision of a better human being. The god of materialism has turned western folk and their carbon copies throughout the world into a greedy, individualistic horde for sale to the highest bidder. People and mother nature have been viewed as a source of wealth to be raped and exploited.

If we are to overcome the strategies of low intensity, and the restrictive systems of greed and hate, then we must raise our struggle to higher levels by struggling during the preparatory phase, and every other phase, for a new definition of people and society. To create a new man and new woman we will have to draw from the best in our ancient past, and the best that arises from our struggle to change ourselves and the society we live in.

LINK THE STRUGGLE FOR IMMEDIATE NEEDS WITH THE STRUGGLE TO CREATE NEW AFRICANS AND NEW PEOPLE

As organizers, we have to link struggles for immediate improvement in our people's lives with the question of transforming our thinking, so that we have a different expectation of the kind of people we want to be, and the kind of society we want to construct. In a society where the key struggle is the maximum production of goods for profit, this value needs to be questioned because it guarantees that people will be used to serve the ends of gaining the maximum production of goods, even if it means that people will not be needed to produce these goods. Cybernation and automation represent the highest achievement of material production through the most efficient scientific means. Yet because the central goal of western society is maximum production and material gain, people find themselves removed from production, without a roof over their heads or food to fill their stomachs. Millions of Black youth, and large numbers of American people as a whole are finding that the maximum production of goods represents no benefit to them.

The organizer must challenge the people to see that we have to create a new culture and new values that create a new framework for change. This framework must make being the best human beings the central task of society. In drawing from the best in our past, we must draw on the collective values of cooperation that reflect the wisdom of mother nature. Mother nature provides to all animals, and humans, without discrimination. She shares her wealth freely, requiring only a necessary effort for survival.

THE UNITY OF THE UNIVERSE

Mother nature and the universe are a great unity, with every small part being tied to the larger whole. People are universes within themselves, and they possess tremendous inherent powers. The people's powers derive from a respect for the dignity of life, the power and wisdom of nature, and the collective power of people to change their conditions when they change their values and priorities.

The people today who find themselves without work or food, or with work and oppression, understand that there is a basic need for social justice. The inner person understands the African-American saying "what goes around comes around." Organizers have to embody truth and justice in their words and actions, because the new society grows out of the new person who makes people the center of life.

During the preparatory phase it is not only important that we raise the question of what kind of new person and new society we want, but it is also important that we are selective in our recruitment so we minimize the chances of being infiltrated by state agents. For most groups this means that we will have to fight against the often popular idea that security measures are unimportant. The strategy of low intensity operations counts on security's laxness during the preparatory phase.

DEVELOP SECURITY CONSCIOUSNESS

Many movement activists think that the government isn't interested in us when our groups are small and financially weak. This may have been true in the sixties, but as the explanations of low intensity strategies proves, the state is now targeting groups that are small but have a potential for gaining mass support.

If you want to survive and have a chance to grow strong then you will have to develop security consciousness and a security system.

The organizer seeks to win the minds and hearts of the people. The people are the great ocean that can drown all of the state's conspiracies from COINTELPRO to low intensity schemes. Winning the people requires that we live with the people and work with them to help them solve their problems. This book has proposed a variety of strategies to win the support of the people.

Here it is important to stress that publicity plays an important part in explaining our goals and creating a positive image among our people. Without good publicity the best programs can go unnoticed. The programs that we implement should be put in the best light possible.

DEFINING OLD/NEW AFRO-CENTRIC VALUES

Low intensity strategists have learned well from the state's successes in coopting militant Black groups in the sixties. This plan proposes a continuation of these strategies described in other parts of this book. What should be clear to us is that there were some concrete reasons why many leaders and followers fell prey to the cooptation and selective repression strategies of the sixties. Most of the rank and file and a large part of the leadership in the Black movement had not defined a clear set of values and revolutionary objectives that would give them a vision beyond reform. In the sixties most leaders and followers were caught up in purely reformist objectives.

And when the system agreed to meet many of the reformist demands from the right to vote, to putting Black politicians into office, many within the rank and file, and some within the leadership believed that the movement's objectives had been achieved. The state then succeeded in separating the followers from the leaders while converting some of the leaders to Black capitalism, and assassinating the most militant leaders.

In all honesty, the state's dual strategy of separating the masses from the leadership through granting reforms while absorbing or removing the militant leadership, is the most dangerous strategy used by the government. At this time we will only have a chance of deflecting this kind of attack if we arm the people and the leadership with an understanding of long term objectives of the struggle. This is why our most important task is raising the cultural question of the type of new person and new society we want to create. Our commitment to collective values that go beyond the individual and speak to the needs of the people as a whole provide the armor of principles that will enable us to exploit the enemies manuevers against us. Collective human values give the people the strength to resist material gain for the few at the expense of the whole.

WEAKNESSES OF LOW INTENSITY STRATEGIES

Still, the cooptation strategy is not a strong as many think. It is vulnerable to cooptation by the people's movement when the leadership and the people understand that the state's resources are not to be used for individual benefit but they are there for use by the movement as a whole. Sometimes a good strategy is to organize the people to capture the policy-making body that administers and identifies groups that will receive government monies.

USING THE JOB AS A RESOURCE FOR THE BLACK COMMUNITY

For organizers who operate under a capitalist system we find ourselves often burning the candle at two ends. On the one hand we have to work for someone else for a living. On the other hand we are members of organizations that are trying to bring about change for our people. For those of us in this position the challenge is to be able to handle both of these responsibilities. What we need to see is that this dual position isn't the liability we make it out to be. Very often the jobs we hold give us access to people, resources, skills, and sometimes legitimacy that can all be used in organizing our people.

Some agencies are good centers for recruitment. Schools, universities, welfare agencies, etc., are good places to recruit. In the case of schools and universities we can use our positions in these institutions to expand the consciousness of our students and fellow workers. Professional jobs carry along with it a degree of legitimacy. We have shown how, during the sixties, COINTELPRO programs attempted to remove militants from jobs that carried prestige and respect among the general population. We need to exploit these positions to add further credibility to the groups that we are organizing in our communities.

Ultimately, reform has a dual cutting edge. One side of the reformist knife cuts against the movement, the other side cuts against the state. For the state, reform is the mother of revolution. For the movement, programs of reform are not designed to fundamentally change the condition of the people as a whole. So no matter how many people these programs buy off, the majority of the people continue to suffer. This continuing suffering, and the expectation that reforms may bring about some genuine change, make it possible for serious organizers to use the reformist process to create more dedicated supporters.

ESTABLISH A SECURITY SECTION

In most Black organizations, there are people who have security talents. These people should be recruited into a security section. Security people should have a high level of political consciousness. They should be physically fit, and they should undergo regular training in intelligence work. Contrary to popular opinion, security people are not all brawn with no brains, because physical security is only one aspect of security, and even physical security requires intelligence and not just physical fitness.

SECURITY CHECKS

A security section is responsible for checking up on new members through conducting background checks, and getting to know the people personally. The security section should maintain a file on each member which contains vital information about him or her. See the sample membership application form in the appendix.

Low intensity strategies are designed to penetrate organizations when they are small. The security section needs to educate members around COINTELPRO and low intensity strategies. Members should understand that just because the organization is small doesn't mean that the government will not try to penetrate the organization. Security education should attempt to overcome the lax attitude surrounding security that often exists in small groups. Sometimes members will resist establishing security procedures because they feel that such measures threaten their individual privacy. Try to show your members that the kind of information that a security section needs to gather is already in the hands of the government. A security system is designed to protect members from government invasions of organizational privacy and organizational existence.

SECURITY RESEARCH

Most of the intelligence work is research that involves clipping articles from newspapers and periodicals and taping radio and TV programs. A subcommittee within your security section should specialize in maintaining updated news clipping files on a variety of topics, including the Black liberation movement, allies, enemies right wing groups, intelligence agencies, big business, organized crime, African liberation movements, Third World nations and liberation movements, the state of the economy, political parties, etc. This section should develop summaries of key information, for the policy-making body of the organization. Under ideal circumstances, if you have enough members, people on this subcommittee should specialize in a specific area such as Black liberation movements, the economy, right wing organizations, etc. Specialists in these areas should develop the ability to predict the behavior of particular groups, or at least predict specific trends.

Everyone in the security section should undergo regular training in physical self-defense and intelligence techniques. People with military or police backgrounds are invaluable here.

Security personnel are needed to secure public rallies, organizational leaders, members, and organizational equipment. A sub-section on physical security should be established which develops plans for securing various types of buildings and events. Security policies should be developed that spell out the do's and don'ts for security personnel. An example of a do is to instruct your security people to be polite to the public. The best security is the security that does not have to use force. You have a good chance of avoiding force if you have a strong visible security presence that is polite and sensitive to the public's needs. The security section should determine policies on visible and invisible security, whether you want to conduct searches, etc.

Members of the organization should be trained in basic organizational security measures. This means that they should develop the habit of being security conscious on a 24-hour basis. A physical training program can be set up in the organization for all members, or members can be encouraged to develop their own physical fitness program. Each member should undergo a basic security training program, which can be integrated with political education.

HANDLING AGENTS

Even with the best security unit and training system for standing members, if your group is above ground it is visible, it can be penetrated by state agents. The security program should assume that, even after you have used every security method you can think of, you have been penetrated. So a part of your program should be designed to control the behavior of agents and non-agents. The organization should have a clear set of by-laws, a clear program and political line, and should insist on members following the organizational program. Whenever any member deviates from the organization program and policies he/she should be immediately approached, talked to, and when necessary disciplined. Tight organizational discipline makes it difficult for agent provocateurs to operate. Agents who are only gathering information will not be obvious in their behavior and will be harder to detect. To detect them you will have to blow their cover, which requires some careful investigation into their backgrounds. Often, agents who are gathering information succeed because we have done nothing to check them out. They are able to win our confidence and rise to influential positions in our organizations, because we ignored the most basic intelligence procedures.

STRENGTHENING BLACK FAMILIES

COINTELPRO and low intensity techniques attack the total person, not just the formal organization. Our families are not free from attack.

FAMILY SECURITY

A favorite intelligence tactic is the disruption of families. As we have seen, families can be disrupted through spreading truths or falsehoods about our nonfamily relationships. Whichever approach is used, for the technique to be effective, there have to be internal weaknesses that the agencies can exploit.

It is wrong to think that most Black families are destroyed because of external attacks or pressures. Black families fall apart because of personal insecurities between family members that boil down to a lack of trust; poor communication; taking each other for granted; outside relationships; a low self-image which leads us to believe that we are not desirable and are not wanted, and a Jones' mentality (wanting what the Joneses have, or believing that what's wrong with the Joneses is wrong with us). This is certainly not a complete list of the problems that separate us; it is only the tip of the iceberg.

Black political organizations have been destroyed as much by negative social relationships, as by important political questions. Until we reverse this backward social reality, our organizations will be like time bombs waiting to explode from within.

Black organizations need to take creative approaches to strengthening the Black family, and mending the torn fences that exist between Black men and Black women. The following are only a few ideas. You will be able to come up with many more by drawing on the creativity of your group.

FORM FAMILY SUPPORT GROUPS

Family support sections can be formed within your group. This section can give counseling to families and single individuals. Your group should operate on an extended family basis, giving parental support to each other's children, and providing support services to all family members. Work to create a situation where all the children see all of the adults as parents, and all parents see each other as brothers and sisters. Black people are family people, and the extended family unit needs to be strengthened among our people.

There are problems that Black women have that can only be solved by them. Conversely, Black men have problems that only they can solve. Black men and women's support groups are good ways to identify and solve problems that exist for both groups.

To be effective, separate Black men and women's groups should be complemented by developing times where both brothers and sisters come together to discuss common problems and solutions. Sometimes you might want to have a social affair where you honor the brothers or sisters.

Blacks who specialize in Black family relationships can be brought in to conduct workshops and lead group discussions. Political education programs can concentrate on studying the Black family so that you can assess its strengths and weaknesses and use some of the positive methods developed in the family to strengthen it. The study of African and New African culture (the culture developed by Blacks in America) should be promoted so that as mothers and fathers we can instill positive values in our youth.

RECOGNIZING AFRICAN WOMEN AS EQUALS

Within the Black liberation movement, we must work to encourage sisters to develop leadership skills. The "Miss Ann" mentality, that sisters should only do sister's work (an artificial distinction,) should be fought against. Where sisters display shyness and a fear to push their ideas in public, we should give them assignments that develop their self-confidence. Sisters should be encouraged to take on leadership responsibilities in heading up committees, initiating programs and taking on top leadership assignments that develop their self-confidence. Where this is not being done, sisters will have to take up the fight to see that trival white distinctions around artificial organizational roles are torn down. The truth is that work knows no sexual distinctions. If a job has to be done, the important thing is that the job gets done. The oppressor does not allow us the luxury of making such meaningless distinctions. The enemy is not reluctant to killing Black women, children, or men. We should therefore have no reluctance to do whatever is necessary to free ourselves. Family relations cannot be separated from community relationships. Our people will find it much easier to relate to us when they see that we maintain normal family relationships, and that we are able to face our problems and solve them, while socializing and enjoying ourselves.

COMMUNITY SECURITY

Your organization is a part of the Black community. Too often, though, we separate ourselves from our community by only associating with organization members, only going to organization functions, and carrying ourselves in a self-righteous way that alienates us from our people. In the section on ORGANIZING, I stressed that the importance of living with the people and feeling their pains and joys. This is not only the requirement for a good organizer, but it is also the soul of security. If you know your community, you will know a great deal about the enemy. The community is your eyes and ears. It lets you know who is right and who isn't. If you are a part of your community, you can keep informed of many of the enemy's moves and intentions.

ESTABLISHING TIES WITH OTHER ORGANIZATIONS

Since we know that "divide and conquer" is the basic tactic of the oppressor, we should build the strongest bonds of unity possible with other Black groups. This means taking time to form personal bonds with the leaders and members of various Black organizations. Personal friendships are the most important bonds, because they are the most difficult to break. Friends are more likely than others to question an anonymous mailing, a derogatory leaflet, or vicious rumors.

ESTABLISH MEDIATION PROCEDURES

To avoid shoot-outs, we should establish mediation procedures to resolve disputes between groups. Where possible, try to get a third party who has the respect of both groups to function as go-between. If various organizations know that the Black press and community groups will publicly criticize any group that violates certain organizational ground rules, then the disputing groups will have an incentive to behave in a positive way.

DEFINE YOUR ORGANIZATIONS IMAGE

The organization's image is an important weapon in the Black liberation movement. The best way to refute FBI slanders is to develop a reputation for honesty and intelligence in the Black community. When the community knows that your members are honest and dedicated, it makes it difficult for them to believe slurs that charge you with criminal activity. The more good your organization is doing for the people, the less likely they are to believe that you are doing wrong.

But a good reputation is not enough. We have to get our ideas and programs to the community. This amounts to defining our own image, rather than letting the enemy define it for us. To do this, we have to have positive relationships with the Black press, the progressive media, and where possible, a few key journalists in the white media.

GET A COLUMN IN THE LOCAL BLACK PRESS

Some of our organizations have been able to get a column in the local Black press. If you can get a column, make it an interesting one, which addresses the people's needs. Use the column as a support builder and as a voice for the people.

Cable television is wide open for community organization involvement. Every cable system has educational programming that community groups can use free of charge, or for a nominal fee. You can either use existing Black media groups to film your program, or you can train your own people. It is best in the long run to have people you can trust and depend on operating your equipment.

OWN YOUR OWN COMMUNICATIONS SYSTEMS

The use of systems controlled by others is all right, but ultimately, we need to control our own communication systems. A newspaper owned by your group is a dynamic communication arm, when it is professionally produced and presents interesting information in the language of the people. A newspaper allows you to print the truth for the people. Even more important, the ownership of a radio station and/or a cable TV channel is a powerful way to communicate your message to the people.

BUILD SUPPORT GROUPS

The government will not only assassinate your image, it may try to tie you up in the court system, and drain your energy and resources. Plan for legal harassment by establishing good relationships with skillful lawyers, who have experience in political defense. Develop ways to build support groups that can raise legal defense funds, thereby freeing your finances for more important things.

DEVELOP LAYERS OF LEADERSHIP

Every Black organization should develop layers of leadership, so that if your primary leadership is imprisoned, exiled or killed, the organization will continue. In the past we have relied on strong, singular, charismatic leadership. When this leadership has been removed, the organizations it led have collapsed. Strong collective leadership gives our movement permanence.

BUILD THE BLOCK STRUCTURE

Real collective leadership is not just three or four co-chairs because three or four collective leaders can be eliminated just as effectively as one. Real collective leadership is rooted on the block level, and it includes thousands and thousands of our people. Mass collective leadership cannot be destroyed.

Collective leadership on the block level is the base for the national movement. The strength of our national security system is determined by the strength of our local organizations and their local security systems.

Our local security systems should share security with their parent organizations on the national level, and national organizations of a progressive or revolutionary nature should share information on an interorganizational basis.

Finally, after you have wracked your brain to develop an efficient security system, remember that often those who act like agents aren't. People who often get labeled as agents aren't agents. They are usually unstable people, or they are people who you have been manipulated into labeling as agents through the use of the snitch label. When you put the agent label on a person, you are doing the kind of damage that cannot be undone. A person with a "snitch jacket" will lose his or her reputation in the movement, and can lose his or her life.

BE COOL AVOID AGENT PHOBIA

The intelligence agencies try to create an agent phobia to sow suspicion within the group. You have to be well-disciplined not to fall for this trap.

When preparing your organization to resist COINTELPRO and low intensity strategies, don't over estimate the government's ability to disrupt movements for social change. Remember that the United States is an extremely large country with a diverse people and culture. It is physically impossible for the national, state, and local intelligence agencies to infiltrate every little grassroots organization that pops up. This fact should not lead you to lower your guard, neither should it leave you shaking with agent fear.

LIMITATIONS OF THE LOW INTENSITY STRATEGY

We should also recognize that the three-stage low intensity strategy is not as simple as the planners may think it is. To date, no Black movement has moved from the preparatory, through the non-violent, to the revolutionary stage of struggle. Some small individual organizations may have moved through these stages, but to date no mass political movement has done so. Some mass movements have moved from the preparatory to the non-violent stage: however, the violent stage (urban rebellions of the sixties) has been spontaneous and unorganized.

MASTERING THE AMERICAN DYNAMIC

There are a lot of reasons why the three stage movement has not emerged on the local or national level. First, and most important, the American political, economic, racial, cultural situation is extremely complex, and the most advanced political formations in the Black Liberation movement have not yet mastered the American dynamic. Therefore, we have a situation where we have individual Black revolutionaries, but we do not have a revolutionary analysis and program that is capable of moving Black people and other oppressed groups through distinct planned stages of struggle that approach the low intensity model. This state of affairs should give none of us comfort. Don't think for one moment that this government is going to ease up on us simply because our organizing campaigns don't have a realizable revolutionary objective. The repressive forces of the government know that as long as progressive movements exist they provide a work shop for gaining a deeper appreciation of the American situation.

As organizers, it should be crystal clear that we have a two-fold responsibility; first, we need practical organizers who understand the mechanics of organizing, and we need organizers who balance practice with a deep theoretical knowledge of the American situation. In the end, the best security against government intelligence operations is a short range and long range strategy that is based on a historical understanding of the entire American situation. This is another way of saying that to win in this battle for liberation, we will have to have a deep understanding of the enemy and of ourselves.

CHAPTER SEVENTEEN
BUILDING THE MASS
ORGANIZATION

As we master the Art of Organizing, we come to understand that Africans in America occupy a strategic position in important American urban centers. As we move to produce change in Washington D.C., New York, Chicago, Atlanta, Los Angeles, Oakland, Philadelphia, Detroit, Houston, and Dallas, to name only a few, we discover that we have the capacity to transform the institutional structure of America. We also have the ability to influence the thinking of every ethnic group.

The great mass movements of the sixties demonstrate that when masses of Blacks begin to move for social change, they have the power to impact on and transform every major American institution. When our people decide to organize and call for deep, profound social changes, we force the presidency to react. Whether it reacts by offering programs of reform, or repression, the mass movement has the capacity to transform the institution of the Presidency. Where it attempts to pacify the mass movement by instituting programs of reform, it runs the likely risk of being viewed by whites as a protector of Blacks. This so-called white "Backlash" creates a counter force that mobilizes large sectors of whites to shift governmental priorities to the agencies of repression, i.e., the military and the police. Other sectors of whites, especially white youth, and people of color, often learn a different message from the Black mass movement. These social forces often become radicalized by the mass movement. Large sectors of white youth learn that its important to rebel against unjust laws and institutions. People of color learn to follow the example of Blacks, by creating militant organizations that speak to their needs.

When the administration chooses the course of repression, it often openly enlists the support of right-wing forces, which are encouraged to become vigilantes. White vigilantes are used to carryout a campaign of law and order. The repressive course of the national government makes it clear to Blacks that the government, or at least the presidential personality, is an enemy of Blacks. The course of repression is one where the presidency leads a campaign to overturn the gains made during the reformists period. Social programs are uprooted, conservative figures are placed on Federal courts and on the Supreme Court.

Whatever course the Presidency chooses in face of the mass movement, it is irrevocably changed. The effort to reform the conditions of Blacks is futile because the reformist measures are never sufficient to change the conditions of the mass of Black people. Ultimately, reformist measures drain the power of the presidency by forcing it to excessively use federal resources, through welfare spending, expenditures on social programs as well as other pacification programs. The demands raised by the mass movement help to educate other social groupings to the correctness of their demands, and these forces, along with Blacks, come to see the Presidency as being unwilling to produce on its promises of reform. In this sense the mass movement serves to radicalize a sector of activists who come to see the government and its institutional representatives as the enemy.

Where the repressive course succeeds in beating down the mass movement, the presidency can become a symbol that unites significant groupings of conservative whites. The presidential ballot box can become the way for many whites to gain a sense of ease and security, which is produced by a presidential figure who promises to end crime in the street (urban rebellions) and welfare stealing. Major economic interests line up to gain federal revenues from a growing defense budget that expands at the expense of the poor. Presidential repression creates great divisions between the rich and the poor, Blacks and whites.

The transformation of the presidency reflects deeper social changes. Social movements led by Blacks bring into question the value of the family, the role of the university, the nature of foreign policy and the relationship between the young and the old. For many Blacks, the mass movements of the sixties reinforced the importance of the patrilineal family, with the Black man serving as the bread winner. By the late seventies and early eighties, the historical research of the great African historian, Cheikh Anta Diop, drove home to conscious African-Americans the need to draw from the equalitarian model of the traditional African matriarchal family. The increased urbanization of Blacks, our increased irrelevance to the American work force,combined with a break down of collective communal African-American values, led to a break down in the African-American family. Among a large sector of whites many began to question the relevance of the monogamous nuclear family. Black mass movements promoted a democratic upsurge throughout society, especially in the citadel of the university. Black students began to raise the demand for Black studies, while white students radicalized by the Civil Rights movement began to demand free speech, and greater student involvement in the operation of the university. The Civil Rights and Black Power movements took the lead in opposing the American war in Vietnam. These Black-led anti-war movements, encouraged white youth, as well as other sectors of white society, to stand up in opposition to the Vietnam war. Black mass movements produce deep social changes that are irrevocable. As the sixties demonstrate, when the state attempts to coopt the mass movement with reforms, while it carries out a international policy of repression, the combined effect can be permanent political and economic decline. The strain on national and international resources can so weaken the state that it finds itself unable to produce the standard of life that worked to pacify large sectors of the working class and middle class. This decline in power, which now occurs at a time when the economy is being transformed from a industrial economy to a service economy, has a devastating effect on the majority of Blacks. The standard of living of Blacks becomes desperate under a low-paying service economy. The Black community comes to face serious breakdown, as the Black standard of living declines, and as Blacks become more closely tied to the American mass culture.

As organizers assess the state of the Black community, it becomes necessary to draw on past cultural and historical strengths to revitalize the Black community and create a sense of African-American community-hood. As we work to rebuild our communities, we have to learn from our past. The sixties represented the Golden Age of Black political struggle. The mass movement innovated creative tactics that kept the national government off balance. The early part of the seventies was the era of Pan Africanism.   Thousands of African-Americans joined with our African brothers and sisters around the world to show solidarity with the liberation movements of South Africa. By the mid-seventies, our movement entered a state of lull. This lull was caused by many forces, including a national leadership that inherited their positions by default. Those Pan Africanists who filled a leadership vacuum at the national level by default, lacked a theoretical understanding of our people's history, and displayed little originality of political thought. These default leaders usually advocated dogmatic positions of a nationalist or Marxist Leninist variety. The dogmatism of the nationalists and the Marxists disrupted three promising organizations of the seventies: the African Liberation Support Committee,   the Congress of African People, and the National Black Political Assembly.

By the eighties, many of those who were involved in the ideological splits of the seventies understood that there was a need to tolerate ideological differences and to rebuild the movement. The formation of the National Black United Front reflected this new political maturity. NBUF grew out of popular movements at the local level. In New York, the Black United Front organized the Black community against police violence.   In Philadelphia, a Black United Front emerged that helped orchestrate a grassroots electoral campaign that unseated a white mayor and elected Goode, a Black mayor. In Mississippi, the United League built a grassroots movement. Surprisingly, in Portland, Oregon, the Black United Front organized an educational movement around curriculum reform.

During the eighties, there have been three significant organizational thrusts coming from the Black community. The first has been the electoral political thrust coming from the grassroots Black community. Tied to this has been the presidential candidacy of Jesse Jackson. Alongside this grassroots electoral thrust has come a Free South Africa Movement, which again initially arose from grassroots Blacks. Finally, during the eighties a less well known educational thrust has come from the Black community. This educational thrust arises from the National Black United Front, which is organizing a national educational program around including an Afro-centric curriculum in the public schools along with after school programs and independent Black schools. The Afro-centric curriculum is tied to programs demanding academic excellence in the areas of reading, math, and science.

The grassroots movement of Blacks in Philadelphia to unseat a law and order mayor, and to replace him with a Black mayor, reflected the beginning of a mass electoral upsurge coming from grassroots Blacks. Unlike the late sixties, when the Ford

Foundation promoted Black political candidates such as Carl Stokes in an effort to create a moderate buffer leadership among Blacks, the electoral motion of the eighties was especially characterized by the effort of grassroot Blacks to overturn white political machines and officials. This grassroots challenge to entrench white political machines was the focus of the Harold Washington mayoral campaign in Chicago. His campaign took on the character of a political movement, with the Chicago Black United Front, under the leadership of Dr. Conrad Worrill playing a key role in shaping a grassroots street campaign. As a result, Black militant, moderate, and conservative forces formed a united front to elect Washington to the office of mayor, ending the white controlled machine system of Daly. With the death of Harold Washington, and the unprincipled alliance of Sawyer, a Black alderman, with the racist white forces who wanted to reinstall the Daly machine, the united front in the Black community has been broken. What the set back in the Washington campaign, as well as some other electoral set backs, should teach us is that first, we should not place our primary emphasis on electoral politics. While it is an arena that we should engage in, it should represent a secondary, not a primary organizing focus. Our primary organizational focus should be the development of solid grassroots block-by-block-organizations. As previously noted, block-by-block organizing gives us a mass organizational base that represents true political empowerment for our people. Electoral politics, issue organizing, and institution building should not be viewed as ends but as means to the end of organizing our whole people. While this political phase of struggle is difficult, the electoral arena is still an important arena for organizing Blacks.

The two presidential candidacies of Jesse Jackson, in 1984 and 1988, grew out of this grassroots electoral motion. Jesse, a resident of Chicago, learned a lot from the Harold Washington campaign. He also learned a lot from the Black Political Assembly, which in the late seventies had proposed running a Black for president of the United States. When Jesse announced his candidacy, he unleashed a fury of energy among grassroots Blacks. Jesse's first presidential candidacy, as I noted earlier, was opposed by the national Black leadership. This made it necessary for Jesse to rely on progressive and radical forces such as the Nation of Islam, and the National Black United Front. Because the electoral thrust came from the grassroots, Jesse with his charismatic appeal, was able to go over the heads of the established Black political leaders, and win the support of grassroots Blacks. Jesse's first presidential campaign can be characterized as a Black presidential campaign. However, Jesse's second Presidential campaign drew heavily on the support of Black elected officials, who did not see a strong Democratic candidate that they could rally behind. In his second campaign, Jesse did not draw on the support of progressive Black organizations such as the Nation of Islam and the National Black United Front. Jesse assumed that he had the support of grassroots Blacks, an assumption that proved to be correct. Jesse addressed his appeal to white farmers, white industrial workers, and other people of color. The end result of this second presidential campaign was on the positive side — the development of a progressive coalition inside the Democratic party. On the negative side, the Democratic party nominated a white southern conservative to the vice presidency, as a way to appeal to southern conservatives. This was an open slap in the face to Jesse and his progressive coalition, which Dukakis considered to be a liability in his presidential campaign. The Dukakis presidential campaign attempted to move to the center of the party by stressing patriotism and a commitment to a strong military defense. The Republicans succeeded in labeling Dukakis a liberal, and keeping him on the defensive. Jesse was hardly heard from during the campaign, as millions of Blacks saw no reason for voting for a Democratic presidential candidate, who was trying to out-conservative the conservatives.

In spite of the defeats suffered by Jesse and his progressive coalition, he did succeed during both campaigns in bringing new activists into the political process. A number of younger Blacks, who had not been previously politically active, began to involve themselves in grassroots politics. In his second campaign, Jesse succeeded in broadening his political base, and winning some significant primaries. Jesse's candidacy, and other electoral thrusts demonstrated that the electoral thrust at the grassroots level is still alive. As organizers we have to relate to this electoral thrust in a positive way. Who occupies the office of mayor is no insignificant issue. For a long time militant Blacks stayed away from electoral politics and permitted moderate Blacks to occupy these offices and to pursue moderate political agendas. Today, the electoral ·arena is one where grassroots organizations can be built, members can be recruited, and progressive political candidates can be elected who speak to a grassroots agenda.

Another significant political movement in the eighties was the Free South Africa movement. Again, the Free South Africa agenda, has its roots in the Nationalist, and Pan Africanist agendas, which mobilized African-Americans to provide political and material support for the liberation movements in Southern Africa. This movement was also a reflection of the international character of the liberation movements of African people. The uprisings by African people in South Africa, demonstrated our people's ability to cause a chain reaction throughout the world. Once again the initiative for the Free South African movement came from grassroots Blacks, who worked as longshoremen in Oakland and San Francisco. Black longshoremen refused to unload South African goods. On the national level, Trans-Africa and other national Black leaders began demonstrations in front of South African embassies. College students began to mount divestment struggles that sought to force their colleges to cease investing in South Africa. The Free South Africa movement succeeded in forcing the United States' government to enact divestment legislation. This represented one of the few victories gained by Blacks and other progressive forces against the conservative Reagan administration. What revolutionary Black nationalists and other militant Black forces should learn from both the Black presidential thrust, and the Free South African thrust, is that the moderate and progressive wings of the Black elite are willing to coopt nationalist's, and Pan Africanists' political thrust, and to freeze the militant nationalists leadership out of the decision making councils. This happened in the second presidential candidacy of Jesse Jackson, and it happened during the Free South Africa campaign. What all of this should teach us is that its absolutely necessary that the nationalist and Pan Africanist sectors of our movement need to not only initiate national grassroots campaigns, but we need to provide the leadership and organization to these movements, so that our people at the grassroots level can achieve serious organization. As long as we fail to achieve national leadership of these movements, we will continue to be in an unorganized position, as we are now, after the Jesse Jackson presidential campaign, and the Free South African Movement.

It is in the new arena of educational struggle that the Nationalist, Pan Africanist, and other progressive sectors have the opportunity to build a truly grassroots movement in the United States. This new arena of political struggle is the arena of education. During the eighties, the Portland Black United Front ignited an educational fire, that is starting to blaze across America. The Portland group organized an educational movement to change the public school curriculum and to bring about other educational reforms. To date, they have succeeded in forcing the Portland Board of Education to hire African-American curriculum experts who have shaped a creative African-centric curriculum. In Oakland, BUFFER (Black United Front for Educational Reform) has built a diverse, grassroots organization that is organizing Blacks in Oakland around African-centric curriculum reform and other educational reforms.

In July of 1988, the National Black United Front adopted the public school program initiated by Portland BUF and organized by BUFFER. To date NBUF chapters in Kansas

City, Dallas, Muskegon, Michigan, Chicago, and San Francisco have started public school curriculum and educational reform movements. In the case of Muskegon, an after school tutorial program is being implemented.

The public school and after-school educational programs are important because they speak to a vital mass issue that concerns most African-Americans throughout the United States. The experience of BUFFER and Portland BUF demonstrates that the issue of African-centric curriculum reform, and other reforms in literacy, math, and science programs are issues around which broad-based community organizations can be built.

During a historical period in which grassroots organizing has occurred, it is essential that the progressive and revolutionary forces begin to build mass-based organizations that have the capacity to organize millions of our people. These grassroots organizations will be launched by organizing around mass issues such as education, however, once broad, mass-based organizations are built, they must respond to broader issues including economic development, electoral politics, self defense, struggles against the drug traffic, and struggles to support the liberation of Southern Africa and other areas of the world. Mass- based organizations will have to develop the capacity to reach out to every sector of the Black population, locally and nationally. Mass-based grassroots organizations must have the capacity to organize on every level of the society. They must be able to organize Black parents, Black community activists, Black businessmen, Black ministers, the Black unemployed, the Black homeless, Black youth, Black professionals, and Blacks of every political persuasion. These organizations must have the capacity to organize our people while they work and after work. We must be able to organize people wherever they are in this society. This is the complex challenge that faces Blacks who are strategically located in the urban centers of the United States.

The BUFFER experience in building a mass organization in Oakland can be instructive in aiding us to build a mass-based movement locally, nationally and internationally. BUFFER has learned that massed-based organizations are built around mass issues. Mass issues are those which cut across large sectors of the Black community. The issue of economic development is a mass issue because it speaks to a fundamental need of Black people — the need to own and control our own businesses. Changing the curriculum, hiring conscious Black teachers, and conscious Black administrators is a key issue because most of our children are in the public schools, where they are being mis-educated. The educational thrust of African-centric curriculum allows us to shape an educational program that can transform the thinking and skills of millions of Black youth. So the mass issue of African-centric curriculum reform, when linked to other educational reforms, such as uniform literacy, math and science programs can serve as the basis for building a mass-based organization. The important thing is that the mass issues must be free of ideological links, because emphasis on ideologies will restrict the organizations appeal to those who agree with the ideology. When the issue of providing a relevant education for Black youth is presented as the educational issue, the organization pushing the educational issue has the capacity to reach to a broad cross section of the Black community. So the first rule in building a mass-based organization is the use of a mass issue which has the power to draw mass support.

As you begin to build an organization around a mass issue, it is essential that a diverse leadership be selected to represent the concerns of the mass organization. Diverse leadership enables an organization to appeal to diverse sections of the Black community. When the mass-based organization includes within it's leadership parents, young and old, reformists and nationalists, Christians and non-Christians, seasoned activists, and newcomers to the struggle--when the mass organization has this kind of broad-based support, it will have the capacity to reach and influence diverse sectors of the Black community. It is important to note that the diversity of the organization is more important than the size of the organization. A diverse organization can be small or large; however, its strength derives from its ability to represent various groupings within the Black community.

Broad-based mass organizations are absolutely essential, because in the complex American environment, which is highly specialized, groups that want to bring about social change have to have the capacity to attack the white Power Structure at many levels simultaneously. We need Blacks, both ministers and lay people, who are part of the Black church structure because they have a political base that influences political policies in our communities. Key Black churches, especially well-organized progressive ones, have the capacity to influence white decision makers. Needless to say, a good organizer understands the importance of having Black church support. It doesn't hurt to have some Black church representation in the mass-based community organization. For broad-based educational organizations, it is essential that Black parents are involved in the leadership and membership of these organizations. Black parents have the power, when organized, to influence PTA's and to transform educational policies at school sites and throughout the school district. Black youth have to be a part of the mass-based community organization, because the youth are our future, and they bring energy and new ideas, along with a no-compromise attitude. The mass-based organization has the important task of educating our youth about our great historical past, and the important role they have to play in the liberation of our people. Many of our Black youth today are politically inactive, and in some cases they are involved in negative social activity, because the no-compromise mass-based community organizations have not been institutionalized in our communities.

If our movements are going to last over the long haul, they must have sufficient finances to base their operations on. Our mass based organizations need Blacks with business skills who can help us shape economic development plans that will enable our groups to be self-reliant. The mass-based community organization needs the involvement and support of Black professionals, because they bring administrative skills to the organization, and they are often strategically placed in white institutions. We need not only professionals in our organizations, but we also need to tap the rich information that many Black professionals have who are working in key white organizations. Here, the mass organization needs to develop the sophistication to use the information of strategically placed professionals without divulging the source of this information. Put another way, the broad-based, diverse community organization needs to understand that those who give us strategic information are just as important as those who give us time and money. Ultimately, the diverse, broad-based community organization, has the capacity to influence the Black community, and the white power structure.

Finally, the secret behind the mass-based diverse community organization is the democratic, consensus-based decision-making structure of the organization. BUFFER's (Black United Front For Educational Reform)experience, and African people's experiences in the African liberation movement worldwide, demonstrate that African people won't support movements that they have not had a voice in shaping. The government of Kwame Nkrumah lost power not only because the West opposed his Pan Africanist policies, but also because he failed to involve his people in the process of shaping governmental policies. Nkrumah made the mistake of assuming that the British system of Parliamentary democracy was a substitute for real African democracy. Had the market women of Ghana, the farmers, chiefs, intellectuals, and other Ghanaians been involved in shaping the policies and programs of Ghana, it is very likely that they would have protected him from the foxy power plays of imperialism. What is true for Ghana is true for the whole African world. Diverse ideas enable the group to shape a diverse program that is able to operate on many levels simultaneously.

If we are to build African people's movements, we must draw on the best historical traditions of our people. Historically, world democracy originated out of African democracy: the chiefless age-grade societies, where the youth, adults, and elders assumed responsibilities based on age, are societies that gave birth to the world's first democracies. These age-grade societies operated on a consensus system that involved all adults in the decision-making process. The consensus system was such a great system because it built it's direction on the best ideas that came from the people. Since every adult had a role in shaping the consensus decisions of the community, the people as a whole worked to implement these decisions as their decisions. BUFFER has learned that the consensus system is the way we build diverse organizations that are centered around mass issues. Consensus decision making encourages diverse ideas. The diversity of ideas attracts diverse people from different religious and political backgrounds to participate in the group. Diverse ideas enable the group to shape a diverse program that is able to operate on many levels simultaneously.

While the consensus process is an essential decision-making system for building diverse organizations, it will only work if the organization shares some common values. Our elder, John Henrik Clarke, notes that for the consensus process to work, the members must have a deep respect for our elders. The respect for elders is at the heart of African culture, and it is the basis for the consensus process.   For in traditional age grade societies,   it   was   the   elders   who recommended decisions to the larger society. Today, during a time that calls for revolutionary struggle, it is important that more than just our elders are involved in shaping community decisions.   In fact, revolutionary periods require that the youth play an important role in the liberation struggle, a role unheard of in traditional African societies. Yet, while our conditions today call for broad involvement of different sectors of our community in shaping decisions, still, the insights of our elders must be given special consideration. Our activist elders bring a wealth of political experience that we ignore only at our own expense.   Sound, solid decisions require that we listen carefully to our elders.   This requirement may seem obvious, but it is not one that is easily achieved in our organizations. In the larger Black community, Black elders are no longer respected.   Our community's general disrespect for elders is carried over into our organizations. If consensus is going to work, we will have to educate our people to the importance of respecting our elders.

Another barrier to the effective operation of the consensus process, as Professor John Henrik Clarke notes, is the decline   of   a   sense   of   African communityhood.   In traditional African societies, those who participated in the consensus process understood that they were deliberating for the living, the dead, and the unborn. Our ancestors had a deep sense of African communityhood. Today, our communities are undergoing breakdown at every level. We have the responsibility to rebuild a sense of African communityhood. African communityhood is not restricted to the African-American community. African communityhood, means building a sense of African communityhood among Africans in America, the Caribbean, South America, Europe, Asia, and Africa. As we deliberate and shape decisions we must act in the interests of Africans everywhere. In creating a sense of communityhood, we must realize that the extended African family is the basis for strong African communities and ultimately strong African nations.

So, in the final years of the twentieth century, we Africans must reach back to our great past and shape a vision for a strong organized race of people. Let us build organizations and institutions that will draw from the strength and creativity of the greatest civilization known to humanity ancient Kemit (Egypt). Let us draw from our great past the lasting values of Maat, (justice) and harmonious complementary dualism. Let us understand that the African man has no future without the African women; that our youth have no future without our elders; that Africans in America have no future without a strong African people throughout the world, and especially in Africa. Let us roll up our sleeves and get down to the task of achieving liberation and power in the 21st century.

APPENDIX

1.   Political Education materials:

   a. Orientation Schedule

   b. Cycles of African Consciousness

   c. Introductory Reading List

   d. Basic Family Bibliography on African and African-AmericanHistory and Culture (compiled by Dr. Asa Hilliard)

   e. Sample Cadre Training Outline

2.   Intelligence Section:

   President Reagan's Memorandum on Intelligence Activities

ORIENTATION SCHEDULE

I.   First Meeting

Discussion of the purpose of political education, the history of PAPO and the Pan Afrikan Secretariat.   Explanation of the structure and rules of PAPO. Discussion of the history of the Black United Front. Show slides on PAPO and ALD. Assign reading of Pan Afrikan values, and cycles   of   Afrikan consciousness. Reading material to be discussed at send meeting.

II.   Second Meeting

Discussion of the Assimilation and the Survival Soul Cultural Awareness stages of consciousness.   Discussion of Pan African Values paper. Discussion of how this material applies to our experiences with assimilation, or the survival soul consciousness stage of awareeness.

III.   Third Meeting

Application of the Disturbance and Exposure stage of consciousness to our own personal experiences.

IV.   Fourth Meeting

Discussion of the transformation process we are undergoing through the Nationaliststage of consciousness. What specific weaknesses are we working on.

V.   Fifth Meeting

Discussion of Afrikan Manhood and Womanhood. The matrileneal family and the Black family in slavery. The status of the Black family today. Causes for the breakdown in Black families. Discussion of how this applied to your family situation. Tie this into Herbert G. Gutman, *The Black Family In Slavery & Freedom, 1750-1925*, New York, Pantheon Books, and Cheikh Anta Diop, *The Cultural Unity of Black Africa*, Chicago, Third World Press, 1959.

VI.   Sixth Meeting

Discussion of Afrikan Manhood and Womanhoods. Stages in the development of a relationship. Responsibilities in a relationship. Developing support systems including building extended families, family advice systems, child rearing support systems, mediation systems, and value sharing systems.

Examination of Afrikan carryovers in the Black family today. Keys to building non-exploitative loving relationships. Divisions of reposnibilities in the family. The family as the foundation unit for the nation. development of sisters in the family and organization.

VII.   Seventh Meeting

Definition of Revolutionary Pan Afrikan Nationalism. Application of the Revolutionary Pan Afrikan Nationalists stage of consciousness to our personal political development. Theoretical summing up of Black political movements i.e., King, SNCC, CORE, the historical development of the civil rights movement. Play taped interview with CLR James on the "Meaning of Pan Afrikanism." Readings include, Clayborne Carson, *In Struggle SNCC and the Black Awakening of the 1960's*, Cambridge Massachussets, Harvard University Press, 1981. Robert Brisbane, *Black Activism*, Valley Forge, Judson Press, 1974, pp. 43-105.

VIII.   Eighth Meeting

Analyze in a theoretical way the significance of Malcolm, the NOI, the OAAU, Black Power, the Urban rebellions, The Black Panther Party, and Cultural Nationalism. Analysis of COINTELPRO strategies. Assessments of strengths and weaknesses, and application to our strategies today.

IX.   Ninth Meeting

Analysis of the S.F. State Strike, Congress of Afrikan People, Afrikan Liberation Support Committee and Black Political Assembly. Examination of causes behind their break up. Analysis of Strategies and Tactics for Black Liberation.

Readings include, William H. Orrick, Jr., "Shut It Down! A College in Crisis", San Francisco State Colege, October 1968 - April 1969, June 1969. Oba T'Shaka, *Strategies and Tactics for Building a National Mass Based Black United Front*, San Francisco, March 1980. Oba T'Shaka, "The San Francisco Strike, A Study of the First Black Studies Strike in the U.S." S.F. 1977.

X.   Tenth Meeting

Self Defense, Soul and Creativity, and Afrikan Nationhood. Focus on Afrikan Nationhood. What do we mean by nationhood? Examination of various positions on the land question, including the PAS position.

Tape on the land panel, third Black United Front Convention: Oba T'shaka, "Analysis of the Black Belt South Position", 1982.

XI.   Eleventh Meeting

Continuation of the discussion on the land question. Discussion of a youth organization project.

XII.   Twelfth Meeting

Discussion of areas of work for new members, meeting dates. Evaluation of prospective members.

I

BASIC BIBLIOGRAPHY
ON
AFRICAN AND AFRICAN-AMERICAN
HISTORY AND CULTURE

Following is a list of recommended basic books on African and African-American history and culture. These are books which should be available on order through most bookstores. Unfortunately, few bookstores, including many African-American bookstores, do not maintain a complete stock of the most significant books in African and African-American history. However, the following books are well worth any temporary inconveniences which may be cause due to a short wait.

The following books should be thought of as a basic reference list, primarily for parents. However, some of the material may be suitable for older children, especially the stories in Joel Rogers' *World's Great Men of Color.*

Armah, A.K. *Two Thousand Seasons.* Chicago: Third World Press, 1979.

Counter, A. and, Evans, D.L. *I Sought My Brother: An Afro-American Reunion.* Cambridge,

Massachussets: MIT Press, 1981.

Diop, C.A. *The African Origin of Civilization: Myth or Reality?* New York: Lawrence Hill, 1974.

Diop, C.A. *The Cultural Unity of Black Africa.* Chicago: Third World Press, 1959.

DuBois, W.E.B. *Black Reconstruction in America: An Essay Toward a History of the Part Which Black Folk Played in the Attempt to Reconstruct Democracy in America, 1860-1880.* New York: Athaeneum, 1973.

Garvey, A.J. *Garvey and Garveyism.* New York: Collier Books, 1968.

Hansberry, W.L. *Africa and Africans as Seen by Classical Writers: The William Leo Hansberry African History Notebooks,* Vol. 2 (J.E. Harris, Ed.). Washington, D.C.: Howard University Press, 1977.

Hansberry, W.L. *Pillars in Eithiopian History: The William Leo Hansberry African History Notebooks,* Vol. 1 (J.E. Harris, Ed.). Washington, D.C.: Howard University Press, 1974.

Herskovits, M.J. *The Myth of the Negro Past.* Boston: Beacon Press, 1958.

Jackson, J.G. *Introduction to African Civilization.* Secaucus, New Jersey: Citadel Press, 1974.

James, G. G.M. *Stolen Legacy.* San Francisco: Julian Richardson, 1976.

Jones, L. *Blues People.* New York: William Morrow, 1963.

Korngold, R. *Citizen Toussaint.* New York: Hill & Wang, 1965.

Price, R. (Ed.). *Maroon Societies: Rebel Slave Communities in the Americas.* New York: Anchor Books, 1973.

Redmond, E.B. Drum Voices: *The Mission of Afro-American Poetry.* New York: Anchor Books, 1976.

Rodney, W. *How Europe Underdeveloped Africa.* Washington, D.C.: Howard University Press, 1974.

Rogers, J.A. *World's Great Men of Color, Vols. 1 and 2.* New York: Collier Books, 1972.

Smitherman, G. *Talkin and Testifyin: The Language of Black America.* Boston: Houghton Mifflin, 1977.

Turner, L. *Africanisms in the Gullah Dialect.* New York: Arno Press, 1969.

Van Sertima, I. *They Came Before Columbus.* New York: Random House, 1976.

Vass, C.W. *The Bantu Speaking Heritage of the United States.* Los Angeles: Center for Afro-American Studies, University of California, 1979.

Williams, C. *The Destruction of Black Civilization: Great Issues of the Race from 4500 B.C. to 2000 A.D.* Chicago: Third World Press, 1974.

Woodson, C.G. *The Miseducation of the Negro.* Washington, D.C.: Associated Publishers, 1969. First published 1933.

JOURNALS

The Journal of African Civilizations. I. Van Sertima, Ed. New Brunswick, New Jersey: Douglass College, Rutgers University.

Black Books Bulletin. H.R. Madhubuti, Ed. Chicago: The Institute for Positive Education, 7524 South Cottage Grove Avenue, Chicago, Illinois 60619

Selected bookstores where some of these materials may be purchased:

The Aquarian Bookstore, Los Angeles

Mamie Clayton's Third World and Ethnic
    Books,
Los Angeles
Marcus Books, San Francisco, Oakland
Liberation Bookstore, Harlem, New York City
The Black Book, Baltimore
Amistad Bookplace, Houston
Hakim's Bookstore, Atlanta
The Shrine of the Black Madonna, Atlanta
Ellis Books, Chicago
The Talking Drum Bookstore, Portland,
    Oregon
Liberation Information, Washington, D.C.

II

EVIDENCE FOR THE AFRICAN ORIGIN OF THE EARLIEST RECORDED CIVILIZATION, FOR THE ANCIENT AFRICANS AS BEING BLACK PEOPLE, AND FOR THE EXISTENCE OF CIVILIZATIONS THROUGHOUT AFRICA BEFORE EUROPEAN COLONIALISM

Adams, William. *Nubia: Corridor to Africa.* Princeton: Princeton University Press, 1977.

Alfred, C. *Art in Ancient Egypt.* London: Alec Tiranti, 1969.

Bain, Mildred and Lewis, Ervin (Eds.). *From Freedom to Freedom: African Roots in American Soil.* New York: Random House, 1977.

Battuta, Ibn. *Travels in Asia and Africa 1325-1354.* New York: Augustus M. Kelley, 1969.

Bell, H. Idris. *Cults and Creeds in Graeco-Roman Egypt.* Chicago: Aries, 1957.

ben-Jochanan, Yosef. *Africa, Mother of Western Civilization.* New York: Alkebu-Lan Books, 1970.

ben-Jochanan, Yosef. *A Chronology of the Bible: Challenge to the Standard*

Version. New York: Alkebu-Lan Books, 1973.

ben-Jochanan, Yosef. *African Origin of the Major "Western Religions".* New York: Alkebu-Lan Books, 1970.

ben-Jochanan, Yosef. *Black Man of the Nile.* New York: Alkebu-Lan Books, 1972.

ben-Jochanan, Yosef. *The Black Man's North and East Africa.* New York: Alkebu-Lan Books, 1971.

ben-Jochanan, Yosef. *The Black Man's Religion: Excerpts and Comments from the Holy Black Bible.* New York: Alkebu-Lan Books, 1970.

Blavatsky, H.P. *Isis Unveiled: A Master Key to the Mysteries of Ancient and Modern Science and Theology.* Pasadena, California: University Press, 1972.

Bovill, E.Q. *The Golden Trade of the Moors.* New York: Oxford University Press, 1980.

Breasted, James Henry. *The Dawn of Conscience.* New York: Charles Scribner, 1978.

Breasted, James Henry. *A History of Egypt from Earliest Times to the Persian Conquest.* New York: Charles Scribner & Sons, 1937. First published 1909.

Brent, Peter. *Black Nile: Mungo Park and the Search for the Niger.* New York: Gordon Cremonisi, 1977.

British Museum. *The Rosetta Stone.* London: British Museum Publications, 1974.

Budge, E.A. Wallis. *Amulets and Talismans.* New York: Collier, 1970. First published 1930.

Budge, E.A. Wallis. *The Book of the Dead, The Papyrus of Ani.* New York: Dover Publications, 1967. First published 1895.

Budge, E.A. Wallis. *The Dwellers on the Nile.* New York: Dover 1977. First published 1926.

Budge, E.A. Wallis. *The Egyptian Heaven and Hell.* Lasalle, Illinois: Open Court Press, 1974. First published 1905.

Budge, E.A. Wallis. *Egyptian Magic.* Secaucus, N.J.: Citadel Press, 1978. First published 1899.

Budge, E.A. Wallis. *Egyptian Religions.* Secaucus, NJ: University Books, 1959. First published 1899.

Budge, E.A. Wallis. *The Gods of the Egyptians: Or, Studies in Egyptian Mythology,* Vols. I and II. New York: Dover, 1969. First published 1904.

Budge, E.A. Wallis. *Osirus and the Egyptian Resurrection.* New York: Dover, 1973. First published 1911.

Carruthers, Jacob H. Maat: *The African Universe.* Unpublished Manuscript.

Carruthers, Jacob H. *Orientation and Problems in the Redemption of Ancient Egypt.* Unpublished Manuscript.

Carruthers, Jacob H. *Tawi: The United Two Lands.* Unpublished Manuscript.

*Churchward, Albert. *The Signs and Symbols of Primordial Man: The Evolution of Religious Doctrines from the Eschatology of the Ancient Egyptians.* Westport, Connecticut: Greenwood Press, 1978. First published 1913.

Clark, J. Desmond. *The Prehistory of Africa.* New York: Praeger, 1971.

Collins, Robert O. *Problems in African History.* Englewood Cliffs: Prentice-Hall, 1968.

Cooley, W.D. *The Negroland of the Arabs Examined and Explained: An Inquiry into the Early History and Geography of Central Africa.* Frank Cass and Co., Ltd., 1966.

Cottrell, Leonard. *Lady of Two Lands: Five Queens of Ancient Egypt.* New York: Bobbs-Merrill, 1967.

Cox, Georgia O. *African Empires and Civilizations.* Washington, D.C.: African Heritage Publishers, 1974.

Davidson, Basil. *African Kingdoms.* New York: Time-Life Books, 1971.

Davidson, Basil. *Discovering Our African Heritage.* Boston: Ginn and Co., 1971.

Davidson, Basil. *Old Africa Rediscovered.* London: Victor Gollancz Ltd., 1970.

*Diop, C.A. *The African Origin of Civilization: Myth or Reality?* New York: Lawrence Hill and Co., 1974. First Published 1955.

*Diop, C.A. *The Cultural Unity of Black Africa.* Chicago: Third World Press, 1978. Originally published 1959.

Doane, T.W. *Bible Myths and Their Parallels in the World's Major Religions: Being a Comparison for the Old and New Testament Myths and Miracles with Those of Heathen Nations of Antiquity, Considering also Their Origins and Meaning.* New York: Truth Seeker Press, 1882. Reprinted 1948.

Dubois, Felix. *Timbuktu the Mysterious.* Longmans, Green & Co., 1896.

DuBois, W.E.B. *The World and Africa: An Inquiry into the Part Which Africa Has Played in*

World History. New York: International
Publishers, 1972. Originally published 1946.

Emery, Walter B. *Lost Land Emerging.* New
York: Charles Scribner, 1967.

Fage, J.D. and Oliver, R.A. *Papers in African
Prehistory.* Cambridge: The University
Press, 1970.

Fazzini, R.A. *Art from the Age of Akhenaten.*
Brooklyn, New York: Brooklyn Museum
Press, 1973.

Fell, Barry. America B.C.: *Ancient Settlers in
the New World.* New York: Wallaby, 1976.

*Fleming, Beatrice J. & Pryde, Marian J.
Distinguished Negroes Abroad.
Washington, D.C.: Associated Publishers,
1946.

Frankfort, Henri. *Ancient Egyptian Religions.*
New York: Harper Torchbooks, 1961. First
published 1948.

Frankfort, Henri. *Kingship and the Gods: A
Study of Ancient Near Eastern Religion as
the Integration of Society and Nature.*
Chicago: University of Chicago Press,
1978. First Published 1948.

Frankfort, Henri, Frankfort, H.A., Wilson, J.A.,
Jacobsen, T., & Irwin, W.A. *The Intellectual
Adventure of Ancient Man: An Essay on
Speculative Thought in the Ancient Near*

East. Chicago: University of Chicago Press, 1977. First published 1946.

Frazer, P.M. *Ptolemaic Alexandria.* Oxford at the Clarendon Press, 1972.

Freud, Sigmund. *Moses and Monotheism.* New York: Vintage, 1967. First published 1939.

Graves, Anna Melissa. *Africa: The Wonder and the Glory.* Baltimore: Black Classic Press, P.O. Box 13414, Baltimore, MD 21203, 1961.

Graves, Kersey. *The World's Sixteen Crucified Saviors: Or Christianity Before Christ.* New York: Truth Seeker Press, 1975. First published 1875.

Griule, Marcel. *Conversation with Ogotemmeli: An Introduction to Dogon Religious Ideas.* Oxford University Press, 1972.

Hall, Manly P. *Free Masonry of the Ancient Egyptians.* Los Angeles: Philosophical Research Society, Inc., 1971. First Published 1937.

Hapgood, Charles H. *Maps of the Ancient Sea Kings: Evidence of Advanced Civilization in the Ice Age.* New York: E.P. Dutton, 1979.

Harris, Joseph E. (Ed.). *Africa and Africans as Seen by Classical Writers: The William Leo Hansberry African History Notebook*, Volume II. Washington, D.C.: Howard University Press, 1977.

Harris, Joseph E. *Africans and Their History.* New York: Mentor, 1972.

*Harris, Joseph E. (Ed.). *Pillars in Eithiopian History: The William Leo Hansberry History Notebook*, Volume I. Washington, D.C.: Howard University Press, 1974.

Higgins, Godfrey. Anacalypsis: *An Attempt to Draw Aside the Veil of the Saitic Ises: Or an Inquiry into the Origin of Languages, Nations and Religions.* London: Longmen, Rees, Oras, Brown; Green, Longman, Paternoster Row, 1836. Reprinted 1972 by Health Research, Mokelume Hill, California.

Hull, Richard W. *African Cities and Towns Before the European Conquest.* New York: W.W. Norton & Co., 1976.

Hurry, Jamieson B. *Imhotep: The Vizier and Physician of King Zoser and Afterwards the Egyptian God of Medicine.* Oxford University Press, 1928.

Hutchinson, Louise D. *Out of Africa: From West African Kingdoms to Colonization.* Washington, D.C.: Smithsonian Institution Press, 1979.

Ions, Veronica. *Eqyptian Mythology.*
  London: Hamlyn, 1965.

Jackson, John G. *Introduction to African
  Civilizations.* NJ: The Citadel Press, 1974.
  First Published 1970.

*Jackson, John G. *Man, God and
  Civilization.* New York: University Books,
  Inc., 1972.

Jairazbhoy, R.A. *Ancient Egyptians and
  Chinese in America.* Totowa, NJ: Roman
  and Littlefield, 1974.

James, George G.M. *Stolen Legacy.* San
  Francisco: Julian Richardson, 1976. First
  published 1954.

Johnson, Samuel. *The History of the Yorubas:
  From Earliest Times to the Beginning of
  the British Protectorate.* Lagos, Nigeria:
  CSS Bookshops, P.O. Box 174, 50 Broad
  Street, Lagos, Nigeria, 1976. First
  published 1921.

Jones, Edward L. Black Zeus: African
  Mythology and History. Seattle: Edward
  L. Jones, Frayn Printing Co., 2518 Western
  Avenue, Seattle,WA 98121, 1977.

*Jones, Edward L. *Profiles in African Heritage.*
  Seattle: Edward L. Jones, Frayn Printing
  Co., 2518 Western Avenue, Seattle, WA
  98121, 1972.

*Jones, Edward L. *Tutankhamon.* Edward L. Jones and Associates, 5517 17th Avenue, N.E., Seattle, WA 98105, 1978 Library of Congress Card #78-61436.

July, Robert W. *A History of the African People.* New York: Charles Scribner & Sons, 1974.

Kandi, Baba Kumasi. *Down the Nile.* Detroit: A Greater Visions Classic, P.O. Box 21606, Detroit, Michigan, 1978.

Leakey, L.S.B. *By the Evidence: Memoirs 1932-1951.* New York: Harcourt Brace Jovanovich, 1974.

Leslau, Wolf. *Falasha Anthology: The Black Jews of Ethiopia.* (Translated from Ethiopic Sources). New York: Schocken, 1951.

Lugard, Lady. *A Tropical Dependency: An Outline of the Ancient History of the Western Sudan with an Account of the Modern Settlement of Northern Nigeria.* Frank Cass & Co. Ltd., 1964.

MacKenzie, Norman. *Secret Societies.* New York: Crescent, 1967.

Maquet, Jacques. *Civilizations of Black Africa.* New York: Oxford University Press, 1972.

Massey, Gerald. *A Book of the Beginnings: Containing an Attempt to Recover and Reconstitute the Lost Origins of the Myths and Mysteries, Types and Symbols, Religion and Language, with Egypt for the Mouthpiece and Africa as the Birthplace.* Secaucus, NJ: University Books, 1974. First published 1881.

Massey, Gerald. *Ancient Egypt, the Light of the World: A Work of Reclamation and Restitution in Twelve Books.* New York: Samuel Weiser, Inc., 1973. Originally published 1907.

*Massey, Gerald. *The Natural Genesis: Or Second Part of a Book of the Beginnings, Containing an Attempt to Recover and Reconstitute the Lost Origins of the Myths and Mysteries, Types and Symbols, Religion and Language, With Egypt for the Mouthpiece and Africa as the Birthplace.* Samuel Weiser, Inc., 1974.

McEvedy, Colin. *The Penguin Atlas of African History.* New York: Penguin Books, 1980.

Means, Sterling M. *Black Egypt and Her Negro Pharaohs.* Baltimore: Black Classic Press, P.O. Box 13414, Baltimore, Maryland, 1978.

Means, Sterling M. *Ethiopia and the Missing Link in African History.* Harrisburg, PA: The

Atlantis Publishing Co., 1980. First published 1945.

Morrell, E.D. *The Black Man's Burden: The White Man in Africa from the Fifteenth Century to World War I.* New York: Modern Reader Paperbacks, 1969. First published 1920.

Murphy, E. Jefferson. *The Bantu Civilization of Southern Africa.* New York: Thomas Y. Crowell, 1974.

Murphy, E. Jefferson. *History of African Civilization.* New York: Dell, 1972.

Nyane, D.T. Sundiata: *An Epic of Old Mali,* London: Longman, 1965.

Obadele, I. and Obadele, A. *Civilization Before the Time of Christ.* New York: Dell, 1972.

Olda, Henry. *From Ancient China to Ancient Greece.* Atlanta: Black Heritage Corporation and The Select Publishing Company, 1981.

Oliver, Roland and Fagin, Brian. *Africa in the Iron Age: c. 500 B.C. to A.D. 1400.* Cambridge: Cambridge University Press, 1975.

Oliver, R. and Oliver Carolyn (Eds.). *Africa in the Days of Exploration.* Englewood Cliffs: Prentice-Hall, 1965.

Osei, J.A., Nwabara, S.N., & Odunsi, A.T.O. *A Short History of West Africa A.D. 1000 to the Present.* New York: Hill and Wang, 1973.

Osei, G.K. *African Contribution to Civilization.* London: The African Publication Society, 1973.

Osei, G.K. *The African: His Antecedents, His Genius, His Destiny.* New Hyde Park: University Books, 1971.

Parker, George Wells. *The Children of the Sun.* The Hamitic League of the World, 1918.

Piankoff, Alexandre, & Rambova, N. *The Shrines of Tut-Ankh-amon.* Princeton, NJ: Princeton University Press, 1977.

Rogers, Joel A. *Africa's Gift to America.* New York: Helga M. Rogers, 1270 Fifth Avenue, New York 10029, 1956.

Rogers, Joel A. *The World's Great Men of Color.* New York: Collier MacMillan, 1972.

Rout, Leslie B., Jr. *The African Experience in Spanish America: 1502 to the Present Day.* Cambridge: Cambridge University Press, 1976.

Samkange, S. African Saga: *A Brief Introduction to African History.* New York: Abingdon Press, 1971.

Samkange, S. *The Origins of Rhodesia.* New York: Praeger, 1968.

Snowden, Frank M., Jr. *Blacks in Antiquity: Ethiopians in the Graeco-Roman Experience.* Cambridge: Harvard University Press, 1971.

Sweeting, Earl, & Lez, Edmond. *African History.* New York: African-American International Press, P.O. Box 775, Flushing, New York 11352, 1973.

UNESCO. *"The Historiography of Southern Africa: Proceedings of the Experts' Meeting Held at Gaborone, Botswana, from 7 to 11 March 1977."* Paris: UNESCO, 1980.

*UNESCO. *"The Peopling of Ancient Egypt and the Deciphering of Meroitic Script: Proceedings of the Symposium Held in Cairo from 28 January to 3 February 1974."* Paris: UNESCO, 1978.

Uya, Okon Edet. *African History: Some Problems in Methodology and Perspective.* Cornell University African Studies and Research Center, 1974.

Volney, C.F. *The Ruins or Meditation on the Revolution of Empires and the Law of Nature.* New York: Truth Seeker Co., 1950. First published 1793.

Walsh, M. *The Ancient Black Christians.* San Francisco: Julian Richardson, 1969.

Weatherwax, John M. *The African Contribution:* Parts I and II. Los Angeles: The John Henry and Mary Louisa Dunn Bryant Foundation, 1968.

Wiener, Leo. *Africa and the Discovery of America.* New York: Kraus Reprint Co., 1971. Originally published 1920.

*Williams, Chancellor. *The Destruction of Black Civilization: Great Issues of A Race 4500 B.C. to 2000 A.D.* Chicago: Third World Press, 1974.

*Williams, John A. (Ed.). *Y'Bird,* Volume 1, No. 2 1978.

Windsor, R.S. *From Babylon to Timbuktu: A History of the Ancient Black Races Including the Black Hebrews.* New York: Oxford University Press, 1966.

Woodson, Carter G. *African Heroes and Heroines.* Washington, D.C.: The Associated Publishers, Inc., 1969.

X, Malcolm. *On African-American History.* New York: Pathfinder Press, 1967.

III

EVIDENCE FOR AFRICAN ANCESTRY IN EUROPEAN

POPULATIONS AND FOR THE CONTINUOUS INTERACTION
OF AFRICANS AND EUROPEANS FROM EARLIEST TIMES

Read, Jan. *The Moors in Spain and Portugal.* London: Faber and Faber, 1974.

*Rogers, Joel, A. *Nature Knows No Color Line: Research Into the Negro Ancestry in the White Race.* New York: Helga M. Rogers, 1270 Fifth Avenue, New York, 1952.

*Rogers, Joel A. *Sex and Race,* Vols. 1, 2, 3. New York: Helga M. Rogers, 1270 Fifth Avenue, New York.

Scobie, Edward. *Black Britannia: A History of Blacks in Britain.* Chicago: Johnson, 1972.

Shyllon, Folarin. *Black People in Britain, 1555 to 1833.* London: Oxford University Press, 1977.

IV

EVIDENCE FOR THE AFRICAN PRESENCE IN AMERICA BEFORE COLUMBUS, AND EVEN BEFORE CHRIST

Clegg, Legrand H. *The Beginning of the African Diaspora: Black Men in Ancient and Medievel America.* Los Angeles: Unpublished manuscript, 1977.

*Van Sertima, Ivan. *They Came Before Columbus.* New York: Random House, 1976.

Von Wuthenau, A. *Unexpected Faces in Ancient America: 1500 B.C. to 1500 A.D., The Historical Testimony of Pre-Columbian Artists.* New York: Crown Publishers, 1975.

V

EVIDENCE FOR HOW EUROPE UNDERDEVELOPED AFRICA WHICH IN MANY PLACES WAS MUCH MORE HIGHLY DEVELOPED THAN EUROPE AT THE TIME OF HER EXPLORATIONS

Ayandale, E.A. *The Missionary Impact on Modern Nigeria, 1914-1942: A Political and Social Analysis.* London: Longman, 1966.

Chineweizu. *The West and the Rest of Us: White Predators, Black Slavers and the African Elite.* New York: Vintage Books, 1975.

Fanon, Frantz. *A Dying Colonialism.* New York: Evergreen, 1965.

Fanon, Frantz. *Black Skin, White Masks.* New York: Grove, 1967.

Farrant, Leda. *Tippu Tip and the East African Slave Trade.* New York: St. Martins Press.

Hallett, Robin (Ed.). *Records of the African Association: 1788 to 1831.* London: Thomas Nelson and Sons, Ltd., 1964.

Mannix, D.P. and Crowley, M. *Black Cargoes: A History of the Atlantic Slave Trade 1518- 1865.* New York: Viking, 1962.

Memmi, Albert. *The Colonizer and the Colonized.* Boston: Beacon, 1965.

Morell, E.D. *The Black Man's Burden: The White Man in Africa from the Fifteenth Century to World War I.* New York: Modern Reader Paperbacks, 1969.

Nkrumah, Kwame. *Neo-Colonialism: The Last Stage of Imperialism.* New York: International Publishers, 1965.

*Rodney, Walter. *How Europe Underdeveloped Africa.* Washington: Howard University Press, 1974.

Rotberg, Robert I. (Ed.). *Africa and Its Explorers: Motives, Methods and Impact.* Cambridge: Harvard University Press, 1973.

VI

EVIDENCE FOR THE AFRICAN-AMERICAN'S IMAPACT ON AMERICA SINCE COLUMBUS

Aptheker, Herbert. *American Negro Slave Revolts.* New York: National Publishers, 1943.

Beasley, Gail. *The Negro Trail Blazers of California: A Compilation of Records from the California Archives in the Bancroft Library at the University of California, in Berkeley, and from the Diaries, Old Papers and Conversations of Old Pioneers in the State of California.* Los Angeles, CA 1919. Reprinted R&E Research Associates, 4843 Mission Street, San Francisco.

Blassingame, John W. *The Slave Community: Plantation Life in the Antebellum South.* London: Oxford University Press, 1972.

Bontemps, Arna. *Great Slave Narratives.* Boston: Beacon, 1969.

Brown, William Wells. *The Negro in the American Rebellion: His Heroism and His Fidelity.* New York: Citadel Press, 1971. First published 1886.

Carwell, Hatti. *Blacks in Science: Astrophysicist to Zoologist.* New York: Exposition Press, 1977.

Crummell, Alex. *Africa and America.* Miami: Mnemosyne Publishing, 1969.

Cunard, Nancy. *Negro Anthology.* New York: Negro Universities Press, 1969. First published 1934.

DuBois, W.E.B. *Black Reconstruction in America: 1850 to 1880.* New York: Athenaeum, 1973. First published 1935.

DuBois, W.E.B. *The Suppression of the African Slave Trade to the United States of America, 1638-1870.* New York: Dover, 1970.

Fon, Horsemann. *Black American Scholars: A Study of Their Beginnings.* Michigan: Detroit Balamp Publishers.

Frazier, E. Franklin, and Lincoln, C. Eric. *The Negro Church in America, the Black Church Since Frazier.* New York: Schocken, 1963.

Genovese, Eugene D. *From Rebellion to Revolution: African-American Slave Revolts in the Making of the New World.* New York: Vintage, 1979.

Jay, James M. *Negroes in Science: Natural Science Doctorates, 1876-1969.* Michigan: Detroit Balamp Publishers, 1971.

Kofsky, Frank. *Black Nationalism and the Revolution in Music.* New York: Pathfinder Press, 1970.

Littlefield, Daniel F., Jr. *Africans and Creeks: From the Colonial Period to the Civil War.* Westport, Connecticut: Greenwood Press, 1979.

Lovell, John, Jr. *Black Song: The Forge and the Flame, The Story of How the Afro-American Spiritual Was Hammered Out.* New York: MacMillan, 1972.

Lynch, John R. *The Facts of Reconstruction.* New York: Arno Press, 1969.

Magdol, Edward. *A Right to the Land: Essays on the Freedmen's Community.* Westport, Connecticut: Greenwood Press, 1977.

Marshall, Herbert and Stock, M. Ira Aldridge: *The Negro Tragedian.* Carbondale, IL: Southern Illinois University Press, 1968.

Martin, Tony. *Race First: The Ideological and Organizational Struggles of Marcus Garvey and the Universal Negro Improvement Association.* Westport, Connecticut: Greenwood Press, 1976.

Nelson, Truman. *Documents of Upheaval: Selections from William Lloyd Garrison's The Liberator, 1831-1865.* New York: Hill and Wang, 1966.

Newell, V.K. , Gipson, J.H., Rich, Waldo, L., & Stubblefield, B. (Eds.). *Black Mathematicians and Their Works.* Ardmore, PA: Dorrance & Co., 1980.

Noble, Jeanne. *Beautiful Also Are the Souls of My Black Sisters: A History of the Black*

Woman in America. Englewood Cliffs: Prentice-Hall, 1978.

Purdue. C.L., Jr., Barden, T.E., & Phillips, R.K. *Weevils in the Wheat: Interviews with Virginia Ex-Slaves.* Bloomington: Indiana University Press, 1980.

Reasons, G. and Patrick S. *They Had a Dream,* Vols. 1-3. Los Angeles: L.A. Times Syndicate, 1971.

Rice, L.D. *The Negro in Texas 1874-1900.* Baton Rouge: Louisiana State University Press, 1971.

Romero, Patricia W. (Ed.). *In Black America.* New York: Books, Incorporated, 1969.

Singletary, Otis A. *Negro Militia and Reconstruction.* New York: McGraw-Hill, 1957.

Southern, Eileen. *The Music of Black Americans: A History.* New York: Norton, 1971.

Tragle, Henry Irving. *The Southhampton Slave Revolt of 1831: A Compilation of Source Material, Including the Full Text of the Confessions of Nat Turner.* New York: Vintage, 1973.

Walls, William J. *The African Methodist Episcopal Church: Reality of the Black*

Church. Charlotte, NC: AME Zion Publishing House, 1974.

Williams, Robert F. *Negroes with Guns.* Chicago: Third World Press, 1973.

Willie, C.V. and Edmonds, R. (Eds.). *Black Colleges in America.* New York: Teachers College Press, 1978.

Woodson, C.G. *The History of the Negro Church.* Washington, D.C.: The Associated Publishers, 1972. First published 1921.

Woodson, C.G. and Wesley, Charles H. *The Negro in Our History.* Washington, D.C.: The Associated Publishers, 1972. First published 1922.

VII

EVIDENCE FOR THE INVENTION OF "RACE" IN EUROPE AS A MATTER OF POLITICS, NOT SCIENCE, AND FOR ITS EVIL CONSEQUENCES IN AMERICA

*Barzun, J. *Race: A Study in Superstition.* New York: Harper, 1965.

*Benedict, Ruth. *Race: Science and Politics.* New York: Viking, 1959.

Biddis, Michael D. *Father of Racist Ideology: The Social and Political Thought of Count*

Gobineau. New York: Weinright and Talley, 1970.

*Chase, Allan. *The Legacy of Malthus: The Social Costs of the New Scientific Racism.* New York: Knopf, 1977.

Curtin, Philip D. *The Image of Africa: British Ideas in Action 1780-1850.* Madison: University of Wisconsin Press, 1964.

Gossett, Thomas F. Race*: The History of an Idea in America.* New York: Schocken, 1973.

Jones, Eldred D. *The Elizabethan Image of Africa.* University Press of Virginia, 1971.

Montagu, Ashley. *Man's Most Dangerous Myth: The Fallacy of Race.* New York: 1974.

Montagu, Ashley (Ed.). *The Concept of Race.* London: Collier, 1964.

Stanton, W. The Leopard's Spots: *Scientific Attitudes Toward Race in America, 1815-1859.* Chicago: University of Chicago Press, 1960.

Weinreich, Max. *Hitler's Professors: The Part of Scholarship in Germany's Crimes Against the Jewish People.* New York: Yiddish Scientific Institute-YIVO 1946.

Wobogo, Vuilinedela. *"Diop's Two Cradle Theory and the Origin of White Racism."* Black Books Bulletin, 4, 1976, 20-37.

VIII

EVIDENCE FOR THE DELIBERATE AND UNCONSCIOUS MANIPULATION OF INFORMATION AND MEDIA TO PRODUCT A "COLORED", "NEGRO", OR "NIGGER", WHO EXISTED ONLY IN THE MINDS OF THEIR EUROPEAN AND EUROPEAN-AMERICAN INVENTORS OF THE TRUE BELIEVERS

Baldwin, James. *The Devil Finds Work.* New York: Dial, 1976.

ben-Jochanan, Yosef. *Cultural Genocide in the Black and African Studies Curriculum.* New York: Alkebu-Lan Books, 1972.

Bogle, Donald. *Toms, Coons, Mulattoes, Mammies, and Bucks: An Interpretive History of Blacks in American Film.* New York: Bantam, 1974.

Bullock, Henry Allen. *A History of Negro Education in the South.* New York: Praeger, 1970.

Cripps, Thomas. *Slow Fade to Black: The Negro in American Film 1900-1942.* New York: Oxford, 1977.

Curtin, Philip D. *The Image of Africa: British Ideas and Action, 1780-1850,* Vols. I and II.

Madison: The University of Wisconsin
Press, 1973.

Gratus, Jack. *The Great White Lie: Slavery,
Emancipation and Changing Racial
Attitudes.* New York: Monthly Review
Press, 1973.

*Gregory, Dick. *No More Lies: The Myth and
Reality of American History.* New York:
Harper and Row, 1971.

Gross, Seymour I. and Hardy, J.E. *Images of
the Negro in American Literature.*
Chicago: The University of Chicago
Press, 1966.

Hodge, J.L., Struckmann, D.K., and Trost, L.D.
*Cultural Bases of Racism and Group
Oppression: An Examination of
Traditional "Western" Concepts, Values
and Institutional Structures Which Supports
Racism, Sexism and Elitism.* Berkeley:
Two Riders Press, P.O. Box 4129, Berkeley,
CA 94704, 1975.

Jones, Eldred D. *The Elizabethan Image of
Africa.* University Press of Virginia, 1971.

Ladner, Joyce (Ed.). *The Death of White
Sociology.* New York: Vintage, 1973.

Leab, Daniel, J. *From Sambo to
Superspade: The Black Experience in
Motion Pictures.* Boston: Houghton-
Mifflin, 1976.

Myrdal, Jan and Kessle, Gun. *Angkor: An Essay on Art and Imperialism.* New York: Pantheon, 1970.

Stoddard, Lothrop. *The Rising Tide of Color Against White World Supremacy.* Westport, Connecticut: Negro University Press. First published 1920.

Toll, Robert C. *Blacking Up: The Minstrel Show in Ninteenth Century America.* New York: Oxford University Press, 1974.

IX

EVIDENCE FOR THE DELIBERATE AND SYSTEMATIC UNDERDEVELOPMENT OF AFRICAN-AMERICANS BY WHITE AMERICANS

Aptheker, Herbert. *A Documentary History of the Negro People in the United States,* Vols. I-III. Secaucus, New Jersey: Citadel Press, 1977.

Bell, Derrick, J. *Race, Racism amd American Law.* Boston: Little, Brown and Co., 1973.

*Burgman, Peter M. and Burgman, Mort N. *The Chronological History of the Negro in America.* New York: Mentor Books, 1969.

Higgenbotham, A. Leon, Jr. *In the Matter of Color: Race and the American Legal*

Process: The Colonial Period. New York: Oxford Press, 1978.

King, Kenneth. *Pan Africanism and Education: A Study of Race, Philanthropy and Education in the Southern States of America and East Africa.* Oxford: Clarendon Press, 1971.

Logan, Rayford W. *The Betrayal of the Negro from Rutherford B. Hayes to Woodrow Wilson.* New York: Collier Books, 1965.

Mellon, Matthew T. *Early American Views on Negro Slavery: From the Letters and Papers of the Founders of the Republic.* New York: Bergman Publishers, 1969. First published 1934.

Purdue, Charles L., Jr., Barden, Thomas E., and Phillips, R.K. *Weevils in the Wheat: Interviews with Virginia Ex-Slaves.* Bloomington, Indiana: Indiana University Press, 1980.

*Woodard, C. Vann. *The Strange Career of Jim Crow.* New York: Oxford, 1966.

X

HEROIC SPOKESPERSONS FOR AFRICANS AND AFRICAN-AMERICANS AND WHAT THEY HAD TO SAY

Arnold, Millard (Ed.). *Steve Biko: Black Consciousness in South Africa.* New York: Random House, 1978.

ben-Jochanan, Yosef. *Our Black Seminarians and Black Clergy Without a Black Theology.* New York: Alkebu-Lan Books, 209 West 125th Street, Suite 218, 1978.

Blyden, J.W. *Christianity, Islam, and Negro Race.* Edinburgh University Press, 1967. First Published 1887.

Breitman, G. *By Any Means Necessary: Speeches, Interviews and a Letter by Malcolm X.* New York: Pathfinder, 1977.

Breitman, G. *Malcolm X. Speaks.* New York: Pathfinder, 1976.

Cabral, Amilcar. *Return to the Source.* New York: Praeger, 1967.

Cesaire, Aime. *Discourse on Colonialism.* New York: Monthly Review Press, 1972.

*Cruse, Harold. *The Crisis of the Negro Intellectual.* New York: Wiliam Morrow, 1967.

Diop, Cheikh A. *Black Africa: The Economic and Cultural Basis for a Federated State.* Westport, Connecticut: Lawrence Hill, 1978.

Garvey, Amy Jacques. *Garvey and Garveyism.* New York: Collier, 1974.

Garvey, Amy Jacques and Essien-Udom, E.U. *More Philosophy and Opinions of Marcus Garvey, Vol. III, previously unpublished papers.* London: Frank Cass, 1977.

Hill, R.A. *Marcus Garvey, the Black Man: A Monthly Magazine of Negro Thought and Opinion.* New York: Kraus-Thompson, 1975.

Hooker, James R. *Black Revolutionary: George Padmore's Path from Communism to Pan-Africanism.* New York: Praeger, 1970.

Jacques-Garvey, Amy (Ed.). *Philosophy and Opinions of Marcus Garvey.* New York: Athenaeum, 1974.

James, C.L.R. *The Black Jacobins: Toussaint L'Ouverture and the San Domingo Revolution.* New York: Random House, 1963.

Korngold, Ralph. *Citizen Toussaint.* New York: Hill and Wang, 1965.

Lamson, Peggy. *The Glorius Failure: Black Congressmen Robert Brown Elliott and the Reconstruction in South Carolina.* New York: Norton, 1973.

Maglangbayan, Shawna. *Garvey, Lumumba, Malcolm: Black Nationalist Separatists.* Chicago: Third World Press, 1972.

Martin, Tony. *Race First: The Ideological and Organizational Struggles of Marcus Garvey and the Universal Negro Imrpovement Association.* London: Greenwood Press, 1976.

Molefi, Kate Asante. *Afrocentricity: The Theory of Social Change.* Buffalo: Amulefi Publishing, 1980.

Nkrumah, Kwame. *Consciencism: Philosophy and Ideology for Decolonization.* New York: Modern Reader, 1970.

Robeson, Paul. *Here I Stand.* Boston: Beacon Press, 1958.

Rogers, Joel A. *From Superman to Man.* New York: Helga Rogers, 1270 Fifth Avenue, New York, 1974.

Walker, David. *Walker's Appeal: An Address to the Slaves of the United States of America.* New York: Arnold Press, 1969. First published 1829.

Williams, Robert L. (Ed.). *Ebonics: The True Language of Black Folks.* St. Louis: Institute of Black Studies.

*Woodson, C.G. *Miseducation of the Negro.* The Associated Publishers, 1969. First published 1933.

XI

AFRICANS IN OTHER PARTS OF THE DIASPORA (THE "NEW WORLD")

Bastide, Roger. *African Civilizations in the New World.* New York: Harper Torchbooks, 1971.

Cole, Hubert. *Christophe, King of Haiti.* New York: Viking, 1967.

Freyre, Gilberto. *The Masters and the Slaves.* New York: Knopf, 1946.

Marshall, Herbert and Stock, Mildred. *Ira Aldridge: the Negro Tragedian.* London: Bifer & Simmons, Inc., 1958.

*Price, R. (Ed.). *Maroon Societies: Rebel Slave Communities in the Americas.* New York: Doubleday, 1973.

Rout, Leslie B. *The African Experience in Spanish America 1502 to the Present Day.* New York: Cambridge, 1976.

Whitten, N.E., Jr. *Black Frontiersmen: A South American Case.* New York: Schenkman, 1974.

XII

DESCRIPTIONS OF AFRICAN CULTURE

Booth, Newell (Ed.). *African Religions: A Symposium.* New York: Nok Publishers, 1977.

Carter, Harold A. *Prayer Tradition of Black People.* Valley Forge: Judson Press, 1976.

d'Azevedo, Warren L. *The Traditional Artist in African Society.* Bloomington: Indiana University Press, 1975.

Jahn, Jahnheinz. *Muntu: The New African Culture.* New York: Grove University Press, 1961.

Mbiti, John S. *Introduction to African Religion.* New York: Praeger, 1975.

Omosade, Awolalu F. *Yoruba Beliefs and Sacrificial Rites.* London: Longman Group, Ltd., 1979.

Shorter, Aylward. *Prayer in the Religious Tradition of Africa.* London: Oxford University Press, 1975.

Wright, Richard A. *African Philosophy: An Introduction.* Washington, D.C.: University Press of America, 1977.

XIII

AFRICAN CULTURAL RETENTIONS IN THE NEW WORLD AS AN EXTENTION OF AFRICA

Alleyne, Mervyn C. *Comparative Afro-American: A Historical Comparative Study of English-based Afro-American Dialects of the New World.* Ann Arbor: Karoma Publishers, 1980.

Anderson, S.E. "Mathematics and the Struggle for Black Liberation." *The Black Scholar,* September, 1970.

Anyanwu, Chukwulozie K. *The Nature of Black Cultural Reality.* Washington, D.C.: University Press of America, 1976.

Christos, Kyle. *Voodoo.* New York: Lippincott, 1976.

Collins, Robert O. *Problems in African History.* Englewood Cliffs: Prentice-Hall, 1968.

Deren, Maya. *Divine Horsemen: Voodoo Gods of Haiti.* New York: Delta, 1970.

Erny, Pierre. *Childhood and Cosmos: The Social Psychology of the Black African Child.* New York: Black Orpheus Press, 1973. First published 1968.

Haskins, J. *Witchcraft, Mysticism and Magic in the Black World.* New York: Dell, 1974.

*Herskovits, Melville J. *The Myth of the Negro Past.* Boston: Beacon, 1969.

Hill, Robert B. *Informal Adoption Among Black Families.* New York: National Urban League, 1977.

Idowu, E. Bolaji. *African Traditional Religion: A Definition.* New York: Orbis Books, 1975.

Jahn, H. Jahnheinz. *Muntu: The New African Culture.* New York: Grove, 1961.

Jenkins, Ulysses Duke. *Ancient African Religion and the African-American Church.* Jacksonville, NC: Flame International, 37 Longstaff St., Jacksonville, NC 28540, 1978.

Johnson J.C. deGraft. *African Glory: The Story of Vanished Negro Civilizations.* New York: Walker, 1954.

Jones, Leroi. *Blues People: The Negro Experience in White America and the Music that Developed from It.* New York: William Morrow, 1963.

Martin, Elmer P. and Martin, Joanne Mitchell. *The Black Extended Family.* Chicago: The University of Chicago Press, 1978.

Mbiti, John S. *African Religions and Philosophy.* New York: Praeger, 1979.

*Mitchell, Henry H. *Black Belief: Fold Belief of Blacks in America and West Africa.* New York: Harper and Row, 1975.

Nettleford, Rex. *Caribbean Cultural Identity: The Case of Jamaica.* Los Angeles: Center for Afro-American Studies and UCLA Latin American Center Publications, University of California, 1979.

Raboteau, Albert J. *Slave Religion: The Invisible Institution in the Antebellum South.* New York: Oxford University Press, 1978.

Sidren, Ben. *Black Talk.* New York: Holt, Rhinehart and Winston, 1971.

Smith, Ernie. *"The Retention of the Phonological, Phonemic, and Morphophonemic Features of Africa in Afro-American Ebonics."* Seminar Paper Series No. 43, Department of Linguistics, Colorado State University, Fullerton, February, 1948.

Turner, Lorenzo. *Africanisms in the Gullah Dialect.* New York: Arno Press, 1969.

*Vass, Winifred. *The Bantu Speaking Heritage of the United States.* Los Angeles: Center for Afro-American Studies, University of California, 1979.

XIV

OF GENERAL INTEREST

Billingsley, Andrew. *Black Families in White America.* Englewood Cliffs: Prentice-Hall, 1968.

BLACK BOOKS BULLETIN

Davidson, Basil. *Old Africa Rediscovered.* London: Victor Gollancz, 1970.

Doblhofer, Ernest. *Voices in Stone: The Decipherment of Ancient Scripts and Writings.* New York:Collier, 1971.

DuBois, W.E.B. *The Philadelphia Negro: A Social Study.* New York: Schocken Books, 1976. First published 1899.

Durham, Philip and Jones, Everett L. *The Western Story.* New York: Harcourt Brace Jovanovich, 1975.

Evans, Judith L. *Children in Africa: A Review of Psychological Research.* New York: Teachers College Press, 1970.

Genovese, Eugene D. *Roll, Jordan, Roll: The World the Slaves Made.* New York: Vintage, 1972.

Gutman, Herbert. *The Black Family in Slavery and Freedom: 1750-1925.* New York: Vintage, 1976.

Hammond, Dorothy and Jablow, Alta. *The Myth of Africa.* New York: Library of Social Science, 1977.

Hill, Robert B. *The Strengths of Black Families.* New York: National Urban League, 1971.

Jairazbhoy, R.A. *Old World Origin of American Civilizations: Ancient Egyptian Chinese in America.* London: George Prior, 1974.

The Journal of African Civilizations. Douglass College, Rutgers University.

The Journal of Negro History. United Publishing Corporation. New York: Association for the Study of Negro Life and History from 1916 to the Present.

Kaiser, Ernest. *In Defense of the People's Black and White History and Culture.* New York: Freedomways, 1970.

King, Kenneth. *Ras Makonnen Pan Africanism from Within.* New York: Oxford, 1973.

King, Lewis M. *African Philosophy: Assumptions and Paradigms for Research on Black Persons.* Los Angeles, California: Fanon Research and Development Center. NIMH Grant # R01MH 255590-01 May 1975.

MacKenzie, Norman. *Secret Societies.* New York: Crescent, 1967.

Rogers, Joel A. *The World's Great Men of Color.* New York: Collier MacMillan, 1972.

Rowland, B. The Ajanta Caves: *Early Buddhist Paintings from India.* New York: Mentor, 1963.

Shepard, Leslie. *Did Jesus Live 100 B.C.?* New York: University Books, Inc., 1967. First published 1903.

Stampp, Kenneth M. *The Peculiar Institution: Slavery in the Antebellum South.* New York: Vintage, 1956.

Turnbull, Colen M. *The Forest People: A Study of the Pygmies of the Congo.* New York: Simon and Schuster, 1961.

Uraeus: *The Journal of Unconscious Life,* Vol. 1 Aquarian Spiritual Center, 1302 West Santa Barbara Avenue, Los Angeles, CA 90037.

Uya, Okon Edet. *African History: Some Problems in Methodology and Perspectives.* Cornell University, New York: Africana Studies and Research Center, 1974.

Vincent, Theodore G. *Black Power in the Garvey Movement.* San Francisco: Ramparts Press, 1976.

Willard. *Lost Worlds of Africa.* New York:
    Dutton, 1967.

Williams, Robert F. *Negroes With Guns.*
    Chicago: Third World Press, 1973.

Wilson, Ellen G. *The Loyal Blacks: The
    Definitive Account of the First American
    Blacks Emancipated in the Revolution,
    Their Return to Africa and Their Creation of
    a New Society There.* New York:
    Capricorn, 1976.

Woodson, Carter G. *Negro Orators and Their
    Orations.* New York: Russell and Russell,
    1969. First published 1925.

Zaslavsky, Claudia. *Africa Counts: Number
    and Pattern in African Culture.* Boston:
    Prindle Weber and Schmidt, 1973.

by Asa G. Hilliard III
Georgia State University

CADRE TRAINING

DEFINITION OF A "CADRE"

The most disciplined, hard working,
ideologically conscious, members, who
operate under the ideological line of
Revolutionary Pan African Nationalism, and
are able to take initiative in carrying out
organizational programs. Cadres are the
backbone of any revolutionary Pan

Africanists organization, and they are the key to the continuity of the movement. The training of cadres is necessary to guarantee that skilled revolutionaries exist who will continue the movement, cadres master the theory and practice of revolutionary Pan African Nationalism through theoretical study, and organizational work, the most important of which requires that they live with the people, feel their joys amd pains, plan with them, and organize with the people for national liberation. Cadres that live with, and serve the people, are the life blood of revolutionary work. The success of our movement for National liberation will largely depend upon the training, care, and organizing work of revolutionary Pan Africanists cadres.

P.A.P.O. AND PAN AFRICAN MOVEMENTS NEED FOR CADRES

1. We need discipline professional cadres.

2. We need cadres who have a clear historical and theorectical outlook.

3. We need cadres that are consistently working in community groups and block by block organizing.

4. We need cadres who consistently work in organizational programs.

5. We need cadres who regularly .

contribute to the organization.

6. We need cadres that can defend the organization's ideology, and program.

7. We need cadres that are skilled in management and coordination of organizational work.

8. We need cadres that are able to help in coordinating secretariat work.

9. We need cadres that understand the process involved in building a national organization and a Pan African mass movement.

10. We need cadres that are good at working with other nationalist groups and individuals.

11. We need cadres that have economic skills, and are good at setting up economic cooperatives.

12. We need cadres that are security conscious.

13. We need cadres that are humble, and accept responsibility without passing the buck.

SUGGESTED FORMAT FOR CADRE TRAINING

I.   Theory and Practice Method;
       Theoretical study should be combined with programmatic work through:

       (a) theoretical and historical

       (b) organizational work projects, where theory is applied, and where new theory is developed through work. Consistenthard work is the most improtant area ofteam appraoch where a cadre's success is determined by the level of development of his partner.

II.   Study groups, where systematic reading is discussed in a collective setting.

III.   Retreats where temporary isolation allows for greater attention on cadre training. retreats can vary from a weekend, to a couple of weeks, to a longer period.

IV.   Lectures and practical examples of certain techniques by people with expertise in a particular area.

V.   Collective training through teams carrying out parts of cadre training.

VI.   Criticism, self-criticism of our work and theoretical development.

VII.   Collective discipline focusing on friendship and detachment.

SUBJECT AREAS OF
CADRE TRAINING

Strategy and tactics for building a mass movement.

1. Theory of opposites or two truths. Understanding the principles that underlay the theory of opposites. Application of this theory as a historical tool for analyzing our struggle. Use of this method in carrying out the internal "*Cultural Revolution*".

2. Analysis of the theory of Revolutionary Pan Africanism. Examination of the historical origin of this theory, and it's historical development, and application to our struggle for national liberation.

3. Study of the theory of Marxism Leninism, Mao Tse Tung thought. Examine the theory of surplus value, commodity production, means of production, class formation and class conflict, money, reserve army, labor, socialism, communism, dialectical materialism and historical

materialism. Maoism, the peasant worker alliance, the Black United Front, wars of national liberation, new democracy, and cultural revolution.

4. Examination of organizational programs of Black and white Marxist groups. These would include SWP (Socialist Workers Party) WU and PFOC (Weather Underground) and Praire Fire Organization Committee, etc.

5. Examination of the ideological lines and programs of the major nationalist organizations. Organizations to be studies include, RNA, AAPRP, APP, APSP, and the Nation of Islam.

6. Analysis of the last 56 years of struggle in the U.S. 1921-1977. Analysis of the Garvey movement, religious movements of the 30s; Communist Party, Civil Rights Movement (Montgomery, local struggles, Selma); urban rebellions; Revolutionary Black Nationalism (Malcolm, Panthers, RAM, RNA, Nation of Islam, US, YOBU); Revolutionary Pan African Nationalism (CAP, ALD, moves of U.S. imperialism, Pan Afrikan Secretariat). Current stage of the

struggle,   projections   and
assessments.

7. What's the long range objectives of
our struggle?   How does a land
objective   relate   to   possible
genocide   moves   by   the   U.S.
government?   What kind of land
objective should our struggle be
based on?   What's the historical
backup for this position?   What are
the programmatic steps for carrying
out this objective?

8. Each chapter of the Secretariat
should prepare a report on the
history of their communities.   What is
the social class structure of our
community?   What are some of the
influential organizational groupings,
(church,   youth,   professional,
women,   political)   in   your
community?   What ties do these
different groupings have to the
colonizer?   How have they acted
when community struggles have
been waged against the colonizer?
(Did they side with the colonizer, or
with the struggling groups in the
community?) What individuals carry
weight in your community?   With
whom?   What's their power based
on?

9. What's the social structure of your
community?   How   do   you

approach various sections of the Black colony in organizing around the Pan Afrikan Secretariat? (1) Black church, (2) Black labor, (3) Black youth, (4) Black women organizations, (5) Black nationalists, (6) Black middle class, (7) Black prisoner groups, (8) Black military, etc.

What appeals do you use to sell each group on the Secretariat? What role should these various grouping play inside the Pan Afrikan Secretariat?

10. Organization of the Black United Front. What have been weakneses and strengths of Black United Fronts in organizing a national liberation struggle? What are the directions of a P.A.S. United Front structure? How do we select various sections (class groupings) from the national and local Black communities, in order to make up a P.A.S. Black United Front? What's the relationship of the United Front to a Black political party? How does the United Front relate to the International programs of the Secretariat? Evaluation of the Secretariat program objectives.

11. Cadre administration and organization.

Steps involved in setting up cadre chapters Developing program objectives which reflect desires and needs of the people.Research techniques to be used indrawing ideas and programs from thepeople. Agitation techniques (public speaking, art of listening); propaganda techniques (laying out leaflets, posters,articles, etc.); mobilizing methods.

Review of Secretariat By-laws.

Correct cadre policies on:

a. handling cadres, assessing strengths and weaknesses, using them where they are best able to work

b. appointment of cadres to positions

c. delegation of cadre authority

d. continuous cadre education

e. cadre accountability

f. recruitment of new cadres

g. methods for handling meetings

h. cadre discipline

i. persuasion techniques, friendships, etc.

j. developing cell structure, using the extended family as the model for the cell structure. Identifying how this method has been used in other countries, and how it can be adapted in the U.S.

12. Cycles in capitalism, which shows comparison between contracting and expanding phases and mass movements among our people.

13. Examination of ancient African history,Kush, Egypt, Sumeria, Ghana, Mali, Songhai, Kanem, Bornu, Monomopata, Zulu, Kongo, Dahomey, etc.

14. Examination of religious cultural systems of ancient Africa.

15. Analysis of triangular trade, plantationslavery in the U.S. and Caribbean, slave revolts, etc.

16. Examine the civil war, reconstruction, and post reconstruction period.

17. Examine movements for national liberation on the continent, the Berlin Conference, colonial annexation, and the independence movements that rose up to resist colonialism.

CIA AND FBI:
A NEW EXECUTIVE ORDER

Reagan administration officials seemed annoyed when a draft of the proposed Executive Order (E.O.) on intelligence agencies was leaked to the media in early March 1981. CIA Deputy Director Bobby Inman told reporters assembled at CIA headquarters that the draft contained "all kinds of ideas." However, Inman acknowledged that a draft for a new E.O. on intelligence is being prepared in response to an explicit order from the White House in January 1981. "The new administration has read a great deal in the years out of office about the state of U.S. intelligence and, particularly questions about our current ability in regard to dealing with terrorism and the whole area of counterintelligence. Inman said the White House requested all intelligence agencies to assess "the impact of current restrictions" and the effect of these restrictions being lifted.

The intelligence working group which drafted the proposed E.O. is headed by CIA general counsel Daniel Silver - which suggests that at least one high ranking official is somewhat in agreement with the draft. Still, Inman emphasized that neither he nor CIA Director William Casey were involved in the drafting and that they were not "actively seeking" some of the changes in the order.

If signed by Reagan, the E.O. would give the CIA wide-ranging powers to use "intrusive" techniques (break-ins, etc.), and to conduct intelligence investigations directed at U.S. citizens and residents (in spite of the clear language of the 1947 National Security Act that the CIA "shall have no police, subpoena, law enforcement powers, or internal security functions). The order would further allow the CIA to conduct physical surveillance operations in the U.S.; to obtain confidential records (e.g. tax returns); infiltrate U.S. organizations, and "affect the activities" (e.g. disruptions, smear campaigns) of organizations headed by foreigners or consisting of U.S. persons which are believed to be working "for or on behalf of a foreign organization or government," even if all the organization's activities are perfectly legal. In the administration's perception, that undoubtedly includes all progressive organizations and solidarity groups.

Several sections of the draft order are contrary even to the recommendations of the Rockerfeller Commission which said that "Presidents should refrain from directing the CIA to perform what are essentially internal security tasks." Ronald Reagan was a member of the Commission and joined in this recommendation.

After considerable public outrage at the draft order, Inman and other administration officials including White House counselor Ed Meese were quick to assert that "the White House is absolutely opposed to the CIA becoming involved in domestic spying." Meese also dismissed the importance of the draft order. However, both Inman and Meese acknowledged that "Reagan soon will issue and executive order meant to improve the CIA's ability to gather intelligence abroad," and Inman added that "some new measures would probably be necessary to control the threat of terrorism." While he maintained that the new E.O. (which will replace Carter's E.O. 12036, signed on January 24, 1978) will not give the CIA greater authority at home, Inman had to acknowledge that "various intelligence agencies had told him that "legal restrictions on domestic spying and very intrusive techniques" diminished the agencies' capabilities. (It should be recalled that Inman headed the National Security Agency before he was appointed CIA Deputy Director by Reagan. The NSA illegally monitors almost all long-distance telecommunications of U.S. citizens.)

Even if the administration were to back away from plans to increase the CIA's domestic power, there are a number of other provisions in the draft order that would bring this country several steps closer to being a Police State. The FBI would be allowed to investigate and "affect the activities" of organizations which <u>may be</u> acting for a foreign power or "engaging in international terrorist activity." under this clause, the FBI's investigfation of political groups could be simply on the basis of an ideological evaluation of an organization by the White House. And given the far-right ideology of the administration, that could, for example, even subject the Catholic Bishops to COINTELPRO type harassment for their opposition to U.S. military intervention in El Salvador.

The draft order and the actual E.O. Reagan will sign do not come in a vaccum. It is only natural that an administration which is trying to expand its military power abroad and is extremely hostile to liberation movements will have to crack down on dissent in the U.S. Already, opposition to Reagan's economic policies of aiding the rich and taking from the poor, and his interventionist policy abroad are encountering increasing opposition in the U.S. Reagan wants to prepare for it by giving more power to the intelligence agencies and stepping up surveillance and repression. Whether or not he will be successful is in the hands of the people.

EXECUTIVE ORDER <u>12036</u>

STANDARDS FOR THE CONDUCT OF UNITED STATES INTELLIGENCE ACTIVITIES

By virtue of the authority vested in me by the Constitution and statutes of the United States of Amierca, including the National Security Act of 1947, as amended, and as President of the United States of America in order to provide for the effective conduct of United States intelligence activities and the protection of constitutional rights, it is hereby ordered as follows.

Section 1

1-1.   Amendment of Section 2 of Executive Order 12036.

1-101. Executive Order 12036 is hereby amended by deleting section 2 entitled "Restriction on Intelligence Activities" and inserting in lieu thereof:

Section 2

Conduct of Intelligence Activities

2-1.   General

2-101. <u>Purpose</u>.   Information about the capabilities, intentions and activities of foreign powers, organizations, or persons is essential to informed decision-making in the areas of national defense and foreign relations. The measures employed to acquire such information should be responsive to legitimate governmental needs and be conducted in a manner that respects established concepts of privacy and civil liberties.

2-102. Principles of Interpretation.
Sections 2-201 through 2-309 set forth governing principles which, in addition to other applicable laws, are intended to achieve the proper balance between protection of individual interests and acquisition of essential information. Those sections govern the conduct of specific activities whithin the Intelligence Community. Those sections shall not be construed as affecting or restricting other lawful activities of intelligence components not otherwise addressed therein. Nothing in this Order shall affect The law enforcement responsibilities of any department or agency. Any collection activity conducted for a law enforcement purpose may be handled in accordance with relevant law enforcement procedures, as appropriate.

2.2. Use of Certain Collection Techniques.

2-201. General Provisions.

(a) The activities described in sections 2-202 through 2-207 shall be undertaken in accordance with this Order and procedures established by the head of the agency concerned and determined by the Attorney General not to violate the constitution or statutes of the United States. Those procedures shall protect constitutional rights, limit use of such information to lawful governmental purposes and, to the extent consistent with the intelligence needs of the United States, accomodate privacy. No agency head shall establish any procedure which the Attorney General determines to be unlawful under the Constitution or statutes of the United States.

(b) The Attorney General hereby is delegated the power to approve the use, for intelligence purposes, of any technique for which a warrant would be required if undertaken for law enforcement purposes, provided that such activities shall not be undertaken in the United States or against a United States person abroad without a judicial warrant, unless the Attorney General has determined that under the circumstances the activity is lawful under the Constitution and statutes of the United States. The Attorney General may approve the use of such techniques by category or delegate authority to the head of any agency within the Intelligence Community to approve the use of such techniques in accordance with procedures approved by the Attorney General.

2-202. <u>Electronic Surveillance</u>. An agency with the Intelligence Community may engage in electronic surveillance directed against a United States person abroad or designed to intercept a communication sent from, or intended for receipt within, the United States, but only in accordance with procedures established pursuant to section 2-201. Any electronic surveillance, as defined in the Foreign Intellligence Surveillance Act of 1978, shall be conducted in accordance with that Act as well as this Order. The CIA may engage in electronic surveillance activity within the United States only for the purpose of assisting, and in coordination with, another agency within the Intelligence Community authorized to conduct such electronic surveillance, but this prohibition shall not apply to the activities described in the remainder of this paragraph. Training of personnel by agencies within the Intelligence Community in the use of electronic surveillance equipment, testing by such agencies of such equipment, and the use of measures to determine the existence and capability of such surveillance equipment being used unlawfully shall notbe prohibited and shall also be governed by such procedures. Such activities shall be limited in scope and duration to those necessary to carry out the training, testing or countermeasures purpose, provided that intelligence information derived during the training of personnel or the testing of electronic surveillance equipment may be disseminated in accordance with procedures developed pursuant to section 2-207.

2-203. <u>Physical Searches</u>. Any unconsented physical search within the United States by an agency wothin the Intelligence Community shall be coordinated with the FBI. All such searches, including those conducted by the FBI, as well as all such searches conducted by any agency within the Intelligence Community outside the United States and directed against United States persons, shall be undertaken only as permitted by procedures established to section 2-201.

2-204. <u>Mail Surveillance</u>. No agency within the Intelligence Community shall open mail or examine envelopes in United States postal channels, except in accordance with applicable statutes and regulations. No agency within the Intelligence Community shall open mail of a United States person that is outside U.S. postal channels except as permitted by procedures established pursuant to section 2-201.

2-205. <u>Physical Surveillance</u>. The FBI may conduct physical surveillance (including the use of monitoring devices for which a warrant would not be required for law enforcement purposes) directed against United States persons or others in the course of a lawful investigation. Other agencies within the Intelligence Community may undertake physical surveillance (including the use of monitoring devices for which a warant would not be required for law enforcement purposes) direvted against a United States person if:

(a) The surveillance is conducted outside the United States in the course of a lawful foreign intelligence, counterintelligence, international narcotics or international terrorism investigation;

(b) That person is being surveilled for the purpose of protecting foreign intelligence and counterintelligence sources and methods from unauthorized disclosure or is the subject of a lawful counterintelligence or personal, physical or communications security investigation; or

(c) The surveillance is conducted solely for the purpose of indentifying a person who is in contact with someone described in subsection (a) or (b) of this section.

Surveillance in the United States shall be coordinated with the FBI if directed at a person other than a present employee, intelligence agency contractor or employee of such contractor, or a military person employed by a non-intelligence element of a military service.

2-206. Undisclosed Participation in Domestic Organizations. In accordance with procedures established under section 2-201, employees within the Intelligence Community may join, or otherwise participate in an organization within the United States on behalf of an agency within the Intelligence Community for any lawful purpose without disclosing their intelligence affiliation to appropriate officials of the organization, provided:

(a) participation by any agency other than the FBI for purposes of acquiring information about the organization or any United States person who is a member thereof is strictly limited in its nature, scope and duration to a lawful purpose related to foreign intelligence and nondisclosure is necessary to achieve that purpose; and

(b) participation by the CIA for purposes of affecting the activities of the organization is limited to attaining legitimate foreign intelligence objectives when the appropriate officials to whom disclosure normally would be made are foreign nationals or the organization involved is owned or controlled by a foreign organization or government or is working for or on behalf of a foreign organization or government and such participation is conducted in a manner that provides due protection for constitutional rights.

2-207. <u>Collection of Nonpublicly Available Information</u>. An agency within the Intelligence Community may collect, retain in files on identifiablle United States persons, or dissimenate information for intelligence or counterintelligence purposes concerning the activities of United States persosn that is not available publicly, or if it does so with their consent or as permitted by procedures established pursuant to section 2-201. Thise procedures shall limit collection, retention in files on identifiable United States persons, and dissemination to the following types of information:

(a) information concerning corporations or other commercial organizations or activities that constitutes foreign intelligence or counterintelligence;

(b) information arising out of a lawful counterintelligence or personnel, physical or communications security investigation;

(c) information concerning persons, derived from any lawful investigation, which is needed to protect foreign intelligence or counterintelligence sources or methods from unauthorized disclosure;

(d) information needed solely to identify individuals in contact with those persons described in paragraph (c) of this section or in contact with someone who is the subject of a lawful foreign intelligence or counterintelligence investigation;

(e) information concerning persons who are reasonably believed to be potential sources or contacts, but only for the purpose of determining the suitability or credibility of such persons;

(f) information constituting foreign intelligence or counterintelligence gathered abroad or from electronic surveillance conducted in compliance with section 2-202 or gathered by lawful means in the United States;

(g) information about a person who has acted or may be acting on behalf of a foreign power, has engaged or may be engaging in international terrorist or narcotics activities, or has endangered the safety of any person protected by the United States Secret Service or the Department of State, or may be endangering the safety of any person;

(h) information acquired by overhead reconnaissance not directed at specific United States persons;

(i) information concerning United States persons abroad that is obtained in response to requests from the Department of State for support of its consular responsibilities relating to the welfare of those persons;

(j) information collected, received, disseminated or stored by the FBI and necessary to fulfil its lawful investigative responsibilities; or

(k) information concerning persons or activitites that pose a credible threat to any facility or personnel of any agency within the

Intelligence Community or any department containing such an agency.

Inaddition, those procedures shall permit an agency within the Intelligence Community to disseminate information, other than information derived from signals intelligence, to another agency within the Intelligence Community for purposes of allowing the recipient agency to determine whether the information is relevant to its lawful responsibilities and can be retained by it.

2.3. Additional Principles

2-301. <u>Tax Information</u>. Agencies within the Intelligence Community may examine tax returns or tax information only as permitted by applicable law.

2-302. <u>Human Experimentation</u>. No agency within the Intelligence Community shall sponsor, contract for, or conduct research on human subjects except in accordance with guidelines issued by the Department of Health and Human Services. The subject's informed consent shall be documented as required by those guidelines.

2-303. <u>Contracting</u>. No agency within the Intelligence Community shall enter into a contract or arrangement for the provision of good and services with privaate companies or institutions in the United States unless the agency sponsorship is known to the appropriate officials of the company or institution. In the case of any company or institution other than an academic institution, intelligence agency sponsorship may be concealed where it is determined, pursuant to procedures approved by the agency head, that such concealment is necessary for authorized intelligence purposes.

2-304. <u>Personnel Assigned to Other Agencies</u>. An employee detailed to another agency within the federal government shall be responsible to the host agency and shall not report to the parent agency on the affairs of the host agency unless so directed by the host agency. The head of the host agency, and any successor, shall be informed of the employee's relationship with the parent agency.

2-305. <u>Prohibition on Assassinations</u>. No person employed by or acting on behalf of the United States Government shall enagage in, or conspire to engage in, assassination.

2-306. <u>Special Activities</u>. No component of the United States Government except an agency within the Intelligence COmmunity may conduct any special activity. No such agency except the CIA (or the military services in wartime) may conduct any special activity unless the President determines, with the SCC's advice, that another agency is more likely to achieve a particular objective.

2-307. <u>Restrictions on Assistance to Law Enforcement Authorities</u>. Agencies within the Intelligence Community other than the FBI shall not, except as expressly authorized by law or section 2-208:

(a)   provide services, equipment personnel or facilities to the Law Enforcement Assistance Administration (or its successor agencies) or to state or local police organizations of the United States; or

(b)   participate in or fund any law enforcement activity within the United States.

2-308. <u>Permissable Assistance to Law Enforcement Authorities</u>. The restrictions in section 2-307 shall not preclude:

(a)   cooperation with appropriate law enforcement agencies for the purpose of protecting the personnel, information and facilities of any agency within the Intelligence Community;

(b)   participation in law enforcement activities in accordance with law and this Order; to investigate or prevent clandestine intelligence activities by foreign powers, or international terrorist or narcotics activities; or

(c)   provision of specialized equipment, technical knowledge, or assistance of expert personnel for use by any department or agency or, when lives are endngered, to support local law enforcement agencies.

2-309. <u>Permission Dissemination and Storage of Information</u>. Nothing in sections 2-201 through 2-308 of this Order shall prohibit:

(a)   dissemination to appropriate law enforcement agencies of information which may indicate involvement in activities that may violate federal, state or foreign laws;

(b) storage of onformation required by law to be retained;

(c) dissemination of information covered by section 2-207 to agencies within the Intelligence Community or entities of cooperating foreign governments; or

(d)   lawful storage or dissemination of information for administrative purposes.

Section 2

2-1. Miscellaneous Amendments.

2-101. Section 1-706 pf Executive Order 12036 is amended to read as follows:

Each agency within the Intelligence Community shall furnish to the FBI and to Fedeal law enforcement agencies information needed by such agencies in the performance of their duties, in accordance with procedures agreed to by the heads of both of the departments or agencies concerned.

2-102. Section 1-801 of Executive Order 12036 is amended by deleting the words "Attorney General" and substituting therefore the words "Director of the Federal Bureau of Investigation.

2-103. Section 1-805 of Executive Order 12036 is amended by deleting the words afer "FBI" and substituting the words "pursuant to procedures agreed upon by the Director of Central Intelligence and the Director of the Federal Bureau of Investigation."

2-104. Sections 3-305 of Executive Order 12036 is amended to read as follows:

"Until the procedures required by amendments to this Order have been established, the activities authorized and regulated herein shall be conducted in accordance with procedures heretofore approved or agreed to by the Attorney general pursuant to this Order shall be established as expeditiously as possible."

2-106. Section 4-202 of Executive Order 12036 is amended by adding a comma after "espoinage," deleting the word "and" after "espionage," and by deleting the word "clandestine."

2-107. Section 4-209 of Executive Order 12036 is amended by inserting the words "occurs in a foreign country or" before the word "transcends" in subsection 4-209(c).

2-108. Section 4-212 of Executive Order 12036 is amended by deleting the words "conducted abroad" after "activities."

2-109. Section 4-214 of Executive Order 12036 is amended to read as follows:

"United States person means a citizen of the United States, an alien physically present in the United States who is known by the intelligence agency concerned to be a permanent resident alien, an unincorporated association substantialy composed of United States citizens, or a corporation incorporated in the United States, unless such corporation is controlled by one or more foreign powers, persons or organizations."

INDEX

A-K

FOOT NOTES

63   Frantz Fanon, <u>The Wretched of the Earth</u>, New York: Grove Press, 1963.

64   Hierocles, The Golden Verses of
     Pythagoras, London: Concord Grove
     Press, 1983, p 64-7.

65   Ajili Hodari, "Proposal for Development
     of a Promotion Campaign for the Pan
     African Center for Progressive
     Education, San Francisco: March 1976,
     p. 1-8.

66   Malcolm X, The Autobiography of
     Malcolm X, New York: Grove Press, 1964
     p. 223.

67   ibid., p. 220

68   ibid., p. 220

69   ibid., p. 220

70   ibid., p. 221

71   Le Duan, This Nation and Socialism are
     One, Chicago: Vanguard Books, 1976,
     p. 19-20.

72   Wilfred Ussery, "The Area Development
     Plan of the Western Addition Target Area,
     plan," San Francisco.

73. Julus Lester, <u>The Seventh Son, The Thought and Writings of W.E.B. Dubois,</u> New York. Random House, 1971, pg 255-56.

74 Cayraud S. Wilmore, <u>Black Religion and Black Radicalism: An interpretation of the religious history of Afro-American people,</u> New York: Orbis Books, 1973, p 8.

75 ibid., p 5.

76 Frederick Douglass, <u>Narrative of the Life of Frederick Douglass an American Slave,</u> Boston: Harvard University Press, 1960 p 102

77 Maya Deren, <u>Divine Horse Men the Living Gods of Haiti,</u> Mc Pherson and Company, 1953, p. 16

78 Dr. Yosef Ben-Jochannan, <u>African Origins of the Major Western Religions,</u> New York: Alkebu-Lan Books, 1970, p. 6.

79 ibid., p. 6-7.

80 ibid., p. 147

81   ibid., p. 146

82   Evelyn Rossiter, The Book of the Dead
     Papyri of Ani, Hunefer, Anhai, British
     Museum, p. 93 and 96.

83   Yosef Ben-Jochannan, African Origins of
     the Major Western Religions, New York.
     Alkebu-Lav Books, 1970, p. 164-165.

84   Gerald Massey, The Historical Jesus and
     the Mythical Christ, Moke Lumne Hill
     California; Heacth Research Unusual
     Books, p. 40

85   ibid., p. 43.

86   ibid., p. 56-57.

87   Dr. Yosef ben-Jochannan African Origins of
     the Major Western Religions, New York:
     Alkebu-Lan Books, 1970, p. 647.

88   ibid., p. 64.

89   ibid., p. 75.

90   ibid., p. 75.

91   ibid., p. 91.

92   ibid., p. 91.

93   ibid., p. 98.

94   ibid., p. 115.

88   ibid., p. 115.

88   ibid., p. 115.

97   ibid., p. 108.

98   Norman R. Yetman, <u>Life Under the Peculiar Institution Selections from the Narrative Collection Holt Rinehart and Winston</u>, 1970, p. 53.

99. ibid., p. 53

100. ibid., p. 95

101. ibid., p. 63

102 Lawrence W. Levine, <u>Black Culture and Black Consciousness,</u> New York, Oxford: Oxford University Press, 1977, p. 43.

103. ibid., p. 43-4

104. Gayraud S. Wilmore, <u>Black Religion and Black Radicalism an interpretation</u>

of the Religious History of Afro-American People, New York: Orbis Books, 1973, p. 41.

105 St. Clair Drake, The Redemption of Africa and Black Religion, Chicago: Third World Press, 1970, p. 49.

106. ibid., p. 45

107. ibid., p. 50

108. Jacob Carruthers, Race Vindication, The Irritated Genie of Haiti, Unpublished Manuscript.

109 John Oliver Killens, The Trial Record of Denmark V esey, Boston: Beacan Press, 1970, p. IV.

110 ibid., p. XV.

111 ibid., p. XV.

112 Cayraud S. Wilmore, Black Religion and Black Radicalism: An Interpretation of the Religious History of Afro-American People, New York: Orbis Books, 1973, p. 9. 64.

113 ibid., p. 64

114. ibid., p. 67

115. ibid., p. 68

116. Lerone Bennett, <u>The Shaping of Black America</u>, Chicago: Johnson Publishing Company, 1969, p. 125.

117. ibid., p. 139-40.

118. Howard Brotz, <u>Negro Social and Political Thought 1850-1920,</u> New York; London: Basic Books Inc. Publishers, 1966, p. 110.

119. John H. Bracey J.R. August Meier and Elliott Rudwick, <u>Black Nationalism in America,</u> New York: The Bobbs-Merrill Company, 1970, p. 172-3.

120. Cayraud S. Wilmore, <u>Black Religion and Black Radicalism</u>: <u>An Interpretation of the Religious History of the Afro-American People</u>, New York: Orbis Books, 1989, p. 138.

121. ibid., p. 140.

122. ibid., p. 141.

123.   "San Francisco Negro Action," San Francisco: San Francisco Examiner, July 24, 1963.

124.   Ollie Bee, "The Black American," July 3rd 9th, 1980.

125.   R.G.E. SIU, <u>The Craft of Power</u>, New York, Chichester, Brisbane, Toronto: 1979, p. 109.

126.   C.L.R. James, <u>The Black Jacobins</u>, New York. Random House, 1963, p. 124.

127.   Marcus Garvey, <u>Philosophy and Opinions of Marcus Garvey</u>, Vol. I, San Francisco: Julian Richardson and Associates, publishers, 1967, p. 15.

128.   Hans T. Morgenthau, <u>Politics Among Nations, the Struggle for Power and Peace</u>, New York Alfred A. Knopf, 1948, 19543, 1960, p. 28-9.

129.   J.A.C. Brown, <u>Techniques of Persuasion from Propaganda to Brainwashing</u>, Dallas: pelican Books, 1963, p. 10-11.

130. New College Edition, <u>The American Heritage Dictionary of the</u>

English,Boston: Houghton Miffcia Company, 1926, p. 12 97.

131. Robert Allen, <u>Black Awakening In Capitalist America, An analytic History</u>, New York: Doubleday, 1969, p. 71, 72 and 73.

132. R.G.H. Siu, <u>The Craft of Power,</u> New York: John Wiley & Sons, 1979, p. 96-8.

133. <u>Supplementary Detailed Staff Reports on Intelligence Activities and the Rights of Americans</u>, Book II. San Francisco: April 213, 1976, p 7.

134. Paul Cowan, Nick Egleson, Nat Hennt off, <u>State Secrets, Police Surveillance In America</u>, New York, Chicago, San Francisco: Holt, Rinehart and Winston, 1974.

135 <u>Supplementary Detailed Staff Reports on Intelligence Activities and the Rights of Americans</u>, Book III Washington D.C., U.S. Government Printing Office, 1976, p. 187.

136 Nat Hentoff, <u>State Secrets Police Surveillance in America</u>, New York,

Chicago San Francisco Holt, Rinehart and Winston.

137 ibid., p. 8

138 ibid., p. 8

139 Supplementary detailed Staff Reports on Intelligence Activities and the Rights of Americans, Book II, San Francisco: April 23, 1976 p. 789.

140 ibid., p. 790.

141 ibid., p. 20.

142 ibid., p. 21-22

144. ibid., p. 36

145   ibid., p. 41

146 Kuwasi Imara, "Pan Afrikan Secretariat Cadre Training," Fresno 1981.

147 Frank Kitson, Low Intensity Operation, Subversions Insurgency, Peace Keeping, U.S.: Archon Books, 1971, p. 67-143.

148 Ken Lawrence, "<u>The New State Repression</u>," Chicago: Summer 1985, p. 9.

149 Kuwasi Imara, "<u>Pan Afrikan Secretarial Cadre Training</u>," Fresno 1981.